This eighth edition was researched and written by **HENRY STEDMAN**. He's been writing guidebooks for more than 25 years and is the author or co-author of over a dozen Trailblazer titles including *Kilimanjaro*, *Inca Trail*, *Coast to Coast Path*, *Hadrian's Wall Path*, *London LOOP* and all three books in the *South-West Coast Path* series. He's usually accompanied by Daisy: two parts trouble to one part Parson's Jack Russell. When not travelling, he lives in Battle, East Sussex, editing and arranging climbs on Africa's highest mountain through his company, Kilimanjaro Experts.

**CHARLIE LORAM** has never found being indoors easy. After he'd broken in his boots on the fells and crags of Snowdonia and the Scottish Highlands, his nomadic tendencies took him to the Himalaya. For five years he wandered the high trails as guidebook writer (author of *Trekking in Ladakh*), wilderness guide and modern-day pilgrim. Insights gained there helped create Trailblazer's British walking guide series which he worked on as author and first series editor. At home on Dartmoor he continues his passion for walking and wilderness, guiding people to a deeper connection with nature and themselves. For more see 🖳 www.the oldway.info or follow him on @the_old_way_ and also @charlie_loram.

Authors

**West Highland Way** First edition: 2003; **this eighth edition 2022**
**Publisher** Trailblazer Publications
The Old Manse, Tower Rd, Hindhead, Surrey, GU26 6SU, UK ⌨ trailblazer-guides.com
**British Library Cataloguing in Publication Data**
A catalogue record for this book is available from the British Library
**ISBN 978-1-912716-29-6**
© Trailblazer 2003, 2006, 2008, 2010, 2013, 2016, 2019, 2022: Text and maps
**Series Editor**: Anna Jacomb-Hood
**Editing and proof-reading**: Nicky Slade, Anna Jacomb-Hood and Jane Thomas
**Cartography**: Jane Thomas and Nick Hill   **Layout**: Nicky Slade   **Index**: Jane Thomas
**Illustrations**: © Nick Hill (pp76-8)   **Photos**: © Henry Stedman unless otherwise indicated

The maps in this guide were prepared from out-of-Crown-
copyright Ordnance Survey maps amended and updated by Trailblazer.

## Acknowledgements

**From Henry**: It's always fun walking in Scotland and a lot of that fun comes from the people you meet. So whether it's for their helpfulness, kindness, or just for their entertaining
company, I would like to thank the following (in no particular order): the staff at Crown Vets
in Fort William for treating Daisy's paw; Helen at the West Highland Way Sleeper, for her
company (and coffee!); Ivor at the (now closed) Anchorage Cottage for the very welcome
drink on a hot day; Melissa and Kevin while waiting for a bus; Adam at Kings House Hotel
for helping when Daisy was hurt; Mark, the exhausted cyclist at Kingshouse; the anonymous
bus driver who allowed Daisy to travel on his bus (even though it went against company policy); Johana Prada, Camilo Audila and Alan Munoz for company on part of the walk; and to
everyone else on the trail who stopped to spend a few minutes chatting to me. Thanks also
to all those readers who've written in with comments and suggestions, in particular, Geert
Ariaans, Heather Bell, Carly Bishop, Roger Coe, Matt Gardiner, Mary Hartman, Tony
Hufton, Zsuzsa Koger, Peter Marshall, Frank Norris, Simon Quinn, Lisa Radel, Paul Scott,
Dave & Angie Walsh and Barbara Winzberg. And, of course, thanks as ever to all at
Trailblazer: Nicky Slade, Jane Thomas, Anna Jacomb-Hood, Nick Hill and Bryn Thomas.
**Dedication – From Henry**: For Zoe, for keeping Henry so royally entertained while I
enjoyed another jolly with my dog; and for just being lovely, of course.

## A request

The author and publisher have tried to ensure that this guide is as accurate and up to date as
possible. Nevertheless, things change. If you notice any changes or omissions that should be
included in the next edition, please contact us at Trailblazer (⌨ info@trailblazer-guides.com).
A free copy of the next edition will be sent to persons making a significant contribution.

## Warning: hill walking can be dangerous

Please read the notes on when to go (pp12-16) and outdoor safety (pp56-61). Every effort
has been made by the author and publisher to ensure that the information contained herein
is as accurate and up to date as possible. However, they are unable to accept responsibility
for any inconvenience, loss or injury sustained by anyone as a result of the advice and information given in this guide.

**Updated information** will be available on: ⌨ **trailblazer-guides.com**

**Photos – This page**: Tackling the long, lonely hike across Rannoch Moor.
**Front cover and overleaf**: Views from the top of the Devil's Staircase (p169),
at 548m (1797ft) the highest point on the West Highland Way.
**Previous page**: Looking towards the iconic Kings House Hotel.
Printed in China; print production by D'Print (☎ +65-6581 3832), Singapore

★ trailblazer

# West Highland
## WAY

### GLASGOW TO FORT WILLIAM

53 large-scale maps & guides to 26 towns and villages

**PLANNING – PLACES TO STAY – PLACES TO EAT**

CHARLIE LORAM

**EIGHTH EDITION UPDATED BY**
**HENRY STEDMAN**

TRAILBLAZER PUBLICATIONS

# Contents

## INTRODUCTION

**West Highland Way**
History 9 – How difficult is it? 10
How long do you need? 12 – When to go 12

## PART 1: PLANNING YOUR WALK

**Practical information for the walker**
Route finding 17 – Accommodation 18 – Food and drink 22
Money 25 – Other services 25 – Walking companies 26 – Walking with
dogs 27 – Information for foreign visitors 28 – Mountain biking 29

**Budgeting** 30

**Itineraries**
Village and town facilities 31 – Which direction? 32
Suggested itineraries 32 – Hillwalking side trips 34
Day and weekend walks 34

**What to take**
Keep your luggage light 35 – How to carry it 36 – Footwear 36
Clothes 37 – Toiletries 38 – First-aid kit 38 – General items 38
Sleeping bag 39 – Camping gear 39 – Money 39 – Sources of further
information 40 – Maps 41 – Recommended reading 41

**Getting to and from the West Highland Way**
National transport 42 – Getting to Britain 43
Local transport 45 – Public transport map 48

## PART 2: MINIMUM IMPACT WALKING & OUTDOOR SAFETY

**Minimum impact walking**
Economic impact 50 – Environmental impact 51 – Access 53

**Outdoor safety**
Avoidance of hazards 56 – Weather forecasts 57 – Water 57
Blisters 58 – Bites 58 – Hypothermia 60 – Hyperthermia 60

## PART 3: THE ENVIRONMENT & NATURE

**Conserving Scotland's nature**
NatureScot 63 – Campaigning & conservation organisations 64
Beyond conservation 65

**Flora and fauna**
Flowers 64 – Trees 68 – Mammals 72 – Reptiles 74
Butterflies 75 – Birds 75

Contents

## ABOUT THIS BOOK

This guidebook contains all the information you need. The hard work has been done for you so you can plan your trip without having to consult numerous websites and other books and maps. When you're all packed and ready to go, there's comprehensive public transport information to get you to and from the trail and detailed maps (1:20,000) to help you find your way along it.

● All standards of accommodation with reviews of campsites, camping barns, hostels, B&Bs, pubs/inns, guesthouses and hotels
● Walking companies if you want an organised tour, and baggage-transfer services if you just want your luggage carried
● Suggested itineraries for all types of walkers
● Answers to all your questions: when to go, degree of difficulty, what to pack, and how much the whole walking holiday will cost
● Walking times in both directions and GPS waypoints
● Cafés, pubs, tearooms, takeaways, restaurants, food shops
● Rail, bus & taxi information for all villages and towns on the path
● Street plans of the main towns and villages both on and off the Way
● Historical, cultural and geographical background

## POST COVID NOTE

This edition of the guide was researched at a time when the entire country was just emerging from restrictions imposed following the Covid pandemic. Most of the hotels, cafés, pubs, restaurants and tourist attractions had reopened but some may not survive the further hardships caused by rising fuel prices and inflation. Do forgive us where your experience on the ground contradicts what is written in the book; please email us – **info@trailblazer-guides.com** – so we can add your information to our updates page on the website.

---

❏ **MINIMUM IMPACT FOR MAXIMUM INSIGHT**

*Nature's peace will flow into you as the sunshine flows into trees. The winds will blow their freshness into you and storms their energy, while cares will drop off like autumn leaves.* **John Muir** (one of the world's earliest and most influential environmentalists, born in 1838)

Walking in wild places is about opening ourselves up to all that is 'green'. Treading lightly and with respect we give ourselves a precious chance to tap into the curative power of the natural world. Physical contact with the land makes us more in tune with it and as a result we feel all the more passionate about protecting it.

By developing a deeper ecological awareness through a better understanding of nature and by supporting rural economies, local businesses, sensitive forms of transport and low-impact methods of farming and land-use we can all do our bit for a brighter future. There can be few activities as 'environmentally friendly' as walking.

# INTRODUCTION

*[Glencoe and Lochaber] had everything: peak, plateau, precipice, the thinnest of ridges, and green valley, all set between the widest of wild moors and a narrow sea-loch.*                    **WH Murray** *Undiscovered Scotland*

WH Murray is not alone in thinking the dramatic concluding stages of the West Highland Way (Glencoe and Lochaber) are equal in beauty to anywhere in the world. The Way has become a pilgrimage for mountain lovers keen to travel simply on foot into the heart of the Scottish Highlands. A better introduction to this stunning region could not have been designed and, what is more, you don't have to wait until the end for the highlights.

**Within a week you will have walked through some of the most fabulous scenery in Britain with relative ease, safety and comfort**

Right from the start the Way gives walkers a taste of the magic of Scotland's wild land and within a week you will have walked through some of the most fabulous scenery in Britain with relative ease, safety and comfort.

The Way begins kindly just 20 minutes by train from the centre of Glasgow, gently undulating through woods and farmland, easing you in to the new demands of long-distance walking. As you stroll along

Approaching Beinn Dorain (Maps 31-2, photo © Bryn Thomas).

the length of Loch Lomond's celebrated wooded shore, lowland subtly transforms into Highlands and rugged mountain grandeur begins to dominate the scene. Ancient tracks previously used by soldiers and drovers lead you north along wide valley bottoms past historical staging posts which still offer sustenance to today's Highland traveller.

**Above**: Looking down from Conic Hill to Loch Lomond and the path to Balmaha (Map 11).

The character of the Way becomes more serious as it climbs across the bleak, remote expanse of Rannoch Moor, skirting the entrance to Glen Coe and climbing over the Devil's Staircase, the highest point on the trail. This is true hillwalking country and the

**Below**: One of the most peaceful sections of the walk is through the woods on the eastern shore of Loch Lomond.

**Above**: This former hunting lodge by Loch Lomond is now Rowardennan Youth Hostel.

INTRODUCTION

extra effort is amply repaid by breathtaking mountain views. As you approach Fort William, the end of the Way, Ben Nevis comes into view rising above the conifer forests. If you have energy left after this superb 96-mile (154km) walk, an ascent of the highest mountain in Britain makes a fitting climax.

# History

The West Highland Way was the first official long-distance footpath in Scotland. The idea was conceived in the 1960s at the height of enthusiasm brought about by the opening of the Pennine Way in England.

It was a massive task to create such an ambitious right of way, requiring investigation of the best route, endless liaising between the various local authorities and the Countryside Commission for Scotland, negotiations with landowners through whose land the Way might pass and then finally, when all was agreed, the construction of the path itself. This may seem simple, yet a flagship route such as the West Highland Way requires information boards,

**Right**: Brightly painted chalet near Carbeth Loch (Map 2).

INTRODUCTION

**Above**: The sculpture at the end of the West Highland Way in Fort William.

**Above**: There are two bothies on the Way, offering basic shelter and somewhere to unroll your sleeping bag. This is Doune Byre Bothy (see p134).

**Above**: This striking war memorial stands beside Loch Lomond at Rowardennan (see p125, photo © BT).

waymarks, sturdy bridges and stiles, and adequate surfacing and drainage to cope with the inevitable high numbers of walkers. As a result it took until 1980 for the Way finally to be declared open. In 2010 the end point of the Way was moved from the roundabout on the A82 to the centre of Fort William, thereby adding one mile to the total route. A bronze sculpture of a seated, weary-looking walker marks the spot.

# How difficult is it?

No great level of experience is needed to walk the West Highland Way as the whole trail is on obvious, well-maintained paths with excellent waymarks where needed. The first half of the route, south of Tyndrum, is across gentle terrain and generally sticks to the bottom of valleys or traverses their sides. Only on a couple of occasions does the trail rise to just over 300m (1000ft) and on the first and hardest instance, the crossing of Conic Hill, this mildly strenuous section can be avoided. On this half you are never far from help and there's plenty of shelter should the weather turn foul.

North of Tyndrum the terrain becomes a little more challenging. With fewer settlements it can even feel quite remote. The trail crosses some high, desolate country: Rannoch Moor (445m/ 1460ft), the Devil's Staircase (548m/1797ft) and the Lairigmor (330m/1082ft), all of which can be exposed in bad weather.

Crossing these magnificent sections gives you a true taste of Highland Scotland and you will require basic outdoor competence to do so safely (see pp55-7 for further advice).

# How long do you need?

During the annual West Highland Way race the entire route is run in less than 35 hours. Admirable though this is, you will probably want to take a little longer. The suggested itineraries (see p33) in this book list various schedules of between six and nine days for walking from Milngavie to Fort William, showing that with a rest day you can easily complete the Way in a week to ten days. If you can afford to take longer you will have the time to climb mountains along the route, explore Glasgow, Glen Coe and Glen Nevis, or simply dawdle when the weather is

**Above**: The 18th-century Bridge of Orchy which gives its name to the tiny village (see p149; photo © Susanne Härtel).

**Above**: Rounding up the sheep near Tyndrum.

**Below**: View over Loch Tulla with Black Mount beyond. Inveroran is to the left.

**Above**: Crossing Rannoch Moor on the old Military Road which was built in the 18th century (see p152).

**Below**: Looking back down the Devil's Staircase towards Kingshouse (Map 40).

kind. If this sort of wandering is more your style a fortnight should be generous enough. Walkers with less time on their hands could conceivably catch a bus or train over the less interesting sections of the Way. For instance, missing out the rather tedious section from Inverarnan to Tyndrum, or even to Bridge of Orchy, would not upset the essential character of the walk and would shorten your time by one or even two days.

There are also some superb **day** and **weekend** walks along the best parts of the Way for those who want to sample the walk in bite-sized chunks; see p34.

# When to go

## SEASONS

The **main walking season** in Scotland is from the Easter holiday (March/April) through to October. Balancing all the variables such as weather, number of other walkers, midges and available accommodation, the best months to walk the West Highland Way are June and September.

**Above**: Ruined farm buildings at Lairigmor (Map 45) beside the Way on the Kinlochleven to Fort William stage.

### Spring

**April** is unpredictable in terms of the weather. It can be warm and sunny, though blustery days with showers are more typical and snow may often still be lying on the hills. On the plus side, the land is just waking up to spring, there won't be many other walkers about and you shouldn't encounter any midges.

As far as the weather is concerned, **May** can be a great time for walking in Scotland; the temperature is warm, the weather is as dry and clear as can be expected, wild flowers are out in their full glory and the midges have yet to reach an intolerable level. However, the Way is exceptionally busy at this time of year and it can be a nightmare finding accommodation if you have not booked in advance. Many B&Bs take bookings in January or earlier for people walking in May. This is not the time to go if you like walking in solitude. You'd be far better off going in **June** which has all the advantages of May without the crowds, though make sure you don't pick the day of the West Highland Way race (see box p14).

**Above**: Blackrock Cottage, a lonely outpost on the northern fringe of Rannoch Moor (see p161; © BT).

## Summer

The arrival of hordes of tourists in **July** and **August** along with warm, muggy weather brings out the worst in the midges. On many days you'll be wondering what all the fuss is about; that's until you encounter a still, overcast evening when you'll swear never to set foot in the Highlands again. Campers are the ones who should really take note of this (see p58) as everyone else can escape the torture behind closed windows and doors. On some weekends it can feel as if the whole world has arrived in the Highlands; traffic is nose to tail on the roads and many hostels and B&Bs are fully booked days in advance. Surprisingly, there can also be a fair amount of rain in these months.

---

### ❑ FESTIVALS AND ANNUAL EVENTS

The following events use part or all of the West Highland Way. They may affect your decision about when to walk.

Note that Conic Hill remains open to walkers year-round now, even during lambing. The exception is for walkers with dogs; see p28 for further information.

In addition to the events below there are several festivals in Glasgow (see p84).

● **Fort William Mountain Festival** (🖥 mountainfestival.co.uk)  A hugely popular event held in **February** or **March** at the Nevis Centre. This week-long extravaganza began life as a mountain film festival but has grown to showcase not just films but all sorts of lectures and exhibitions.

● **Scottish Motorcycle Trials** (🖥 ssdt.org)  Parts of the trail between Bridge of Orchy and Fort William are used for these six-day trials each year. This usually takes place over the first full week in **May**. Walkers can continue using the trail at this time but there's obviously some disturbance. There's also lots of competition for the accommodation, particularly in Kinlochleven.

● **West Highland Way Race** (🖥 westhighlandwayrace.org)  This takes place in **June** and the idea is to race from Milngavie Station to Fort William Leisure Centre, setting off at 1am and hopefully finishing before noon next day, ie to complete the entire West Highland Way in just 35 hours. The record for men was broken in 2017 by Rob Sinclair who did the route in 13 hours 41 minutes and 8 seconds. Lucy Colquhoun holds the women's record, taking 17 hours 16 minutes and 20 seconds in 2007.

● **Ben Race** (🖥 bennevisrace.co.uk)  If you are in the Ben Nevis area on the first Saturday in **September** try to watch the Ben Race when up to 600 fell-runners reach the summit and return to the glen in ludicrously short times. This spectacle began in 1895 when William Swan ran to the top and back down in 2 hours 41 minutes. Today the men's record stands at 1 hour 25 minutes 34 seconds, and the women's 1 hour 43 minutes and 25 seconds (both set in 1984, by Kenny Stuart and Pauline Haworth).

## Autumn

A slower pace of life returns when the school holidays come to an end. Early **September** is a wonderful and often neglected time for walking, with fewer visitors and the midges' appetites largely sated.

Towards the end of the month and into **early October** the vivid autumn colours are at their best in the woods and on the hills but you are starting to run the risk of encountering more rain and stronger winds. The air temperature, however, is still quite mild.

## Winter

**Late October** and **early November** can occasionally be glorious with crisp clear days, but this is also the start of winter; the days are shortening, the temperature has dropped noticeably and many seasonal B&Bs, hostels, campsites and shops have closed.

You need to be pretty hardy to walk between **late November** and **mid March**. True, some days can be fantastically bright and sunny and your appreciation will be heightened by snow on the hills and few people around. You are far more likely, however, to encounter the weather the Highlands are famous for; driving rain and snow for days on end on the back of freezing northerly winds.

## TEMPERATURE

January temperatures are on average 1-6°C and July temperatures are on average 10-18°C. See table overleaf.

**Above**: Rowchoish Bothy (see p128) offers basic free shelter for the night. There's a fireplace so you can cook and keep warm if it's cold. The photo above was taken in January (© BT).

**Below**: Cottage below Buachaille Etive Mor, the 'Great Herdsman of Etive', standing guard at the entrance to Glen Coe (see p165).

**Above**: Climbing Ben Nevis (see p180) after you've walked the West Highland Way makes a fitting grand finale. (Photo © Joel Newton).

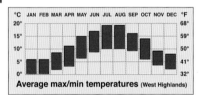

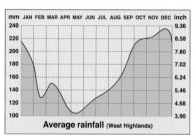

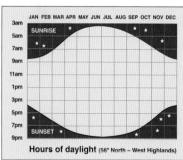

## RAINFALL

The annual rainfall for the West Highlands is about 2000mm (80 inches). As you progress north you are likely to encounter wetter weather. The annual average for Glasgow is 1000mm, while in Glen Nevis it can be as much as 3000mm. The good news is that more than half of this precipitation falls as snow in winter.

## DAYLIGHT HOURS

If walking in autumn, winter and early spring, you must take account of how far you can walk in the available light. It may not be possible to cover as many miles as you would in summer. The table gives the sunrise and sunset times for each month at latitude 56° North. This runs across the southern tip of Loch Lomond, giving an accurate picture of daylight for the West Highland Way. Depending on the weather you will get a further 30-45 minutes of usable light before sunrise and after sunset.

**Above**: By the Way north of Kingshouse.

# PLANNING YOUR WALK

# 1

## Practical information for the walker

### ROUTE FINDING

The West Highland Way has been way-marked with signposts and wooden posts in appropriate places. Each of these is marked with a white thistle within a hexagon or the newer WHW logo to confirm the line of the trail. They have an additional yellow arrow when indicating a change in direction. Used in combination with the detailed trail maps and directions in this book you have no excuse for getting lost.

### Using GPS with this book

Whilst modern Wainwrights will scoff, more open-minded walkers will accept that GPS technology can be an inexpensive, well-established if non-essential, navigational aid. In no time at all a GPS receiver, given a clear view of the sky, will establish your position and altitude in a variety of formats to within a few metres. These days, most **smartphones** have a GPS receiver built in and mapping software available to run on them (see p41).

Most of the maps throughout the book include **numbered waypoints** along the route. These correlate to the list on p195 which gives the latitude and longitude and a description. You'll find more waypoints where the path is indistinct or there are several options as to which way to go. You can download the complete list for free as a GPS-readable file (that doesn't include the text descriptions) from the Trailblazer website: 🖥 **trailblazer-guides.com/gps-waypoints**. State-of-the-art digital mapping to import into your GPS unit (see p41) is also available, but it's not the most reliable way of navigating and the small screen on your phone or pocket-sized GPS unit will invariably fail to put places into context or give you the 'big picture'. Traditional OS paper maps (see p40) whilst bulkier, are preferable.

Another way of using a GPS unit is to download a **track log** of the route from the internet. Where waypoints are single points like cairns, a track log is a continuous line-like a path that appears on

❏ **BOOK ACCOMMODATION IN ADVANCE!**
Always book your accommodation in advance. Not only does this ensure you have a
bed for the night but it gives you an opportunity to find out more about the place,
check the price and see what's included. Most B&Bs and hotels can now also be
booked through a website, either their own or an agency's; however, phoning is probably best because you can check details more easily. If you have to cancel please telephone your hosts; it will save a lot of worry and possibly allow them to provide a bed
for someone else.

You may also want to consider using the services of one of the walking companies listed on pp26-7 who will happily book your accommodation for you, for a small
fee, saving you a considerable amount of work.

your screen as on a car sat-nav; all you have to do is keep on that line. If you
lose it on the screen you can zoom out until it reappears and walk towards it.
While it's impressive to see the trail unfold as a track log on a calibrated map
or Google Earth, many of these 'user-generated' track logs available online are
imperfect because it takes an extremely trail-savvy and committed person to
record a perfect track log without any gaps or confusing diversions.

It's worth repeating that most people who have walked the West Highland
Way did so without GPS.

## ACCOMMODATION

Places to stay are relatively numerous and well spaced along most of the Way,
allowing for some flexibility in itineraries. All bunkhouses/wigwams, hostels
and B&Bs should, however, be booked ahead (see box above) if possible, especially from May to August when some get booked up weeks in advance. You
can avoid a lot of this accommodation mayhem at the busy times of the year by
starting your walk mid week, rather than opting for the usual Saturday start
from Milngavie. Note also that many places are closed during the winter.

### Camping
*There is pleasure in camping in mountains inexplicable to the unbeliever, but will at once
be apparent to anyone of imagination.* **WH Murray**

Even in the crowded British Isles camping can nurture a sense of freedom and
simplicity which beautifully complements the act of walking. Your rucksack
will of course be heavier, but carrying all the necessary equipment for sleeping
out and cooking your own meals lightens the load in other ways: there's no need
to book accommodation, you can make and change your plans as you go and
it's by far the cheapest option (see p30). However, pitching your tent wherever
you like is not allowed along the Way – see p53 for Loch Lomond restrictions.
Realising that many backpackers prefer to camp in the wild, several informal
free sites with no facilities have been provided where you can pitch for one
night as long as you leave no trace of being there and above all never light a
fire. More information on how to camp with minimal impact is given on p53.

Official sites along the Way range from those with a basic toilet and little else to luxurious establishments with shop, laundrette, restaurant and even swimming pool and sauna.

If you want to camp but not carry your tent, note that the baggage carriers listed on p26 will visit campsites.

## Bothies

Bothies are simple unlocked huts with sleeping platform and fireplace. In terms of comfort, they give shelter somewhere between a tent and a bunkhouse, providing very basic, free accommodation for walkers who are happy to follow the 'Bothy Code' (see box below). If you are camping it can mean a welcome night without having to pitch a tent. But if you intend to stay mainly in bunkhouses/hostels remember to bring a sleeping bag and mat for your night in a bothy.

Bothies are cared for by the Mountain Bothies Association (💻 mountain bothies.org.uk). On the Way there are two (Rowchoish and Doune) on the eastern shore of Loch Lomond. Visit the website to check that they are open for your trek as they are sometimes closed for maintenance.

## Bunkhouses and hostels

There is a wide range of comfortable and interesting bunkhouses and hostels along the West Highland Way enabling walkers to travel on a small budget without having to carry bulky and heavy camping equipment. All have mattresses or beds to sleep on and bed linen is usually available, either to hire or included in the price. Many have full cooking facilities (cooker, pans, crockery and cutlery) which you can use for free and some even provide good-value cooked meals. If

### THE BOTHY CODE OF RESPECT

**For other users**
● Leave the bothy clean, tidy and with dry kindling for the next visitors

**For the bothy**
● Guard against fire risk and don't cause vandalism or graffiti
● Please take out all rubbish which you don't burn
● Avoid burying rubbish: this pollutes the environment
● Please don't leave perishable food: this encourages mice and rats
● Make sure the doors and windows are properly closed when you leave

**For the surroundings**
● If there is no toilet, human waste must be buried carefully out of sight; please use the spade provided

● For health reasons never use the vicinity of the bothy as a toilet
● Keep well away from the water supply
● Conserve fuel; never cut live wood

**For the agreement with the estate**
● Observe any restrictions on use of the bothy, eg during stag stalking or at lambing time
● Please remember bothies are available for short stays only

**For the restriction on numbers**
Because of overcrowding and lack of facilities, large groups (six or more) should not use a bothy nor camp near a bothy without first seeking permission from the owner. Bothies are not available for commercial groups.

Camping cabins at Beinglas Farm
Campsite (see p134)

Microlodge at Glencoe Mountain
Resort (see p156)

not, there is invariably somewhere close by where you can eat.

It is recommended that you take your own sleeping bag and make breakfast where possible, otherwise your trip won't be much cheaper than staying in B&Bs. You may also want to take a stove and pan to give yourself more flexibility when cooking facilities aren't available.

Simplest of all the bunkhouses are the innovative, low-impact wooden '**wigwams**' and **camping cabins** or **micro-lodges**. They sleep between two and six people, are insulated and occasionally heated. The other **bunkhouses** are more like hostels with dormitory accommodation or occasionally small rooms sleeping two to four people.

**Independent hostels** (⌨ hostel-scotland .co.uk) are privately owned and are as diverse as their owners. They all have full cooking facilities, dormitory accommodation and differ from SYHA hostels in that you don't pay more if you are not a member.

To stay at a SYHA hostel you either need to be a member of the Youth Hostel Association (Hostelling International) of your home country or you can join the **Scottish Youth Hostels Association** (aka Hostelling Scotland; ⌨ hostellingscotland.org.uk) at any of their hostels; it costs from £20 for a year. Beds can be booked online through the SYHA website or by phone either by calling the central number (☎ 0345-293 7373) or the relevant hostel direct. Despite their name there is no upper age restriction for membership.

### Bed and breakfast (B&B)

B&Bs are a great British institution. For anyone unfamiliar with the concept, you get a bedroom in someone's home along with an enormous cooked breakfast the following morning; in many respects it is like being a guest of the family. Staying in B&Bs is a brilliant way to walk in Scotland as you can travel with a light pack and gain a fascinating insight into the local culture. One night you may be staying in a suburban 'semi', the next on a remote hill farm.

**What to expect**  For the long-distance walker tourist-board recommendations and star-rating systems have little meaning. At the end of a long day you will simply be glad of the closest place with hot water and a smiling face to welcome you. If they have somewhere to hang your wet and muddy clothes so much the better. It is these criteria that have been used for places mentioned in this guide, rather than whether a room has a shaver point or TV. B&B owners are often proud to boast that all rooms are **en suite**. This enthusiasm has led some to squeeze a cramped shower and loo cubicle into the corner of a bedroom. Establishments without en suite rooms are sometimes preferable as you may get sole use of a bathroom (**private facilities**) across the corridor and a hot bath is often just what you need after a hard day on the trail. In some cases you may need to share the bathroom (**shared facilities**) with other guests.

**Single** rooms are usually poky rooms with barely enough room for the bed and certainly not enough to swing the proverbial cat. **Twin** rooms have two single beds while a **double** is supposed to have one double bed, although just to confuse things, some twins are also called doubles if the beds can be moved together. **Family** rooms sleep three or more (either with one double and one single bed, or with three single beds, or a double bed with bunk beds).

Some B&Bs provide an **evening meal** (£10-15), particularly if there is no pub or restaurant nearby, but generally you will need to have requested this in advance; check what the procedure is when you book. If an evening meal is not served, or you prefer to eat elsewhere, they may offer you a lift to a local eatery, though some places expect you to make your own arrangements anyhow.

Other services offered by many B&Bs along the Way are a **packed lunch** (£5-7) if you request one the night before, and a **pick-up/drop-off service** enabling you to stay at their establishment even if your day's walking doesn't deposit you at the front door. There's sometimes an extra charge (£3-15) for this.

**Rates** B&B tariffs are either quoted per room (based on two sharing) or per person per night; per person rates range from £25 per person for a simple room with a shared bathroom to over £50 per person for a very comfortable room with private bathroom, or en suite facilities, and all mod cons. Note that rates are sometimes discounted if you stay for more than one day.

If you're travelling by yourself then the rates for single occupancy of a double/twin room will probably be higher than the per person rate for two people. Conversely, the per person rate for three or more people sharing a room will usually be lower than if two people are sharing the room.

Unless specified, rates are for bed and breakfast. At some places, particularly the chain hotels such as Travelodge or Premier Inn, the only option is a **room rate**; this will be the same whether one or two people (or more if permissible) use the room.

Most places listed in this guide are around £35-50 per person. The rates we quote in this guide tend to be for the summer high season, when most people will be walking. Owners sometimes change their tariffs at a moment's notice in response to the number of visitors, so **use the rates in this book only as a rough guide**. In the low season (September to March) rates tend to come down. See also p30.

### Guest houses, hotels, pubs and inns

The B&B concept has been carried through into other more upmarket establishments such as **guest houses** (and hotels). These businesses are much less personal and generally slightly more expensive but do offer more space, an evening meal and a comfortable lounge for guests.

**Pubs** and **inns** often turn their hand to mid-range B&B accommodation in country areas. They can be good fun if you plan to drink in the bar until closing time, though possibly a bit noisy if you want an early night.

**Hotels** in the true sense of the word do not attract many walkers because of their genteel surroundings and comparatively high prices; £50-90 per person, usually inclusive of breakfast. However, they can be fantastic places with great character and some walkers feel they deserve a special treat for one night of their holiday, particularly to celebrate their achievement at the end.

The Way is also bookended by hotels belonging to the Premier Inn and Travelodge chains at both Milngavie and Fort William (as well as in Glasgow); prices at these places vary according to demand and can fluctuate enormously, but if you're lucky you may get a double/twin room for as little as £25, which represents very good value indeed.

### Holiday cottages

Self-catering cottages make sense for a group walking part of the Way and returning to the same base each night. They are normally let on a weekly basis. Cottages haven't been listed in this book; there are numerous websites dealing with holiday rentals or you could contact the local Tourist Information Centre (see p40).

### Airbnb

The rise and rise of Airbnb (🖥 airbnb.co.uk) has seen private homes and apartments opened up to overnight travellers on an informal basis. While accommodation is primarily based in cities, the concept is spreading to tourist hotspots in more rural areas, but do check thoroughly what you are getting and the precise location.

Be aware that these places are not registered B&Bs, so standards may vary, yet prices may not necessarily be any lower than the norm.

## FOOD AND DRINK

### Breakfast and lunch

Although you may expect a bowl of Scottish porridge for your B&B **breakfast**, you're more likely to be offered a bowl of cereal or muesli followed by a full plate of bacon, eggs, black pudding and baked beans as well as toast and marmalade; ideal for setting you up for a day on the trail. If you prefer something lighter, continental breakfasts are normally available.

You will need to carry a packed **lunch** with you some days; your accommodation host may well be able to prepare one. However, there are a number of village shops and bakeries en route enabling you to buy your lunch as you pass by. There are also several cafés, pubs, hotels and teahouses on or near the trail, especially on the southern half, but not always where you need them. Use the information in the village and town facilities table (see p31) and in Part 5 to plan ahead.

## ❏ SCOTTISH FOOD

For too long Scotland, and most of Britain for that matter, neglected its once fine local food culture but things are starting to change although there is still little regional differentiation on many menus along the Way. As highly subsidised mass-produced food enters Britain from across the globe, local small-scale producers find it hard to compete. Pub grub bows to the economic dictates of freezer and microwave, rather than the sanity of home-grown specialities. At the end of a hard day on the trail your staple diet is more likely to be scampi and chips or lasagne, than cock-a-leekie or crappit heids. This is a shame; one of the great joys of travel is to embrace the spirit of a place and there is no better way of doing this than by sampling food that is grown and produced locally. By doing so you feed the local economy and strengthen regional identity; a direct benefit to the locality that is giving you, the traveller, so much. Now and then you will come across brave places attempting to breathe life back into rural culinary traditions and these should be actively supported. Keep an eye out for **Taste of Scotland** (🖳 taste-of-scotland.com) signs indicating places serving good quality, fresh Scottish produce.

Some traditional dishes include:
● **Arbroath smokies** – smoked haddock
● **Bannocks** – oatcakes baked in an oven and served with cheese
● **Bridies** – minced beef pies
● **Cock-a-leekie** – chicken and leek soup with prunes
● **Clapshot/tatties and neeps** – originating from Orkney, this is a combination of mashed potatoes, turnips, chives and butter or dripping; it usually accompanies haggis
● **Crappit heids** – lobster-stuffed haddock heads
● **Cullen skink** – smoked haddock and potato soup
● **Haggis** – minced lamb's or deer's liver and a collection of other meaty offal bits
● **Porridge** – boiled oats, often eaten for breakfast
● **Rumbledethumps** – mashed potato, swede and cabbage oven-baked with a cheesy topping
● **Scotch broth** – a thick soup of lamb, vegetables, barley, lentils and split peas
● **Stovies** – fried potatoes and onion mixed with left-over meat and baked in an oven

PLANNING YOUR WALK

### Evening meals

Stumbling across a good **pub** when you're on a long walk is like manna from heaven. There are some unique and interesting ones along the West Highland Way all used to the idiosyncrasies of walkers and sometimes having a separate 'boots' or 'climbers' bar where you won't be out of place with muddy boots and a rucksack. Not only a good place to revive flagging spirits in the middle of the day or early afternoon, the local pub (or 'hotel') is often your only choice for an evening meal. Many have à la carte restaurants, but most walkers choose something from the cheaper bar menu washed down by a pint of real ale and perhaps a nip of malt whisky to bring the day to a contented close. Menus include at least one vegetarian option.

In the larger villages and towns you'll have a wider choice with **takeaways** serving anything as long as it's fried, and good **restaurants** dishing up culinary selections from round the world.

### Buying camping supplies

There are enough shops along the Way to allow campers to buy **food** supplies frequently when cooking for themselves. All the shops are listed in Part 5. The longest you should need to carry food for is two days. Village shops are open year-round (though not always daily/all day) but those on campsites are typically only open in the main holiday season.

Getting **fuel** for camp stoves requires a little more planning. Gas canisters and methylated spirits are available in many general stores and campsite shops; Coleman Fuel is not so widely distributed. Special mention has been made in Part 5 of shops which sell fuel and the types they generally stock.

### Whisky, beer and water

Scotland is world famous for its alcohol production and most pubs and hotel bars have a good selection of whisky and beer. Scotch **whisky**, 'the water of life', is distilled from malted barley and other cereals and is either a blend, or a single malt made in one distillery. A connoisseur can tell the difference between single malts distilled in different parts of the country such as the West Coast, East Coast, Lowlands, Highlands, Isle of Islay, the list goes on, and many happy evenings can be spent brushing up on this neglected skill without coming to any conclusion about which is best. There can be little argument about which is the most appropriate whisky for walkers, however: the **Highland Way** is distilled, casked, matured, blended and bottled by the company of the same name, who took the trail as their inspiration, explaining that the stuff 'delicately captures the flavours of the glens, lochs and mountains that are unique to its heritage.' Ian Macleod is another distiller associated with the Way, with the **Glengoyne** distillery (🖳 www.glengoyne.com) only a few hundred metres from the trail near Dumgoyne.

Traditional **British ale**, beer, bitter, call it what you like, is the product of small-scale regional breweries who have created a huge diversity of strengths and flavours through skill and craftsmanship. Real ale continues to ferment in the cask so can be drawn off by hand pump or a simple tap in the cask itself. It

should not be confused with characteristically, industrially produced beer whose fermentation is stopped by pasteurisation and therefore needs the addition of gas to give it some life and fizz. Traditionally the Highlands have not been a happy hunting ground for the real ale enthusiast. In the last few years, however, there seems to have been a resurgence in craft brewing and the walker in Scotland shouldn't find it hard to track down a few quality pints, with over a hundred breweries (some of them tiny craft breweries) and more than a thousand micro-breweries now operating north of the border.

The West Highland Way goes right past the door of River Leven Ales in Kinlochleven, one of Scotland's popular craft breweries. Perhaps missing

Glengoyne Distillery (see p106) can easily be visited as it's near the Way.

a trick, however, the brewery have yet to name a beer after the trail, allowing the Loch Lomond Brewery (🖳 www.lochlomondbrewery.com) to attract the walker with their pale ale called West Highland Way (3.7%).

Recent winners of CAMRA's champion beer of Scotland include Weizen (5.2%ABV), brewed by Windswept Brewing (🖳 windsweptbrewing.com) who are based in Lossiemouth, and Jarle (3.8%ABV) from family-owned farm brewery Fyne Ales (🖳 fyneales.com). Another particularly interesting pint to try is Fraoch Heather Ale (🖳 www.williamsbrosbrew.com), which is flavoured with heather flowers to give you a real taste of the country you're walking over.

**Spring water**, 'a noble, royal, pleasant drink' as the Highland poet Duncan Ban Macintyre would have it, is readily available for the taking along much of the West Highland Way from Rowardennan northwards, gushing in trickles and torrents off the mountainsides. In the lowland parts of the Way you can fill up your water bottle in public toilets, or alternatively ask in shops, cafés or pubs if they would mind filling it up; most people are happy to do so.

See pp57-8 for further information on when and how to purify water.

## MONEY

Plan your money needs carefully. In the past, you needed to carry a fair amount of **cash** with you on the middle part of the walk as there are no banks or cash machines between Drymen and Tyndrum (though there is a post office with an ATM at Crianlarich, 20 minutes off the path). However, that has changed post-pandemic and many more businesses now accept **credit or debit card** payments. Nevertheless, it's a good idea to carry some cash as back up for those that don't. Larger shops and supermarkets may have a **cashback** service so you can obtain cash but often only if you buy something at the same time. Note that some cash machines/ATMs (not those at banks) charge you for making a cash withdrawal (usually the Link machines that are sometimes found in shops and post offices; some readers using cards issued by banks abroad have had them rejected by Link machines). Note that very few places will accept a **cheque** now. The table on p31 indicates the locations of post offices and banks. See also p39.

### Getting cash from a Post Office
Most banks in Britain have agreements with the Post Office allowing customers to make cash withdrawals using their debit card at post offices throughout the country. This is a useful facility on the West Highland Way where there are more post offices than banks. To find branches and check their services contact the Post Office (☎ 0345-611 2970, 🖳 postoffice.co.uk/branch-finder).

## OTHER SERVICES

Most of the settlements through which the Way passes have little more than a **general store** and a **post office** (which may have limited opening hours/days). The post office might be useful if you have discovered you are carrying too much in your rucksack and want to send unnecessary items home to lighten your load.

Where they exist, special mention has also been made in Part 5 of other services which are of use to walkers such as **banks**, **cash machines**, **outdoor equipment shops**, **laundrettes**, **pharmacies/chemists**, **medical/health centres** and **tourist information centres**.

## WALKING COMPANIES

For walkers wanting to make their holiday as easy and trouble free as possible there are several specialist companies offering a range of services from accommodation booking to fully guided group tours.

### Accommodation booking
Arranging all the accommodation for your walk can take a considerable amount of time but these companies will do it for you:

- Easyways (☎ 01324-714132, 🖳 easyways.com)
- Sherpa Van Project (☎ 01748-826917, 🖳 sherpavan.com)

### Baggage carriers
This is one service that's well worth the money! The following companies offer a baggage-carrying service either direct to your campsite/accommodation each night or to a drop-off point in each village from about £35 per rucksack for the whole Way; all you need to carry is a small daypack with essentials in it. If you are finding the walk harder than expected you can always join one of these services at a later stage. Note that they will take camping gear and visit campsites.

Some of the taxi firms listed in this guide (see Part 5) provide a similar service within a local area if you are having problems carrying your bags.

- AMS Scotland Ltd (☎ 01360-312840, 🖳 amsscotland.co.uk)
- Sherpa Van Project (☎ 01748-826917, 🖳 sherpavan.com)
- Travel-Lite (☎ 0141-956 7890, 🖳 travel-lite-uk.com)

### Self-guided holidays
The following companies provide all-in customised packages which usually include detailed advice and notes on itineraries and routes, maps, accommodation booking, daily baggage transfer, and transport arrangements at the start and end of your walk. Most companies offer a range of itineraries (taking from three to ten days) and offer the walk from south to north. However, almost all are flexible and will also tailor-make holidays including from north to south. If you don't want the whole package deal some companies can arrange accommodation-booking or baggage-carrying services on their own (see above).

- Absolute Escapes (☎ 0131-610 1210, 🖳 absoluteescapes.com), Edinburgh
- Alpine Exploratory (☎ 0131 214 1144, 🖳 alpineexploratory.com), Edinburgh
- Celtic Trails (☎ 01291-689774, 🖳 celtictrailswalkingholidays.co.uk), Chepstow
- Contours Holidays (☎ 01629-821900, 🖳 contours.co.uk), Derbyshire
- Discovery Travel (☎ 01983-301133, 🖳 discoverytravel.co.uk), Isle of Wight
- Easyways (☎ 01324-714132, 🖳 easyways.com), Falkirk
- Gemini Walks (☎ 01324-410260, 🖳 geminiwalks.com), Stirlingshire

- Great British Walks (☎ 01600-713008, 💻 great-british-walks.com), Monmouth
- Hillwalk Tours (☎ +353 91-763994, 💻 hillwalktours.com), Ireland
- Let's Go Walking (☎ 01837-880075, 💻 letsgowalking.co.uk), Devon
- Macs Adventure (☎ 0141-530 8886, 💻 macsadventure.com), Glasgow
- Mickledore Travel (☎ 017687-72335, 💻 mickledore.co.uk), Keswick
- North-West Frontiers (☎ 01997-421474, 💻 nwfrontiers.com), Strathpeffer
- NorthWest Walks (☎ 01257-424889, 💻 northwestwalks.co.uk), Wigan
- The Natural Adventure (☎ 0203-962 1455, 💻 thenaturaladventure.com), London
- Thistle Trekking (☎ 07375-789173, 💻 thistletrekking.co.uk), Cumbria
- Transcotland Holidays (☎ 01887-820848, 💻 transcotland.com), Perthshire
- Walkabout Scotland (☎ 0131-261 6470, 💻 walkaboutscotland.com), Edinburgh
- Walkers' Britain (☎ 0208-875 5070, 💻 walkersbritain.co.uk), London
- Walkers Ways (☎ 07971-815248, 💻 walkersways.co.uk), Stirlingshire
- Wilderness Scotland (☎ 01479-420020, 💻 wildernessscotland.com), Aviemore

### Group/guided walking tours

Fully guided tours are ideal for individuals wanting to travel with others and for groups of friends wanting to be guided. Packages usually include meals, accommodation, transport arrangements, mini-bus backup, baggage transfer, as well as a qualified guide. Companies' specialities differ with varying size of groups, standards of accommodation, age range of clients, distances walked and professionalism of guides; it's worth checking out several before making a booking.

- Adventure Solos (☎ 080011-23411 , 💻 adventuresolos.com) Small groups of solo walkers with accommodation a mix of hostels and camping.
- Alpine Exploratory (☎ 0131-214 1144, 💻 alpineexploratory.com) Happy to arrange on request.
- HF Holidays (☎ 0345-470 7558, 💻 hfholidays.co.uk) runs a 9-day full-board package with the last four nights at their own country house hotel, Altshellach
- NorthWest Walks (☎ 01257-424889, 💻 northwestwalks.co.uk) offers a 9-day holiday, south to north.
- Thistle Trekking (☎ 07375-789173, 💻 thistletrekking.co.uk) offers a 7 days walking/8 nights' accommodation holiday.
- Tracks and Trails Ltd (☎ 0208-144 6442, 💻 tracks-and-trails.com) offers a 7 days walking/8 nights accommodation holiday.
- Walkabout Scotland (☎ 0131-261 6470, 💻 walkaboutscotland.com) offers 7 days' walking on scheduled departures and bespoke as required.
- Wilderness Scotland (☎ 01479-420020, 💻 wildernessscotland.com) offer a 7 nights/8-days walking holiday.

### WALKING WITH DOGS                            (see also pp198-9)

You can take your dog with you along all of the West Highland Way for most of the year. The old restrictions around Conic Hill, Inversnaid to Crianlarich and

PLANNING YOUR WALK

Tyndrum to Bridge of Orchy no longer apply, provided that your dog is kept under proper control. The only exception to this is on the eastern side of Conic Hill where there are two enclosed lambing fields, which may be closed for up to six weeks (though usually for about four weeks) between mid April and mid May. Precisely when the trail in this section is closed to dogs is announced only in March. If you do come with your dog at this time, you will be sent on a diversion via Milton of Buchanan.

Though the path is now open to dogs for most of the year, owners are still expected to keep their dogs under close control on a short lead in areas of farmland, in public places, and in moorland, forests and grasslands during the bird breeding season that runs from April to July. You should also always clear up after your dog when it defecates on the walk. A number of guest houses and B&Bs accept dogs, though in many cases this is by arrangement; look for the 🐕 symbol in the accommodation information in Parts 4 & 5. See also pp198-9.

---

❏ INFORMATION FOR FOREIGN VISITORS

● **Currency** The British pound (£) comes in notes of £50, £20, £10 and £5, and coins of £2 and £1. The pound is divided into 100 pence (usually referred to as 'p', pronounced 'pee') which comes in silver coins of 50p, 20p, 10p and 5p, and copper coins of 2p and 1p.

● **Money** Up-to-date **rates of exchange** can be found on 🖳 xe.com/ucc, at some post offices, or at any bank or travel agent.

● **Business hours** Most **shops** and main **post offices** are open at least from Monday to Friday 9am-5pm and Saturday 9am-12.30pm. Many choose longer hours and some open on Sundays as well. Scottish **banks** open Monday to Friday from as early as 9am to as late as 5.30pm; some also open on Saturday from 9am to 12.30pm. As a rule of thumb most are open from at least 10am to 4pm Monday to Friday. **Pubs** are generally open 11am-11pm Monday to Saturday and 12.30-3pm & 7-10.30pm on Sunday. However, opening hours are flexible so some remain open until 1am although mostly in urban rather than rural areas.

● **National (bank) holidays** Most businesses in Scotland are shut on Jan 1st and 2nd, Good Friday (Mar/Apr), the first and last Mondays in May, the first Monday in Aug, Dec 25th and 26th. Some businesses also close on St Andrew's Day, Nov 30th.

● **School holidays** School holidays in Scotland are generally: a one-/two-week break mid October, two weeks around Christmas and the New Year, up to a week mid February, 2-3 weeks around Easter, and from late June/early July to mid August.

● **EHICs and travel insurance** Although the UK's National Health Service (NHS) is free at the point of use, that is only the case for residents. All visitors to Britain should be properly insured, including comprehensive health coverage. Though the UK has left the EU, the European Health Insurance Card (EHIC) does still entitle EU nationals (on production of the EHIC, so ensure you bring it with you) to necessary medical treatment under the NHS while on a temporary visit here. To make sure this is still the case when you visit, however, contact your national social security institution. Also note that the EHIC is not a substitute for proper medical cover on your travel insurance for unforeseen bills and for getting you home should that be necessary. Also consider cover for loss and theft of personal belongings, especially if you are camping or staying in hostels, as there may be times when you'll have to leave your luggage unattended.

You can find out the latest information about walking with your dog by visiting 🖳 outdooraccess-scotland.com.

## MOUNTAIN BIKING

The West Highland Way is designed and maintained as a walking route. There are a few sections which would be suitable for mountain biking, particularly some parts of the old military and drove roads in the north. However, they are interspersed with lengthy, unrideable parts making it impractical and unfulfilling to plan a ride of anything longer than a couple of hours or so along the trail. Tackling longer sections of the Way is really not an option.

The number of people walking also detracts from the Way's suitability as an off-road route. You'll be constantly slowing down to pass walkers and be unable to ride as hard as you might like. Rather than stir up antagonism, why not use the mountain bike's potential to really get off the beaten track.

---

• **Weights and measures** In Britain, milk can still be sold in pints (1 pint = 568ml), as can beer in pubs, though most other liquid including petrol (gasoline) and diesel is sold in litres. Distances on road and path signs will continue to be given in miles (1 mile = 1.61km) rather than kilometres, and yards (1yd = 0.9m) rather than metres. The population remains divided between those who still use inches (1 inch = 2.5cm), feet (1ft = 0.3m) and yards and those who are happy with millimetres, centimetres and metres; you'll often be told that 'it's only a hundred yards or so' to somewhere, rather than a hundred metres or so.

Most food is sold in metric weights (g and kg) but the imperial weights of pounds (lb: 1lb = 453g) and ounces (oz: 1oz = 28g) are frequently displayed too. The weather – a frequent topic of conversation – is also an issue: while most forecasts predict temperatures in Celsius (C), many people continue to think in terms of Fahrenheit (F; see the temperature chart on p16 for conversions).

• **Smoking** The ban on smoking in public places relates not only to pubs and restaurants, but also to B&Bs, hostels and hotels. These latter have the right to designate one or more bedrooms where the occupants can smoke, but the ban is in force in all enclosed areas open to the public – even if they are in a private home such as a B&B. Should you be foolhardy enough to light up in a no-smoking area, which includes pretty much any indoor public place, you could be fined £50, but it's the owners of the premises who carry the can if they fail to stop you, with a potential fine of £2500.

• **Time** During the winter, the whole of Britain is on Greenwich Mean Time (GMT). The clocks move one hour forward on the last Sunday in March, remaining on British Summer Time (BST) until the last Sunday in October.

• **Telephone** From outside Britain the international country access code for Britain is ☎ 44 followed by the area code minus the first 0, and then the number you require. Within Britain, to call a landline number with the same code as the landline phone you are calling from, the code can be omitted: dial the number only. If you're using a mobile phone that is registered overseas, consider buying a local SIM card to keep costs down.

• **Emergency services** For police, ambulance, fire or coastguard dial either ☎ 999 or ☎ 112.

PLANNING YOUR WALK

# Budgeting

If you're **camping**, most sites charge around £7-10 per person so you can get by on as little as £15-20 per person per day using the cheapest sites and the free 'wild' sites/bothies as often as possible. This assumes you would be cooking all your own food from staple ingredients rather than eating convenience food. Most people find that the best-laid plans to survive on the bare minimum fall flat after a couple of hard days' walking or in bad weather. Assuming the odd end-of-day drink and the occasional pub meal or takeaway, a budget of £20-25 is more realistic.

A **bunkhouse/hostel** bed costs from about £18 to £25 per person. Every SYHA hostel has a self-catering kitchen (but not all independent hostels/bunkhouses do) and the larger ones offer breakfast (£5-7), packed lunches (£5-7) and evening meals (about £10-12). Allowing £35-45 per day will enable you to have the occasional meal out and enjoy sampling a few of the local brews. If you don't want to carry a stove, cook in a hostel's kitchen or are planning on eating out most nights add another £15 per day.

If you're staying in **B&Bs**, you won't be cooking for yourself. Bearing in mind that B&B prices vary enormously, £60-75 per person per day is a rough guide based on spending £25-35 on a packed lunch, evening pub meal and a couple of drinks. If staying in a **guesthouse** or **hotel** expect to spend £65-85 per day. If you are travelling alone you must also expect to pay a single occupancy supplement. See also p21.

Don't forget to set some money aside, perhaps £100-150, for the inevitable extras: postcards, bus/train fares, taxis, cream teas, whisky and beer, using a baggage-carrying service, or any changes of plan.

**Note also that in 2022 the UK entered a period of increased inflation at a rate higher than for many years. Prices in this book, though correct as we go to press, will inevitably rise.**

# Itineraries

Walkers are individuals. Some like to cover large distances as quickly as possible, others are happy to stroll along stopping whenever the fancy takes them. You may want to walk the West Highland Way all in one go, tackle it over a series of weekends or use the trail for linear day walks; the choice is yours. To accommodate these differences this guidebook has not been divided into rigid daily stages which often leads to a fixed mindset of how you should walk. Instead, it's been designed to make it easy for you to plan your own perfect itinerary.

## VILLAGE AND TOWN FACILITIES

| PLACE* | DISTANCE* MILES/KM | BANK (ATM) | POST OFFICE* | TOURIST INFO* | EATING PLACE* | FOOD SHOP* | CAMP-SITE* | BUNK/ HOSTEL* | B&B* |
|---|---|---|---|---|---|---|---|---|---|
| (Glasgow) | | ✓✓ | ✓✓✓ | TIC | ✓✓✓ | ✓✓✓ | | YHA/H | ✓✓✓ |
| Milngavie | WHW start | ✓✓ | ✓ | | ✓✓✓ | ✓✓✓ | | | ✓✓ |
| (Blanefield) | | ATM | | | ✓✓ | ✓ | | | |
| Strathblane | | | | | ✓ | | | | ✓ |
| Dumgoyne | 7/11.5 | | ✓ | | ✓✓✓ | | | | |
| (Killearn) | | ATM | | | ✓✓ | ✓ | | | |
| Easter Drumquhassle | 4/6.5 | | | | | | ✓✓ | | ✓ |
| Drymen | 1/1.5 | ATM | ✓ | | ✓✓✓ | ✓ | | B | ✓✓✓ |
| Balmaha | 11/17 | | | NPC | ✓✓ | ✓ | ✓ | | ✓✓✓ |
| Cashel | 3/5 | | | | | | ✓✓✓ | | |
| Rowardennan | 4/6 | | | | ✓ | | | YHA/B | ✓ |
| | | | | | | | | (Rowchoish bothy) | |
| Inversnaid | 7/11 | | | | ✓✓ | | (✓) | B | ✓✓ |
| | | | | | | | (Doune Byre bothy) | | |
| (Ardlui) | | | | | ✓ | | | B | ✓ |
| Inverarnan | 6.5/10 | | | | ✓✓ | (✓) | ✓ | B | ✓✓✓ |
| Crianlarich | 6.5/10 | ATM | ✓ | | ✓✓✓ | ✓ | | YHA | ✓✓✓ |
| Strathfillan | 3.5/6 | | | | ✓✓ | ✓ | ✓ | B | ✓✓ |
| Tyndrum | 2.5/4 | ATM | ✓ | | ✓✓✓ | ✓✓ | ✓ | B/H | ✓✓✓ |
| Bridge of Orchy | 7/11 | | (✓) | | ✓ | | (✓) | B | ✓ |
| Inveroran | 3/5 | | | | ✓ | | (✓) | | ✓ |
| Glencoe Ski Ctr | 8/10 | | | | ✓ | | ✓ | B | |
| Kingshouse | 2/3 | | | | ✓ | | | B | ✓ |
| (Glencoe) | | ATM | ✓ | VC | ✓✓ | ✓ | ✓ | YHA/H/B | ✓✓✓ |
| Kinlochleven | 8.5/14 | ATM | ✓ | VC | ✓✓✓ | ✓✓ | ✓ | B/H | ✓✓✓ |
| Glen Nevis | 12.5/20 | | | VC | ✓✓ | (✓) | ✓ | YHA/H/B | ✓ |
| Fort William | 2/3 | ✓✓ | ✓ | TIC | ✓✓✓ | ✓✓✓ | | B/H | ✓✓✓ |

PLANNING YOUR WALK

### *NOTES

**PLACE**  Places in brackets (eg Blanefield) are a short walk off the route. Glencoe, however, is 9 miles/14.5km off the West Highland Way.

**DISTANCE**  Distances given are between places directly on the West Highland Way. Gartness, for example, is 10 miles/16km from Milngavie.

**TOURIST INFO**  TIC = Tourist information centre; VC = visitor centre; NPC = national park centre

**POST OFFICE**  (✓) = only open a few hours a week

**EATING PLACE**  ✓ = one place, 𝗪 = two, 𝗪𝗪 = three or more; (✓) = seasonal

**FOOD SHOP**  (✓) = seasonal    **CAMPSITE**  (✓) = wild camping

**BUNK/HOSTEL**  YHA = Youth hostel, H = independent hostel, B = bunkhouse/cabins

**B&B**  ✓ = one place, 𝗪 = two, 𝗪𝗪 = three or more

❑ WALKING FROM GLASGOW TO MILNGAVIE

Highly recommended is to add an extra (short) day to your itinerary and walk from the centre of Glasgow to Milngavie and the official start of the West Highland Way. Far from trudging along pavements beside busy streets, as you might imagine a walk out of a city might entail, you follow two rivers, the Kelvin and the Allander, through parks and then beside fields. Two official footpaths, the **Kelvin Walkway** and the **Allander Walkway**, follow the rivers and if you stay overnight near Kelvingrove Park, you can join the route right there.

From Kelvingrove Park to Milngavie is approximately 10 miles (16km) and this easy day's walk is a great way to start; see pp94-8.

The **overview map** and **stage maps** (see end of the book) and **table of village and town facilities** (p31) summarise the essential information.

Alternatively, to make it even easier, have a look at the **suggested itineraries** (see opposite) and simply choose your preferred type of accommodation and speed of walking.

There are also suggestions on p34 for those who want to experience the best of the trail over a day or a weekend. The **public transport map and table** on pp46-9 may also be useful at this stage.

Having made a rough plan, turn to **Part 5**, where you will find summaries of the route; full descriptions of accommodation, places to eat and other services in each village and town; as well as detailed trail maps.

## WHICH DIRECTION?

Most walkers find the lure of the Highlands, and Ben Nevis in particular, more appealing than the suburbs of Glasgow so walk the Way south to north. This traditional northern direction of travel has been followed in the layout of this book. There are other practical reasons for heading north rather than south; the prevailing wind and rain (south-westerly) is behind you, as is the sun, and the gentler walking is at the start giving you time to warm up before tackling the steeper climbs of the last few days.

That said, there is no reason why you shouldn't walk in the other direction, especially if just tackling a part of the Way. The maps in Part 5 give timings for both directions and, as route-finding instructions are on the maps rather than in blocks of text, it is straightforward using this guide back to front.

## SUGGESTED ITINERARIES

These itineraries (opposite) are suggestions only; adapt them to your needs. They have been divided into different accommodation types and each table has different itineraries to encompass different walking paces. **Don't forget to add your travelling time before and after the walk**.

## CAMPING

| Night | Relaxed Place | Distance miles/km | Medium Place | Distance miles/km | Fast Place | Distance miles/km |
|---|---|---|---|---|---|---|
| 0 | Milngavie | | Milngavie | | Milngavie | |
| 1 | E Drumquhassle | 10/16 | E Drumquhassle | 10/16 | E Drumquhassle | 10/16 |
| 2 | Loch Lomond | 11/18 | Sallochy | 14.5/23.5 | Sallochy | 14.5/23.5 |
| 3 | Rowchoish Bothy | 8.5/13.5 | Inverarnan | 15/24 | Inverarnan | 15/24 |
| 4 | Inverarnan | 13.5/22 | Strathfillan | 9/14.5 | Bridge of Orchy | 19.5/31.5 |
| 5 | Strathfillan | 9/14.5 | Bridge of Orchy | 10/16 | Glencoe Mt Ctr* | 11/18 |
| 6 | Bridge of Orchy | 10/16 | Glencoe Mt Ctr* | 11/18 | Kinlochleven | 10.5/17 |
| 7 | Glencoe Mt Ctr* | 11/18 | Kinlochleven | 10.5/17 | Glen Nevis | 12.5/20 |
| 8 | Kinlochleven | 10.5/17 | Glen Nevis | 12.5/20 | | |
| 9 | Glen Nevis | 12.5/20 | | | | |

*Note that the extra weight of camping equipment is likely to add a day onto your trip compared with staying in hostels or B&Bs. See p53: Loch Lomond camping restrictions.*
*\* or walk 2 miles further on to Kingshouse and take the bus to Glencoe.*

## STAYING IN BUNKHOUSES & HOSTELS

| Night | Relaxed Place | Distance miles/km | Medium Place | Distance miles/km | Fast Place | Distance miles/km |
|---|---|---|---|---|---|---|
| 0 | Milngavie | | Milngavie | | Milngavie | |
| 1 | Drymen | 12/19.5 | Drymen | 12/19.5 | Balmaha | 19/30.5 |
| 2 | Rowardennan | 14/22.5 | Rowardennan | 14/22.5 | Rowardennan | 7/11.5 |
| 3 | Inverarnan | 13.5/22 | Inverarnan | 13.5/22 | Inverarnan | 13.5/22 |
| 4 | Tyndrum | 12.5/20 | Bridge of Orchy | 19.5/31.5 | Bridge of Orchy | 19.5/31.5 |
| 5 | Bridge of Orchy | 7/11.5 | Kingshouse* | 13/21 | Kinlochleven | 21.5/34.5 |
| 6 | Kingshouse* | 13/21 | Kinlochleven | 8.5/13.5 | Fort William** | 15/24 |
| 7 | Kinlochleven | 8.5/13.5 | Fort William** | 15/24 | | |
| 8 | Fort William** | 15/24 | | | | |

*\* or in Glencoe, 9 miles (14.5km) off the Way. Catch a bus or hitchhike from Kingshouse to Glencoe and back again.*
*\*\* or Glen Nevis – 12.5miles (20km) from Kinlochleven.*

## STAYING IN B&Bs

| Night | Relaxed Place | Distance miles/km | Medium Place | Distance miles/km | Fast Place | Distance miles/km |
|---|---|---|---|---|---|---|
| 0 | Milngavie | | Milngavie | | Milngavie | |
| 1 | Drymen | 12/19.5 | Drymen | 12/19.5 | Balmaha | 19/30.5 |
| 2 | Rowardennan | 14/22.5 | Rowardennan | 14/22.5 | Inversnaid | 14/22.5 |
| 3 | Inverarnan | 13.5/22 | Inverarnan | 13.5/22 | Tyndrum | 19/30.5 |
| 4 | Strathfillan | 9/14.5 | Tyndrum | 12.5/20 | Kingshouse | 20/32 |
| 5 | Bridge of Orchy | 10/16 | Kingshouse | 20/32 | Kinlochleven | 8.5/13.5 |
| 6 | Kingshouse | 13/21 | Kinlochleven | 8.5/13.5 | Fort William | 15/24 |
| 7 | Kinlochleven | 8.5/13.5 | Fort William | 15/24 | | |
| 8 | Fort William | 15/24 | | | | |

## HILLWALKING SIDE TRIPS

The majesty of the Highlands can only be fully grasped by climbing out of the valleys and onto the summits. The West Highland Way passes below many of the best-loved mountains in Scotland presenting the well-equipped walker with a wonderful opportunity for a few days' hillwalking. There are detailed route descriptions in Part 5 for climbing the two most popular peaks, Ben Lomond and Ben Nevis, and planning information for a few other convenient peaks above Bridge of Orchy, between Inveroran and Kingshouse, and in Glen Coe.

Popular routes to the top of over 40 Munros (see box opposite) leave either from or near the West Highland Way so there's ample scope for peak bagging if

❏ DAY AND WEEKEND WALKS

There's nothing quite like walking a whole long-distance footpath from beginning to end but some people just don't have the time. The following highlights offer outstanding walking and scenery coupled with good public transport (see pp46-9) at the start and finish. If you are fit and experienced and like the idea of a challenge, each of the weekend walks can be walked in a long day.

### Day walks

● **Milngavie to Killearn**  An easy 9-mile (14.5km) walk straight out of the city into beautiful countryside with buses from Killearn to get you back; see pp103-11.

● **Drymen to Balmaha via Conic Hill**  A spectacular 7-mile (11.5km) walk climbing to the top of Conic Hill with wonderful views over Loch Lomond; see pp116-21.

● **Rowardennan to Inversnaid**  A 7-mile (11.5km) walk along the pretty eastern shore of Loch Lomond and taking a boat back (see p132 and pp125-6); see pp128-33.

● **Rowardennan to Inverarnan**  An extension of the above suggestion taking in the wildest stretch of Loch Lomond, 13½ miles (22km); see pp128-39.

● **Bridge of Orchy to Kingshouse**  A beautiful and challenging 13-mile (21km) walk across Rannoch Moor, see pp155-62.

● **Kingshouse to Kinlochleven**  A wonderful 8½-mile (13.5km) mountain walk up the Devil's Staircase packed with stunning views – Glen Coe, the Mamores, Ben Nevis, Blackwater Reservoir and Loch Leven; see pp166-76.

### Weekend walks

● **Balmaha to Inverarnan**  A lovely 20½-mile (33km) walk along the eastern shore of Loch Lomond staying overnight at Rowardennan, Rowchoish Bothy or Inversnaid; see pp121-39. If you want to add a few extra miles either start at Drymen or climb Ben Lomond en route.

● **Inverarnan south to Rowardennan**  A wild walk along Loch Lomond (13½ miles, 22km) on the first day, with a fitting finish **climbing Ben Lomond**, Scotland's most southerly Munro, the next day; see from p134 back to p125.

● **Bridge of Orchy to Kinlochleven**  21½ miles (34.5km) combining two of the most spectacular day walks above; see pp155-76.

● **Kingshouse to Fort William**  A strenuous 23-mile (37km) mountain walk through the heart of the Highlands finishing at the foot of Ben Nevis, Britain's highest mountain. If you have an extra day you could climb 'the Ben' as well; see pp166-86

❏ **MUNROS**

In 1891 Sir Hugh Munro, soldier, diplomat and founder member of the Scottish Mountaineering Club (SMC), published a list of all Scottish mountains over the magical height of 3000ft (or the rather clumsy metric equivalent of 914m). He had been aware that many peaks had gone unrecognised and his new tables came up with 538 'tops' over 3000ft, 283 of which, because of certain distinguishing features, merited the status of 'separate mountains'. Unwittingly he had given birth to the mountaineering equivalent of train-spotting; ticking off as many 'Munros' as possible by climbing to their summit. The craze caught on quickly. By 1901 Reverend Robertson was the first to climb them all and since then over 6000 hill walkers have followed his lead.

'Munro-bagging' has encouraged many walkers to explore some of the finest country in Scotland, luring them away from the popular honey-pot areas to reach a specific hill. Yet when it becomes an obsession, as it frequently does, there is a danger that other equally wonderful areas of wild land are ignored and the true esoteric reasons for walking are lost. Much to the dismay of purists the goalposts occasionally shift as the tables are revised following the latest surveying data. The number of Munros currently stands at 282. Interestingly Sir Hugh never completed his own round, failing repeatedly to climb the Inaccessible Pinnacle on Skye before he died at the age of 63.

you are bitten by that bug. See some of the walking guidebooks, including Trailblazer's *Scottish Highlands Hillwalking Guide*, on p42 for more information.

Although not particularly high when compared with other mountains round the world, the Scottish mountains can be dangerous for the unprepared at any time of year. Read 'Mountain Safety' on p57, and also 'Access' on pp53-5 to make sure your planned walk doesn't interfere with other users of the hills.

# What to take

How much you take with you is a very personal decision which takes experience to get right. For those new to long-distance walking the suggestions below will help you strike a sensible balance between comfort, safety and minimal weight.

## KEEP YOUR LUGGAGE LIGHT

In these days of huge material wealth it can be a liberating experience to travel **as light as possible** to learn how few possessions we really need to be safe and comfortable. It is all too easy to take things along 'just in case' and these little items can soon mount up. If you are in any doubt about anything on your packing list, be ruthless and leave it at home.

To liberate themselves entirely from their luggage, many people now make use of **baggage-carrying companies** (see p26).

PLANNING YOUR WALK

## HOW TO CARRY IT

The size of your **rucksack** depends on how you plan to walk. If you are camping along the Way you will need a pack large enough to hold a tent, sleeping bag, cooking equipment and food; 65 to 75 litres' capacity should be ample. This should have a stiffened back system and either be fully adjustable, or exactly the right size for your back. If you carry the main part of the load high and close to your body with a large proportion of the weight carried on your hips (not on your shoulders) by means of the padded hip belt you should be able to walk in comfort for days on end. Play around with different ways of packing your gear and adjusting all those straps until you get it just right. It's also handy to have a **bum/waist bag** or a very light **day pack** in which you can carry your camera, guidebook and other essentials when you go off sightseeing or for a day walk.

If you are staying in bunkhouses or wigwams you may want to carry a sleeping bag (see p39) and possibly a small stove and pan, though arguably neither of these is essential (see p19); a 40- to 60-litre pack should be fine. If you are indulging in the luxury of B&Bs you should be able to get all you need into a 30- to 40-litre pack.

Pack similar things in different-coloured **stuff sacks** so they are easier to pull out of the dark recesses of your pack. Put these inside **waterproof rucksack liners**, or tough plastic sacks, that can be slipped inside your pack to protect everything from the inevitable rain. It's also worth taking a **waterproof rucksack cover**; most rucksacks these days have them 'built in' to the sack, but you can also buy them separately for less than a tenner.

Of course, if you decide to use one of the baggage-carrying services you can pack most of your things in a **suitcase** and simply carry a small day-pack with the essentials you need for the day's walking.

## FOOTWEAR

### Boots

Your boots are the **single most important item** that can affect the enjoyment of your walk. In summer you could get by with a light pair of trail shoes if you're carrying only a small pack, although they don't give much support for your ankles and you'll get wet, cold feet if there is any rain. Some of the terrain is rough so a good pair of walking boots would be a safer option. They must fit well and be properly broken in. A week's walk is not the time to try out a new pair of boots. Refer to p58 for some blister-avoidance strategies.

If you plan to climb any of the mountains along the Way, good boots are essential. For winter hillwalking side-trips your boots must be able to take crampons.

### Socks

The traditional wearing of a thin liner sock under a thicker wool sock is no longer necessary if you choose a high-quality sock specially designed for walking. A high proportion of natural fibres makes them much more comfortable. Three pairs are ample. Some people, however, still prefer to use thin liner socks (silk being best) as these are much easier to wash than thick socks, so you can change them more regularly.

### Extra footwear
Some walkers like to have a second pair of shoes to wear when they are not on the trail. Trainers, sport sandals or flip-flops are all suitable as long as they are light.

## CLOTHES

Scotland's wet and cold weather is notorious; even in summer you should come prepared for wintry conditions. It can also be spectacularly glorious so clothes to cope with these wide variations are needed. Experienced walkers pick their clothes according to the versatile layering system: a base layer to transport sweat from your skin; a mid-layer or two to keep you warm; and an outer layer or 'shell' to protect you from any wind, rain or snow.

### Base layer
Cotton absorbs sweat, trapping it next to the skin which will chill you rapidly when you stop exercising. A thin lightweight **thermal top** made from synthetic material is better as it draws moisture away keeping you dry. It will be cool if worn on its own in hot weather and warm when worn under other clothes in cooler conditions. A spare would be sensible. You may also like to bring a **shirt** for wearing in the evening.

### Mid-layers
From May to September a woollen jumper or mid-weight polyester **fleece** will suffice. For the rest of the year you will need an extra layer to keep you warm. Both wool and fleece, unlike cotton, stay reasonably warm when wet.

### Outer layer
A **waterproof jacket** is essential year-round and will be much more comfortable (but also more expensive) if it's also 'breathable' to prevent the build-up of condensation on the inside. This layer can also be worn to keep the wind off.

### Leg wear
Whatever you wear on your legs it should be light, quick-drying and not restricting. Many British walkers find polyester tracksuit bottoms comfortable. Poly-cotton or microfibre trousers are excellent. Denim jeans should never be worn; if they get wet they become heavy and cold, and bind to your legs.

A pair of **shorts** is nice to have on sunny days. Thermal **longjohns** or thick tights are cosy if you're camping and necessary for winter walking.

**Waterproof trousers** are necessary most of the year but in summer could be left behind if your main pair of trousers is reasonably windproof and quick-drying. **Gaiters** are not needed unless you come across a lot of snow in winter.

### Underwear

Three changes of what you normally wear is fine. Women may find a **sports bra** more comfortable because pack straps can cause bra straps to dig into your shoulders.

### Other clothes

A **warm hat** and **gloves** should be carried at all times of the year. Take two pairs of gloves in winter. In summer you should carry a **sun hat** and possibly a **swimsuit** if you enjoy swimming in cold lochs and rivers (or one of the heated pools along the way). There are also a few swimming pools along the route which can be good at the end of a hot day. A small **towel** will be needed if you are not staying in B&Bs. If camping in summer a **head net** to protect you from the midges can be invaluable. These can be bought at various places along the Way.

## TOILETRIES

Only take the minimum: a small bar of **soap** in a plastic container (unless staying in B&Bs) which can also be used instead of shaving cream and for washing clothes; a tiny tube of **toothpaste** and a **toothbrush**; and one roll of **loo paper** in a plastic bag. If you are planning to defecate outdoors a lightweight **trowel** for burying the evidence (see p52 for further tips) can be helpful.

In addition a **razor**; **tampons/sanitary towels**; **deodorant**; a high-factor **sun screen**; and a good **insect repellent** for the midges (see pp58-9) should cover all your needs.

## FIRST-AID KIT

You need only a small kit to cover common problems and emergencies; pack it in a waterproof container.

A basic kit will contain **Ibuprofen** or **paracetamol** for treating mild to moderate pain and fever; **plasters/Band Aids** for minor cuts; 'moleskin', 'Compeed', or 'Second Skin' for blisters; a **bandage** for holding dressings, splints, or limbs in place and for supporting a sprained ankle; an **elastic knee support** (tubigrip) for a weak knee; a small selection of different-sized **sterile dressings** for wounds; **porous adhesive tape**; **antiseptic wipes**; **antiseptic cream**; **safety pins**; **tweezers**; **scissors**.

## GENERAL ITEMS

### Essential

Most walkers carry **mobile/cell phones** (don't forget to bring the charger) but it is important to remember that the network may not provide full coverage of the area through which you are walking owing to the terrain. Anyone walking in the mountains should carry a 'Silva' type **compass** and understand how to use it; the modern equivalent, a **GPS** (see pp17-18) or **GPS-enabled smartphone**, can be just as useful though again you need to know how to use GPS properly and to make sure it's fully charged when you leave. An emergency **whistle** for summoning assistance is a good idea, as are the following: a **water bottle** or **pouch** holding at least one litre; a **torch** (flashlight) in case you end up walking after dark and want to save the battery on your mobile phone by not using the phone's flashlight; **emergency food** which your body can quickly convert into energy (see p56); a **penknife**; a **watch** with an alarm; and several degradable **plastic bags** for packing out any rubbish you accumulate.

If you're not carrying a sleeping bag or tent you should also carry an emergency plastic **bivvy bag**.

## Useful

The quality of the **camera** on a smartphone these days is impressive, though most serious photographers would still prefer to use an **SLR**. That said, it can be liberating to travel without one once in a while; a **notebook** can be a more accurate way of recording your impressions; a **book** to pass the time on train and bus journeys or for the evenings; a pair of **sunglasses** in summer or when there's snow on the ground; **binoculars** for observing wildlife; a **walking stick** or **walking poles** to take the shock off your knees; and a **vacuum flask** for carrying hot drinks.

## SLEEPING BAG

Unless you are staying in B&Bs all the way you will find a sleeping bag useful. Bunkhouses and hostels always have some bedding but you'll keep your costs down if you don't have to hire it. A three-season bag will cope with most eventualities although many walkers will be able to make do with one rated for one or two seasons; it's a personal choice.

## CAMPING GEAR

If you're camping you will need a decent **tent** (or bivvy bag if you enjoy travelling light) able to withstand wet and windy weather with netting on the entrance to keep the midges at bay; a **sleeping mat** (also invaluable for anyone planning to stay in a bothy); a **stove** and **fuel** (there is special mention in Part 5 of which shops stock which fuel; bottles of meths and the various gas cylinders are readily available, Coleman fuel is sometimes harder to find); a **pan** with a lid that can double as a frying pan/plate is fine for two people; a **pan handle**; a **mug**; a **spoon**; and a wire/plastic **scrubber** for washing up (there's no need for washing-up liquid and, anyway, it should never be used in streams, lochs or rivers). **Incense sticks** to burn by your tent have been recommended as a midge repellent.

## MONEY

There are few banks on the West Highland Way so you will need to carry some **cash**, especially if you do not have an account with a bank that has an agreement with the Post Office (see p25). A **debit card** is the easiest way to draw money either from banks or cash machines and that or a **credit card** can often

**❏ SOURCES OF FURTHER INFORMATION**

**Trail information**
● **West Highland Way website** The latest information on the trail can be found on the West Highland Way's dedicated website: 🖳 **www.westhighlandway.org** which also sells maps and books. It is run by the Loch Lomond & the Trossachs National Park Authority whose main website is also useful: 🖳 lochlomond-trossachs.org.
● **Rangers** (🖳 outdoorhighlands.co.uk)  West Highland Way rangers can provide knowledgeable advice and information about all aspects of the trail.
● 🖳 **tyndrumbytheway.com**  The website for Tyndrum By The Way Hostel and Campsite (see p146) has some good links.

**Tourist information**
● **Tourist information centres (TICs)**  Provide all manner of locally specific information for visitors. A few also still offer accommodation booking (usually for a fee), though this has mostly been surpassed by the rise of websites such as 🖳 booking.com and 🖳 hotels.com. There are TICs at either end of the Way in **Glasgow** (see p82) and **Fort William** (see p188), plus a national park centre at **Balmaha** (see p116) and visitor centres at **Glencoe** (see p164) and **Glen Nevis** (see p174).

**Tourist boards** For general information on the whole of Scotland see **VisitScotland** (🖳 www.visitscotland.com), formerly the Scottish Tourist Board. There are links to the regions, some of which have their own websites – eg **Glasgow** (🖳 peoplemake-glasgow.com). However, for accommodation along the Way their listings are not as comprehensive as this guidebook's since they include only paying members.

**Organisations for walkers**
● **Backpackers Club** (🖳 backpackersclub.co.uk)  Aimed at people who are involved or interested in lightweight camping through walking, cycling, skiing, canoeing, etc. They produce a quarterly magazine, provide members with a comprehensive advisory and information service on all aspects of backpacking and also publish a farm-pitch directory. Membership is £20/30 individual/family per year.
● **British Mountaineering Council** (🖳 thebmc.co.uk)  Promotes the interests of British hillwalkers, climbers and mountaineers. Among the many benefits of membership are an excellent information service, a quarterly magazine and travel insurance designed for mountain sports. Annual membership is £40, though they are currently offering 25% off the first year of membership if paying by direct debit.
● **The Long Distance Walkers' Association** (🖳 ldwa.org.uk)  Annual membership, at £18/25.50 individual/family, with £3 discount if paying by direct debit; membership includes three copies of *Strider* magazine a year giving details of challenge events and local group walks as well as articles on the subject. Information on 1600 long-distance paths is presented in their *UK Trailwalker's Handbook*.
● **Mountaineering Scotland** (🖳 mountaineering.scot)  The main representative body for mountaineers and hillwalkers in Scotland. Among the many benefits of membership are discounts at outdoor stores, subscription to their quarterly magazine and access to mountaineering workshops and events. Membership is £33/£16.75 adult/youth, or from £35 for families. Discounts are on offer for your first year if applying online.
● **Ramblers** (🖳 ramblers.org.uk)  Looks after the interests of walkers throughout Britain. They publish lots of useful information including their quarterly *Walk* magazine, and have an extensive map library and an app with 3000 walking routes, both free to members. Membership costs £36.60/49 individual/joint. Their website also has information about walking in Scotland (🖳 ramblers.org.uk/scotland).

be used to pay in larger shops, restaurants and hotels. Post-pandemic, an increasing number of smaller business also now accept card payments but it's best to check in advance rather than relying on this.

## MAPS

### Printed maps

The hand-drawn maps in this book cover the trail at a scale of 1:20,000, which is a better scale than any other map currently available, and we've also included plenty of detail and information so you should not need any other map if you're walking just the Way.

If you want to climb any of the mountains along the route, however, you must also take a map from Ordnance Survey or Harvey so that you can navigate accurately with a compass. The best-buy map of the Way is published by **Harvey** (🖥 harveymaps.co.uk; £14.95) with the trail arranged in strips at a scale of 1:40,000. Its coverage either side of the trail is limited though it extends to Ben Lomond, Ben Dorain and Ben Nevis.

The **Ordnance Survey** (🖥 ordnancesurvey.co.uk) publishes both paper maps (£9.99) and weatherproof ones (£15.99) in two scales. The 1:25,000 scale Explorer maps (orange cover) are excellent but you need six maps (Nos 348, OL38, OL39, 377, 384 and 392) to cover the whole trail. Alternatively, there are the Landranger maps (pink cover), Nos 64, 56, 50 and 41 at a scale of 1:50,000. Other possible maps for use on hillwalking side trips are listed in the relevant route descriptions.

### Digital maps

There are numerous software packages now available that provide Ordnance Survey (OS) maps for a PC, smartphone, tablet or GPS. Maps are downloaded into an app from where you can view, print and create routes on them.

**Memory Map** (🖥 memory-map.co.uk) currently sell OS Explorer 1:25,000 and Landranger 1:50,000 mapping covering the whole of Britain with prices from £15 for a one year subscription.

**Anquet** (🖥 anquet.com) has the full range of OS 1:25,000 maps covering all of the UK for £24 per year annual subscription. Or you can go to the original source itself: for a subscription of £2.99 for one month or £23.99 for a year (on their current offer) **Ordnance Survey** (🖥 ordnancesurvey.co.uk) allows you to download and use their UK maps (1:25,000 scale) on a mobile or tablet without a data connection for a specific period.

**Harvey** (🖥 harveymaps.co.uk) sell their West Highland Way map (1:40,000 scale) as a download for £20.49 for use on any device.

## RECOMMENDED READING

### General guidebooks

Rough Guides and Lonely Planet both produce a *Scotland* guide for the whole country and also publish guidebooks to the Scottish Highlands and Islands for travelling in the remoter parts of west Scotland.

## Walking guidebooks

*Scottish Highlands Hillwalking Guide* by Jim Manthorpe (Trailblazer) has detailed route descriptions and maps for the ascents of some of Scotland's best-known, and some less well-known, mountains.

The Pathfinder guides, such as the one to *Loch Lomond, the Trossachs & Stirling* are useful area guidebooks with a selection of low- and high-level day walks, each illustrated with OS map excerpts.

If the West Highland Way has fired your enthusiasm for walking long-distance trails check out the other titles in this Trailblazer series: see p208. These include the *Great Glen Way* which continues from where the West Highland Way ends at Fort William north along Loch Ness to Inverness.

## Flora and fauna field guides

*Scottish Birds* by Valerie Thom (Collins) and *Scottish Wild Flowers* by Michael Scott (Birlinn Ltd)) are ideal pocket-sized field guides to take with you. The RSPB also publish their own *Handbook of Scottish Birds*, by Peter Holden and Stuart Housden.

# Getting to and from the West Highland Way

Travelling to the start of the West Highland Way by public transport makes sense. There's no need to worry about the safety of your temporarily abandoned vehicle while walking, there are no logistical headaches about how to return to your car after the walk and it's obviously one of the biggest steps you can take towards minimising your ecological footprint. Quite apart from that, you'll simply feel your holiday has begun the moment you step out of your front door, rather than having to wait until you've slammed the car door behind you.

## NATIONAL TRANSPORT

Glasgow, only 20 minutes from the official start of the West Highland Way at Milngavie, is easily reached by rail, road, or air from the rest of Britain. For information on getting from Glasgow to Milngavie see p80.

### By rail

**Glasgow** (Glasgow Central) is on the West Coast rail line (operated by Avanti West Coast at the time of writing) and the Cross Country line from Leeds via Edinburgh and the Trans Pennine Express line from both Manchester and Liverpool, so it is served by frequent trains making it easy to get to the start of the West Highland Way letting the train take the strain.

**Fort William** is on the stunning West Highland Line from where you can either go north to Mallaig or south to Glasgow.

Timetable and fare information can be obtained from **National Rail Enquiries** (☎ 03457-484950; 24hrs; 🖳 nationalrail.co.uk) or the relevant train companies, particularly **Avanti West Coast** (☎ 0345-528 0253, 🖳 www.avan tiwestcoast.co.uk) and **Scotrail** (see box p47). Tickets can be bought direct from the train companies, railway stations, or from websites such as 🖳 thetrain-line.com but they may have additional charges such as a booking fee.

If you plan to take a bus when you arrive consider getting a **plusbus** (🖳 plusbus.info) ticket when you buy your train ticket. If you want to book a taxi **Traintaxi**'s website (🖳 traintaxi.co.uk) gives details of the companies operating at railway stations.

Of particular use if you're travelling from the south of England is the comfortable overnight (Sunday to Friday only) **sleeper service from London** (Euston) with accommodation in seats and twin (bunk-bed) or double cabins.

The **Lowlander** service operates to Glasgow/Edinburgh and the **Highlander** services to other destinations in Scotland including one to Fort William stopping en route at Glasgow, Arrochar & Tarbet, Ardlui (on request only), Crianlarich, Upper Tyndrum and Bridge of Orchy. These are therefore very convenient for West Highland Way walkers. For further details contact

---

❑ **GETTING TO BRITAIN**

● **By air**  There are plenty of cheap flights from around the world to London's airports: Heathrow, Gatwick, Luton, London City and Stansted; these are all about 5½ hours by train from Glasgow. However, Glasgow airport (🖳 glasgowairport.com), right at the start of the Way, Prestwick (🖳 glasgowprestwick.com), near Glasgow, and Edinburgh (🖳 edinburghairport.com), only one hour by train from Glasgow, have a limited number of international flights from North America and Europe and would be far more convenient. For details about airlines that fly to Glasgow and Edinburgh, and destinations served, visit the respective airport's website.

● **From Europe by train**  Eurostar (🖳 eurostar.com) operates a high-speed passenger service via the Channel Tunnel between Paris/Brussels/Amsterdam and London. The Eurostar terminal in London is at St Pancras International station which has connections to the London Underground and to all other main railway stations in London.

For more information about rail services from Europe contact your national rail service provider, or Railteam (🖳 railteam.eu).

● **From Europe by coach**  Eurolines (🖳 eurolines.de) works with various long-distance coach operators across mainland Europe to provide an integrated network connecting hundreds of destinations to the UK, where it links with the National Express network (see p44). FlixBus (🖳 global.flixbus.com) also provides services from destinations in mainland Europe to London.

● **From Europe by ferry (with or without a car)**  There are numerous ferries plying routes between the major North Sea ports, as well as across the Irish Sea and the English Channel. A useful website for information about the routes and the ferry operators is 🖳 directferries.com.

● **From Europe by car**  Eurotunnel (🖳 eurotunnel.com) operates '**le shuttle**' train service for vehicles via the Channel Tunnel between Calais and Folkestone taking one hour between the motorway in France and the motorway in Britain.

---

❏ **NATIONAL EXPRESS COACH SERVICES**
**National Express** (☎ 0871-781 8181, lines open 24 hours; 🖥 nationalexpress.com)
Note: the services listed below operate daily but not all stops are included. At the time
of writing the timetable was still limited owing to the pandemic; as restrictions ease,
more services will resume.

**181** Birmingham to **Glasgow** overnight via Manchester & Carlisle,1/day
**182** Birmingham to Edinburgh via Manchester & **Glasgow**, 1/day
**183** Birmingham to **Glasgow** via Leeds, Newcastle & Edinburgh, 1/day
**590** London to **Glasgow** via Birmingham & Carlisle, 1/day
**591** London to **Glasgow** via Leeds, Newcastle & Edinburgh, 1/day
**595** London to **Glasgow** overnight via Heathrow Airport, 1/day

Caledonian Sleeper (🖥 sleeper.scot, ☎ 0330-060 0500 or from overseas ☎ +44
141-555 0888). Tickets can be booked a year in advance.
    Tickets for all other rail services can be bought about 12 weeks in advance.
Buy a ticket as early as possible. Only a limited number of tickets are sold at discounted prices. It helps if you can be flexible and don't forget that most of these
tickets carry some restrictions, so check what they are before you buy your ticket. Travel in peak hours and on a Friday may be more expensive than at other
times.

## By coach

Travel by coach (long-distance bus) is usually cheaper than by rail but takes
longer. For discounts be sure to book at least a week ahead. If you don't mind
an uncomfortable night there are overnight services on some routes.
    **National Express** (see box above) is the main coach operator in Britain. To
get the cheapest fares you need to book seven days ahead. You can purchase tickets from coach and bus station ticket offices, National Express agents, directly
from the driver (though not always, so do check in advance), with their app,
online or by phone (note that phone bookings are subject to an additional fee).
Allow at least four working days for posted tickets.
    Another company to consider is **Megabus** (🖥 uk.megabus.com) which has
several services a day between London and Glasgow via Manchester (5/day,
from around £9.99 one way).
    For coach travel within Scotland the main operator is **Scottish Citylink** (☎
0871-266 3333, 🖥 citylink.co.uk).

## By car

Milngavie is simple to get to by car using the motorway network via Glasgow.
There is free parking outside Milngavie station with CCTV in operation, or you
can leave your car on the road outside the police station. Please let them know
if you decide to do this and give them your registration number.
    Some B&Bs will let you park outside for the duration of your walk. This is
the best option if leaving your car in Fort William. At the other end, Croftburn

B&B in Croftamie (see p110) is one that offers week-long parking space; others may if you enquire.

## By air

With many bargain tickets to **Glasgow Airport** (see box p43) available from the rest of Britain and short flight times this can seem an alluring way to cover large dis-

> ❏ **TRAVELINE SCOTLAND**
> The best way to plan local travel to and from the West Highland Way is by using the 'Journey planner' tab on 🖳 **travelinescotland.com**. Also available as a mobile app.

tances. Bear in mind, however, the time and expense of travelling to and from the airports and the extra time you need to allow for check-in. Glasgow Airport is nine miles west of the city; **Prestwick Airport** (see box p43), used by some budget airlines, is 29 miles to the west.

Air travel is by far the least environmentally sound option (see 🖳 choose climate.org for the true costs of flying).

## LOCAL TRANSPORT

Getting to and from most parts of the West Highland Way is relatively simple thanks to a comprehensive public transport network including trains, coaches and bus services. The **public transport maps** (pp48-9) give an overview of routes which are of particular use to walkers. The **public transport table** on pp46-7 gives the approximate frequency of services, the relevant stops, and contacts for detailed timetable information. However, the best way to plan local travel here is by using the **Traveline Scotland** website – 🖳 travelinescotland.com – or by phoning traveline ☎ 0871-200 2233 (but note that phone charges for 0871 numbers are high).

Because of its proximity to Glasgow the southern section of the Way is well served by buses and trains. As you progress north the most useful services are trains, which run on the West Highland line parallel to the trail until Bridge of Orchy, and Scottish Citylink coaches along the A82 also never far from the Way. Ferries in summer can get you to the less accessible eastern shore of Loch Lomond. The reasonably frequent public transport services in the area open up the potential for linear walks from an hour to several days without the worry of where to park your car and how to get back to it. See p34 for ideas.

> ❏ **DEMAND RESPONSIVE TRANSPORT SERVICE**
> For places where there are few or no regular bus services – such as Blanefield, Croftamie, Easter Drumquhassle & Drymen – there is a **demand responsive transport service** (🖳 stirling.gov.uk/drt). This 'bus' service uses taxis with fares based on distance. They tend to cost slightly more than they would be on an actual bus though holders of an Older Persons Bus Pass travel for free. Prior booking is essential – from 30 days in advance and up to two hours before travel if booked online through the website, or 24 hours in advance if booked by phone (Mon-Fri 9am-3pm, ☎ 01786 237800). The service is very popular so book early. The various operators listed on the website can tell you what the fare will be – it must be paid to the driver in cash.

## ❑ PUBLIC TRANSPORT SERVICES

### Bus services

**Notes**: The details below were correct at the time of writing but services and operators change so it is essential to check before travelling.

Many of the services listed operate year-round; however, they may operate less frequently in the winter months (generally November to March/April).

Services operate with the same frequency in the opposite direction.

Bus Times (🖥 bustimes.org) is a very useful website for finding bus stops.

- **FSE**    **First Scotland East** (South East and Central Scotland; 🖥 www.firstbus.co.uk/south-east-and-central-scotland)
- **FG**    **First Glasgow** (Greater Glasgow; 🖥 firstbus .co.uk/greater-glasgow)
- **GC**    **Garelochhead Coaches** (☎ 01436-810200, 🖥 garelochheadcoaches.co.uk)
- **GCB**    **Glasgow Citybus** (operated by West Coast Motors ☎ 01586-552319, 🖥 westcoastmotors.co.uk/glasgow-citybus)
- **McC**    **McColls** (☎ 01389-754321, 🖥 mccolls.org.uk)
- **SC**    **Scottish Citylink** (🖥 citylink.co.uk)
- **SB**    **Shiel Buses** (☎ 01397-700700, 🖥 shielbuses.co.uk)
- **WCM**    **West Coast Motors** (☎ 01586-555885, 🖥 westcoastmotors.co.uk)
- **WR**    **Wilson's of Rhu** (🖥 wilsonsof rhu.co.uk)

| | | |
|---|---|---|
| **N41** | Glen Nevis Youth Hostel to Roy Bridge via Fort William, Mon-Sat 2/day | **SB** |
| **N42** | Fort William to Glen Nevis Lower Falls via Glen Nevis Youth Hostel, early May to early Oct 6/day | **SB** |
| **N44** | Kinlochleven to Fort William via Glencoe Junction, Mon-Sat 6-7/day, Sun 4/day | **SB** |
| **X10** | Glasgow to Stirling via Milngavie, Strathblane, Killearn, Balfron& Kippen, Mon-Fri 6/day, Sat 4/day, Sun Glasgow to Balfron 5/day plus Balfron to Stirling 5/day | **FSE** |
| **X10A** | Glasgow to Stirling via Milngavie, Strathblane, Killearn, Balfron, Gartmore & Thornhill, Mon-Fri 6/day, Sat 4/day *X10 & X10A have some additional services between Glasgow and Balfron* | **FSE** |
| **1/1A** | Glasgow to Balloch via Alexandria (different stops en route), Mon-Sat 1-4/hr, Sun 1-2/hr | **FG** |
| **1E** | Glasgow to Balloch, Mon-Fri 3/day (4-6pm; morns only to Glasgow) | **FG** |
| **15** | Glasgow to Milngavie, Mon-Sat 1/hr during the day | **GCB/WCM** |
| **60A** | Easterhouse to Castlemains via Glasgow & Milngavie, daily 1-3/hr | **FG** |
| **302** | Helensburgh to Carrick Castle via Luss, Inverbeg, Tarbet & Succoth, Mon-Sat 2/day, Mon-Sat plus 1-2/day to Succoth | **GC** |
| **305** | Alexandria to Luss via Balloch & Arden, Mon-Fri 8/day, Sat 10/day, Sun 9/day | **McC** |
| **306** | Alexandria to Helensburgh, Mon-Fri 7/day, Sat 5/day, Sun 2/day | **McC** |
| **309** | Alexandria to Balmaha via Balloch & Drymen, Mon-Sat 10/day, Sun 9/day | **McC** |
| **316** | Helensburgh to Coulport via Garelochhead, Mon-Sat 1/hr plus 1/hr to Garelochhead, Sun 6-7/day plus 2/day to Garelochhead | **GC/WR** |
| **500** | Glasgow to Glasgow Airport, daily 3-4/hr | **FG** |

| | | |
|---|---|---|
| **500/505** | Fort William to Mallaig, Mon-Fri 4/day | **SB** |
| **534** | Fort William to Mallaig, Sat 1/day | **SB** |
| **913** | Tyndrum to Fort William via Bridge of Orchy & Glencoe, May-Sep 1/day | **SC** |
| **914** | Glasgow to Fort William via Balloch, Luss, Inverbeg, Tarbet, Sloy (power station) for Inveruglas, Ardlui, Inverarnan, Crianlarich, Tyndrum, Bridge of Orchy & Glencoe, 1-3/day | **SC** |
| **915/916** | route as 914 but continues to Portree (Skye) 3/day with 1-2/day continuing to Uig | **SC** |
| **918** | Fort William to Oban, Mon-Sat 2/day | **WCM** |
| **919** | Fort William to Inverness, May-Sep daily 10-11/day, rest of year, Mon-Sat 4/day, daily 2/day | **SC** |
| **926** | Glasgow to C'beltown via Luss, Inverbeg & Tarbet, 5/day | **WCM** |
| **975** | Glasgow to Oban via Balloch, Luss, Inverbeg, Tarbet, Sloy (power station) for Inveruglas, Ardlui, Inverarnan, Crianlarich & Tyndrum, daily 1/day | **WCM** |
| **976** | Glasgow to Oban via Balloch, Luss, Inverbeg & Tarbet, daily 3/day | **WCM** |
| **977** | Glasgow to Oban via Balloch, Luss, Inverbeg, Tarbet, Sloy (power station) for Inveruglas, Ardlui, Inverarnan, Crianlarich & Tyndrum, daily 1/day | **SC** |

## Train services

**Scotrail (☎ 0344 811 0141, 🖥 scotrail.co.uk) Note**: not all stops are listed
At the time of writing Scotrail introduced a temporary timetable with reduced services. The details below reflect this but check before travelling as services may improve.

● Springburn to Milngavie via Glasgow Queen Street Low Level, Charing Cross, Partick & Hyndland, Mon-Sat 1-2/hr
● Motherwell to Milngavie via Glasgow Queen Street Low Level, Partick & Hyndland, Sun 1/hr
● Airdrie to Balloch via Glasgow Queen Street, Charing Cross, Partick, Hyndland & Alexandria, Mon-Sat 1-2/hr
● Larkhall to Balloch via Glasgow Queen Street Low Level, Partick, Hyndland & Alexandria, Sun 1/hr
● Glasgow Queen Street to Oban/Mallaig via Helensburgh Upper, Garelochhead, Arrochar & Tarbet, Ardlui & Crianlarich
At Crianlarich the trains divide: to **Oban** via Tyndrum Lower, Mon-Sat 3/day, Sun 2/day; to **Mallaig** via Upper Tyndrum, Bridge of Orchy, Rannoch, Roy Bridge & Fort William, Mon-Sat 2/day, Sun 1/day
● Glasgow Queen Street to Inverness via Stirling & Perth, Mon-Sat 5/day, Sun 3/day

## Water bus/ferry services

**Cruise Loch Lomond (☎ 01301-702356,**
🖥 **cruiselochlomond.co.uk/waterbus-ferries)**
Contact them for details of seasonal services from Luss to Balmaha, Inchcailloch, Rowardennan and Tarbet.
● Tarbet to Inversnaid, early Apr-early Nov 4/day
● Tarbet to Rowardennan, early Apr-early Nov 1/day

PLANNING YOUR WALK

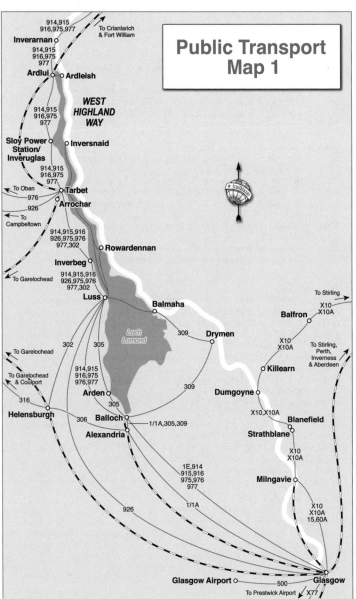

**Public Transport Map 1**

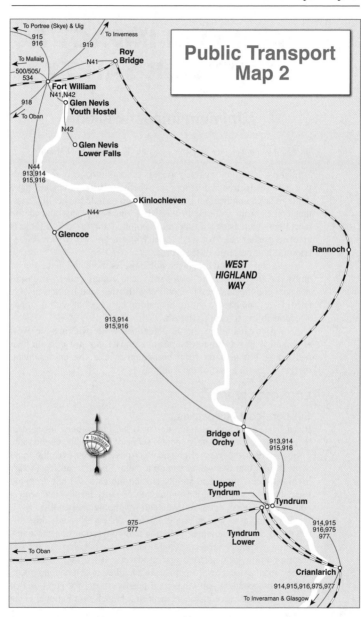

**Public Transport Map 2**

To Portree (Skye) & Uig
915
916
919
To Inverness

**Roy Bridge**

To Mallaig
500/505/
534

N41

**Fort William**
N41,N42

**Glen Nevis Youth Hostel**

918
To Oban

N42

**Glen Nevis Lower Falls**

N44
913,914
915,916

**Kinlochleven**

N44

**Glencoe**

**Rannoch**

*WEST HIGHLAND WAY*

913,914
915,916

**Bridge of Orchy**

913,914
915,916

**Upper Tyndrum**

**Tyndrum**

975
977

**Tyndrum Lower**

914,915
916,975
977

To Oban

**Crianlarich**

914,915,916,975,977

To Inverarnan & Glasgow

PLANNING YOUR WALK

# 2

# MINIMUM IMPACT & OUTDOOR SAFETY

## Minimum impact walking

*Walk as if you are kissing the Earth with your feet*  **Thich Nhat Hanh**

Scotland's large and sparsely populated countryside is the closest you can get to true wilderness anywhere in Britain. Visitors have come in large numbers for over a century to sample the healing balm that comes from walking in these less touched places and as the world gets increasingly faster, more polluted and urbanised there is an even greater need for wild country where you can go for re-creation in the true sense of the word.

Inevitably this too brings its problems. As more and more people enjoy the freedom of the hills so the land comes under increasing pressure and the potential for conflict with other land-users is heightened. Everyone has a right to this natural heritage but with it comes a responsibility to care for it, too.

By following some simple guidelines while walking the West Highland Way you can have a positive impact, not just on your own well-being but also on local communities and the environment, thereby becoming part of the solution.

### ECONOMIC IMPACT

#### Support local businesses

Rural businesses and communities in Britain have been hit hard in recent years by a seemingly endless series of crises. The countryside through which the West Highland Way passes is no exception and there is a lot that the walker can do to help. Playing your part today involves much more than simply closing the gate and not dropping litter; there is something else you can do – **buy local** – and with it comes huge social, environmental and psychological benefits.

Look and ask for local produce to buy and eat. Not only does this cut down on the amount of pollution and congestion that the transportation of food creates, so-called 'food miles', but also ensures you are supporting local farmers and producers. It's a fact of life that money spent at local level – perhaps in a market, or at the greengrocer, or in an independent pub – has a far greater impact for good on that community than the equivalent spent in a branch of a national chain store or restaurant. If you can find local food which is also organic so much the better. While no-one would advocate that walkers should boycott the larger supermarkets, which after all do provide local employment, it's worth remembering that businesses in rural communities rely heavily on visitors for their very existence. If we want to keep these shops and post offices, we need to use them.

## ENVIRONMENTAL IMPACT

By choosing a walking holiday you have already made a positive step towards minimising your impact on the wider environment. By following these suggestions you can also tread lightly along the West Highland Way.

### Use public transport
Traffic congestion in the Highlands at peak holiday times is becoming more and more of a nightmare. Yet public

A REQUEST
FROM THE HOLIDAY FELLOWSHIP

FRIEND, WHEN YOU STRAY, OR SIT AND TAKE YOUR EASE
ON MOOR, OR FELL, OR UNDER SPREADING TREES
PRAY, LEAVE NO TRACES OF YOUR WAYSIDE MEAL
NO PAPER BAG, NO SCATTERED ORANGE PEEL;
NOR DAILY JOURNAL LITTERED ON THE GRASS,
OTHERS MAY VIEW THESE WITH DISTASTE, AND PASS.
LET NO ONE SAY, AND SAY IT TO YOUR SHAME,
THAT ALL WAS BEAUTY HERE UNTIL YOU CAME.

THE HOLIDAY FELLOWSHIP LTD

The Holiday Fellowship, who supplied this plaque with its gentle reminder to its holidaymakers to take their litter home, is still going strong, its name abbreviated to HF Holidays. Dating from the 1930s, the plaque is set in the wall of the Rowardennan Hotel, right beside the Way.

transport to and along the West Highland Way is excellent and the more people who use it the better services will become. This not only benefits visitors but also local people and the environment.

### Never leave litter
Leaving litter shows a total disrespect for the natural world and others coming after you. As well as being unsightly, litter kills wildlife, pollutes the environment and can be dangerous to farm animals.

**Please** carry a degradable bag so you can dispose of your rubbish in a bin in the next village. It would be very helpful if you could pick up litter left by other people too.

● **Is it OK if it's biodegradable?**  Not really. Apple cores, banana skins, orange peel and the like are unsightly, encourage flies and wasps and ruin a picnic spot for others. Using the excuse that they are natural and biodegradable just doesn't cut any ice. When was the last time you saw a banana tree in Scotland?
● **The lasting impact of litter**  A piece of orange peel left on the ground takes six months to decompose; silver foil 18 months; a plastic bag 10 years; clothes 15 years; and an aluminium drinks can 85 years.

### Erosion
● **Stay on the main trail**  The effect of your footsteps may seem minuscule but when they are multiplied by several thousand walkers each year they

become rather more significant. Avoid taking shortcuts, widening the trail or creating more than one path; your boots will be followed by many others.

● **Consider walking out of season** Maximum disturbance by walkers coincides with the time of year when nature wants to do most of its growth and repair. In high-use areas, like that along much of the Way, the trail never recovers. Walking at less busy times eases this pressure while also generating year-round income for the local economy. Not only that, but it may make the walk a more relaxing experience for you as there are fewer people on the path and there's less competition for accommodation.

## Respect all wildlife
Care for all wildlife you come across on the Way; it has just as much of a right to be there as you. Tempting as it may be to pick wild flowers leave them so the next people who pass can enjoy them too. Don't break branches off trees.

If you come across wildlife keep your distance and don't watch for too long. Your presence can cause considerable stress particularly if the adults are with young or in winter when the weather is harsh and food scarce. Young animals are rarely abandoned. If you come across deer calves or young birds keep away so that their mother can return.

## The code of the outdoor loo
'Going' in the outdoors is a lost art worth reclaiming, for your sake and everyone else's. As more and more people discover the joys of the outdoors this is becoming an important issue. In some parts of the world where visitor pressure is higher than in Britain walkers and climbers are required to pack out their excrement. This could one day be necessary here. Human excrement is not only offensive to our senses but, more importantly, can infect water sources.

● **Where to go** Wherever possible **use a toilet**. Public toilets are marked on the trail maps in this guide and you will also find facilities in pubs, cafés and campsites. The West Highland Way is not a wilderness area and the thousands of walkers using it each year mean you need to be as sensitive as possible.

If you do have to go outdoors choose a site at least **30 metres away from running water** and 200 metres away from high-use areas such as huts and bothies. Carry a small trowel and **dig a hole** about 15cm (6") deep to bury your excrement in. It decomposes quicker when in contact with the top layer of soil or leaf mould. Use a stick to stir loose soil into your deposit as well as this speeds up decomposition even more. Do not squash it under rocks as this slows down the composting process. If you have to use rocks to hide it make sure they are not in contact with your faeces. Make sure you do not dig any holes on ground that is, or could be, of historic or archaeological interest.

● **Toilet paper and tampons** Toilet paper takes a long time to decompose whether buried or not. It is easily dug up by animals and can then blow into water sources or onto the trail. The best method for dealing with it is to **pack it out**. Put the used paper inside a paper bag which you place inside a (degradable) plastic bag (or two). Then simply empty the contents of the paper bag at the next toilet you come across and throw the bag away. You should also pack out **tampons** and **sanitary towels** in a similar way; they take years to decompose and may be dug up and scattered about by animals.

## Wild camping

Along the West Highland Way there are a number of informal sites where you are allowed to camp wild. There is deep, lasting pleasure to be gained from living outdoors close to nature but all too often people ruin that enjoyment for those who come after them.

☐ **WILD CAMPING PERMITS**
Note, between 1st March and 30th September local bylaws create Camping Management Zones around parts of Loch Lomond & The Trossachs National Park. To camp in these zones you must have a permit (£4 per tent; apply online) or stay in a campsite. See ☐ lochlomond-trossachs.org for details.

Camping without any facilities provides a valuable lesson in simple, sustainable living where the results of all your actions, from going to the loo to washing your plates in a stream, can be seen. Follow these suggestions for minimising your impact and encourage others to do likewise.

● **Be discreet** Camp alone or in small groups, spend only one night in each place and pitch your tent late and move off early.

● **Never light a fire** The deep burn caused by camp fires, no matter how small, seriously damages the turf and can take years to recover. Cook on a camp stove instead. Be aware that accidental fire is a great fear for farmers and foresters; take matches and cigarette butts out with you to dispose of safely.

● **Don't use soap or detergent** There is no need to use soap; even biodegradable soaps and detergents pollute streams and lochs. You won't be away from a shower for more than a couple of days. Wash up without detergent; use a plastic or metal scourer, or failing that, a handful of fine pebbles from the stream or some bracken or grass.

● **Leave no trace** Enjoy the skill of moving on without leaving any sign of having been there: no moved boulders, ripped up vegetation or dug drainage ditches. Before heading off; pick up any litter that you or anyone else has left, so leaving it in at least as good a state as you found it, if not better.

## ACCESS

The West Highland Way, as a designated 'Long Distance Footpath', is a right of way with open access to the public. Access laws in Scotland were for many years very different from those in England and Wales largely due to an uneasy tradition of 'freedom to roam' going back many centuries. This freedom to roam was, until recently, little more than a moral right rather than a legal one. This changed with the Land Reform (Scotland) Act 2003 that established statutory rights of access to land and inland water for outdoor recreation which came into

MINIMUM IMPACT & OUTDOOR SAFETY

## ❏ THE SCOTTISH OUTDOOR ACCESS CODE

Scotland has its own 'Countryside code' for those looking to enjoy the outdoors. The full code runs to 67 pages, a copy of which can be found on their website 🖳 outdooraccess-scotland.scot. However, they also publish a brief summary of the code, the main points of which are listed below.

### Take personal responsibility for your own actions
You can do this by:
● Caring for your own safety by recognising that the outdoors is a working environment and by taking account of natural hazards;
● Taking special care if you are responsible for children as a parent, teacher or guide to ensure that they enjoy the outdoors responsibly and safely.

### Respect people's privacy and peace of mind
● Use a path or track, if there is one, when you are close to a house or garden;
● If there is no path or track, keep a sensible distance from houses and avoid ground that overlooks them from close by;
● Take care not to act in ways which might annoy or alarm people living in a house; and at night, take extra care by keeping away from buildings where people might not be expecting to see anyone and by following paths and tracks.

### Help land managers and others to work safely and effectively
You can do this by:
● Following any precautions taken or reasonable recommendations made by the land manager, such as to avoid an area or route when hazardous operations, such as tree felling and crop spraying, are underway;
● Checking to see what alternatives there are, such as neighbouring land, before entering a field of animals;
● Never feeding farm animals;
● Avoiding causing damage to crops by using paths or tracks, by going round the margins of the field, by going on any unsown ground or by considering alternative routes on neighbouring ground; and by leaving all gates as you find them;
● Not hindering a land management operation, by keeping a safe distance and following any reasonable advice from the land manager.

### Care for your environment
You can do this by:
● Not intentionally or recklessly disturbing or destroying plants, birds and other animals, or geological features;
● Following any voluntary agreements between land managers and recreation bodies;
● Not damaging or disturbing cultural heritage sites;
● Not causing any pollution and by taking all your litter away with you.

### Keep your dog under proper control
● Never let it worry or attack livestock;
● Never take it into a field where there are calves or lambs;
● Keep it on a short lead or under close control in fields with farm animals;
● If cattle react aggressively and move towards you, keep calm, let the dog go and take the shortest, safest route out of the field;
● Keep it on a short lead or under close control during the bird breeding season (usually April to July) in areas such as moorland, forests, grassland and loch shores;
● Pick up and remove any faeces if your dog defecates in a public open place.

efect in February 2005. The law now states that there is a right of access to land that is considered, among other designations, moorland and mountain.

Walkers need to be aware of the wider access situation, especially if planning to leave the Way to explore some of the remoter country around it. In the past there has been some conflict between the interests of large sporting estates and walkers. The new access legislation relies on an attitude of co-operation between landowners and those wishing to use the land for peaceful recreation. Hillwalkers therefore have a responsibility to be considerate to those using the land for other purposes such as farming, forestry and field sports. This means following the Scottish Outdoor Access Code (see box opposite) and respecting the lambing and deer-stalking seasons (see below).

For more information see **Scottish Rights of Way Society** (🖳 scotways.com), a charity that works to develop and protect public rights of way.

## Other points to consider on the West Highland Way

● All along the Way there are stiles and kissing gates through boundaries. If you have to climb over a gate which you can't open, always do so at the hinged end.
● Walkers should take special care on country roads. Cars travel dangerously fast on narrow winding lanes. To be safe, walk facing the oncoming traffic and carry a torch or wear highly visible clothing when it's getting dark. Conversely, if you are driving, go carefully on country roads and park your car with consideration for others' needs; never block a gateway.
● Make no unnecessary noise. Enjoy the peace and solitude of the outdoors by staying in small groups and acting unobtrusively. Avoid noisy and disruptive behaviour which might annoy residents and other visitors and frighten farm animals and wildlife.

### Lambing
This takes place from mid March to mid May and is a critical economic time for the hard-pressed hill farmers. Please do not interfere with livestock farming in any way. If a ewe or lamb seems to be in distress contact the nearest farmer. See also p28.

Dogs should be kept off land where sheep are grazing throughout this season so that the pregnant ewes are not disturbed.

### Deer-stalking
Large areas of the Highlands have been actively managed for deer shooting, or stalking as it is known, since the 19th century when it became fashionable for the aristocracy and the newly

> **❏ THE SHEEP-FARMER'S YEAR**
> **May** – lambing
> **June** – young rams (*tups*) are clipped and dosed against parasites; sheep are gathered to mark lambs; clipping of year-old lambs (*hogs*) and ewes with no lambs
> **July** – ewes with lambs clipped
> **August** – lambs gathered and sold
> **October** – sheep gathered for marking, counting, dosing and dipping against ticks; ewes older than six years are sold; hogs are taken to winter pastures on the east coast
> **November** – tups put out with ewes (three tups per hundred ewes)
> **January** – tups gathered and those older than four or five years sold
> **February** – sheep gathered for dosing
> **March** – sheep dipped; lambing begins
> **April** – hogs return from winter pastures to be dipped and dosed.

rich industrialists to partake in all forms of field sports. Little has changed today except that the wealthy now come from all over the world and contribute £30 million to the Highland economy every year providing much-needed income for many estates.

Stalking is partly responsible for the deer population spiralling out of control, doubling in number since the early 1960s, which has ironically enabled stalkers to play a more legitimate role in culling the deer. As red deer have no natural predators other than man this is a necessary activity. In addition, no matter what one's ethical stance on the sport may be, while our laws and methods of land ownership remain as they are, alternative means for estates to generate an income, such as conifer plantations, ski developments and the like, would be far worse for both walkers and the environment. Deer stalking is also an important conservation measure; it maintains a healthier herd of deer and aids vegetation recovery and habitat improvement.

Access restrictions during the deer-culling seasons should therefore be respected when walking on land owned by sporting estates and you should try to cause the minimum of disturbance. Stags are culled between July 1st and October 20th, hinds are culled between October 21st and February 15th. Details of access restrictions are usually posted on signs in the vicinity of stalking activities and on the internet at 🖳 www.outdooraccess-scotland.scot/practical-guide-all/heading-scottish-hills.

# Outdoor safety

The West Highland Way is not a particularly difficult or dangerous walk and with common sense, some planning and basic preparation most hazards and hassles can easily be avoided. The information given here is just as valid for walkers out on a day walk as for those walking the entire Way.

## AVOIDANCE OF HAZARDS

Always make sure you have suitable **clothes** (see pp37-8) to keep you warm and dry, whatever the conditions, and a spare change of inner clothes. A **compass**, **whistle**, **torch** and **first-aid kit** should also be carried. Take plenty of **food** and **water** (see opposite) with you for the day. You will eat far more walking than you do normally so make sure you have enough, as well as some high-energy snacks, such as chocolate, dried fruit or biscuits, in the bottom of your pack for an emergency. Stay alert and know exactly where you are throughout the day. The easiest way to do this is to **regularly check your position** on the map. If visibility suddenly decreases with mist and cloud, or there is an accident, you will be able to make a sensible decision about what action to take based on your location.

## Walking alone

If you are walking alone you must appreciate and be prepared for the increased risk. It is always a good idea to leave word with somebody about where you are going; you can always ring ahead to your accommodation and let them know you are walking alone and what time you expect to arrive. Don't forget to contact whoever you have left word with to let them know you've arrived safely. Carrying a mobile phone can be useful though you cannot rely on getting good reception.

## Mountain safety

If you plan to climb any of the mountains along the West Highland Way there are further precautions you need to take. You must always take a **map** and **compass** with you on the Scottish mountains and be able to navigate accurately with them as paths are rare and visibility often poor. In addition to the emergency equipment, food and clothes you would normally carry, you may also want to take a **survival bag**.

In summer the temperature on the summits of Scottish mountains can be as much as 12°C lower than in the valley so take an extra warm layer and always pack a **hat** and **gloves**. Gales carrying sleet, hail and snow can blow in with little warning at any time of the year; be prepared.

In **winter** you should not venture onto the hills unless you are a competent mountaineer. The typical Arctic conditions require crampons, ice axe and specialist clothing as well as knowledge of snow conditions, avalanche and cornices.

## Mountain guides

If you feel your skills need polishing there are a number of experienced mountain guides and instructors in the region who run courses (and also provide accommodation) such as **West Coast Mountain Guides** (☎ 01397-532022, 🖳 westcoast-mountainguides.co.uk).

## WEATHER FORECASTS

The weather in Scotland can change with incredible speed. At any time of the year you must be prepared for the worst. Most hotels, some B&Bs and TICs will have pinned up somewhere a summary of the **weather forecast**. Alternatively you can get a forecast through Mountain Weather Information Service (🖳 mwis.org.uk/forecasts/scottish/west-highlands, Winterhighland 🖳 winterhighland.info) or reports that also take in the whole country: 🖳 bbc.co.uk/weather, or 🖳 metoffice.gov.uk.

## WATER

You need to drink lots of water while walking; 2-4 litres a day depending on the weather. If you're feeling drained, lethargic or just out of sorts it may well be that you haven't drunk enough. Thirst is not a reliable indicator of how much you should drink. The frequency and colour of your urine is better and the maxim, 'a happy mountaineer always pees clear' is worth following.

Tap water is safe to drink unless a sign specifies otherwise. In upland areas above habitation and away from intensively farmed land walkers have traditionally drunk straight from the stream and many continue to do so with no problems. It must be said, however, that there is a very small but steadily increasing risk of catching giardia from doing this. Just a few years ago this disease was only a threat to travellers in the developing world. As more people travel some are returning to the UK with the disease. If one of these individuals defecates too close to a stream or loch that water source can become infected and the disease transmitted to others who drink from it. If you want to minimise the risk either purify the water using a filter or iodine tablets, or collect water only from a tap.

Far more dangerous to health is drinking from natural water sources in the lowlands. The water may have run off roads, housing or agricultural fields picking up heavy metals, pesticides and other chemical contaminants that we humans use liberally. Such water should not be drunk; find a tap instead.

## BLISTERS

You will prevent blisters by wearing worn-in, comfortable boots and looking after your feet; air them at lunchtime, keep them clean and change your socks regularly. If you feel any 'hot spots' on your feet while you are walking, stop immediately and apply a few strips of zinc oxide tape and leaving them on until it is pain free or the tape starts to come off.

If you've left it too late and a blister has developed, surround it with 'moleskin' or any other 'blister kit' such as Compeed to protect it from abrasion. Popping it can lead to infection. If the skin is broken keep the area clean with antiseptic and cover it with a non-adhesive dressing material held in place with tape.

## BITES

For the summer-time walker these few bugs are more irritating than dangerous.

### Midges

The Gaelic name for this annoying blood-sucker is *meanbh-chuileag* – tiny fly. When you see its diminutive size it's inconceivable to think that it can cause such misery, but it never works alone. The culprits are the pregnant females who critically need a regular supply of fresh blood to develop their eggs. On finding a victim she sends out a chemical invitation to other hungry females and you are soon enveloped in a black gyrating cloud. A single bite would pass unnoticed, but concurrent bites are itchy and occasionally mildly painful.

The key to dealing with this wee beastie is understanding its habits. The main biting season is from June to August, so planning a holiday outside this time obviously makes sense. For many though, this is not an option. It's worth knowing that the midge is also extremely sensitive to light and only comes out when the sun's radiation is below a certain intensity; dawn, dusk, long summer twilight hours and dull overcast days are its favourite hunting times. The message for campers is to get into your tent early, get up late and not to camp in conifer forests which can often be dark enough to trigger a feeding frenzy.

The other factor on your side is wind. It only needs a gentle breeze of 5½ mph to keep the midge grounded. Try to camp on raised ground which will catch any hint of a breeze or, if you're walking on a still, overcast day, keep moving. The apparent wind created is often enough to keep them away. Insect repellents vary in effectiveness with different brands working for different people. The simplest methods are often the best: long-sleeved shirts, trousers and midge-proof headnets are all worth wearing, preferably in a light colour which the midges find less attractive. Weirdly, Avon Skin So Soft, a moisturising body lotion, has proved to be the most effective repellent against midges and is even now sold in many camping shops along the way.

When all is lost and there is nothing you can do to keep them away, try to seek solace from the final words of George Hendry's fascinating little book, *Midges in Scotland*, '... the Scottish Highlands remain one of the most underpopulated landscapes with a timelessness difficult to find anywhere at the start of the twenty-first century ... If, as seems likely, the biting midge is a significant factor in limiting our grossest capacities for unsustainable exploitation then this diminutive guardian of the Highlands deserves our lasting respect.'

### Ticks

Ticks are small, wingless creatures with eight legs which painlessly bury their heads under your skin to feed on your blood. After a couple of days' feasting they will have grown to about 10mm and drop off.

There is a very small risk that they can infect you with **Lyme Disease**. Because of this you should check your body thoroughly after a walk through long grass, heather or bracken; the tick's favoured habitat. If you find a tick, remove it promptly. Use fine point tweezers and grasp the tick where its head pierces your skin; do not squeeze its body. Tug gently and repeatedly until the tick lets go and falls off. Be patient, this will take time. Keep the area clean with disinfectant and over the next month watch for any flu-like symptoms, a spreading rash or lasting irritation at the site of the bite which could indicate Lyme Disease. If any of these symptoms appear see a doctor and let them know you suspect Lyme Disease. It is treatable with antibiotics but the sooner you catch it the easier this will be.

Prevention is always better than cure so wear boots, socks and trousers when walking through or sitting on long grass, heather and bracken.

For further information look up 💻 lymediseaseaction.org.uk.

### Horseflies and mosquitoes

In July and August **horseflies**, or *clegs*, can be a nuisance on warm bright days. Their bite is painful and may stay inflamed for a few days.

There are several species of **mosquito** in Scotland which tend to bite at night leaving an itchy, painful mark. Insect repellents such as Jungle Formula or Autan may help deter horse flies and mosquitoes but they do not offer a permanent solution. You can take other preventative measures such as wearing a midge net over your head (available from outdoor shops and local village shops throughout the Highlands) and wearing light-coloured clothing: most insects are attracted to dark colours. If you are bitten, rest assured that Scottish mosquitoes and horse flies carry no nasty viruses or diseases. The worst that will happen is that the bite will become itchy and swollen for a day or two. To soothe the affected area, cover it with an antihistamine gel.

### Adders

The adder is the only venomous snake present in the British Isles. It is very rare to be bitten by one and deaths are even rarer, although children and pets are more vulnerable. In the unlikely event of a bite you should stay calm and try to move as little as possible to prevent the venom circulating quickly. Send a companion to call for help.

Prevention is better than cure. If you see an adder, give it a wide berth and move on. It will only attack if you provoke it. Adders are active on warm, sunny days, so look out for them in open, grassy areas. See also p75.

## HYPOTHERMIA

Also known as exposure, this occurs when the body can't generate enough heat to maintain its normal temperature, usually as a result of being wet, cold, unprotected from the wind, tired and hungry. It is easily avoided by wearing suitable clothing, carrying and eating enough food and drink, being aware of the weather conditions and checking the morale of your companions.

Early signs to watch for are feeling cold and tired with involuntary shivering. Find some shelter as soon as possible and warm the victim up with a hot drink and some chocolate or other high-energy food. If possible give them another warm layer of clothing and allow them to rest until feeling better.

If allowed to worsen, strange behaviour, slurring of speech and poor co-ordination will become apparent and the victim can quickly progress into unconsciousness, followed by coma and death. Quickly get the victim out of wind and rain, improvising a shelter if necessary. Rapid restoration of bodily warmth is essential and best achieved by bare-skin contact: someone should get into the same sleeping bag as the patient, both having stripped to their underwear, with any spare clothing under or over them to build up heat. Send urgently for help.

## HYPERTHERMIA

Hyperthermia occurs when the body generates too much heat, eg heat exhaustion and heatstroke. Not ailments that you would normally associate with the Highlands of Scotland, these are serious problems nonetheless.

Symptoms of **heat exhaustion** include thirst, fatigue, giddiness, a rapid pulse, raised body temperature, low urine output and, if not treated, delirium and finally a coma. The best cure is to drink plenty of water.

**Heatstroke** is more serious. A high body temperature and an absence of sweating are early indications, followed by symptoms similar to hypothermia (see opposite) such as a lack of coordination, convulsions and coma. Death will follow if treatment is not given instantly. Sponge the victim down, wrap them in wet towels, fan them and get help immediately.

## DEALING WITH AN ACCIDENT

● Use basic first aid to treat any injuries to the best of your ability.
● Work out exactly where you are.
● Try to attract the attention of anybody else who may be in the area. The **emergency signal** is six blasts on a whistle, or six flashes with a torch.
● If possible leave someone with the casualty while others go for help. If there is nobody else, you have a dilemma. If you decide to get help leave all spare clothing and food with the casualty.
● Call ☎ **999** for the police who will alert the mountain rescue team.
● Report the exact position of the casualty and their condition.

---

❑ SCOTLAND'S NATIONAL PARKS
*Thousands of tired, nerve-shaken, over-civilized people are beginning to find out that going to the mountains is going home; that wildness is a necessity; and that mountain parks and reservations are useful not only as fountains of timber and irrigating rivers, but as fountains of life.*　　**John Muir** *Our National Parks*

Right up to the end of the 20th century Scotland was one of only a handful of countries yet to embrace the concept of national parks. This despite the Scotsman John Muir instigating the first national parks in North America over 100 years ago and England and Wales bowing to pressure from walkers by granting ten national parks in the 1950s (the current number is 13). Objectors included both landowners and local planning authorities who view the national park system as unnecessary bureaucracy heaped on top of an already mountainous pile of landscape and wildlife designations. When such places are still threatened, however, it can only be right to grant these outstandingly beautiful areas the highest level of landscape protection available.

**Loch Lomond and the Trossachs** (🖳 lochlomond-trossachs.org), through which the West Highland Way passes, was the first national park, opened in 2002 and followed by the **Cairngorms** (🖳 cairngorms.co.uk) in 2003. As a result resources are being made available to manage the parks in an integrated way for conservation, quiet recreation and sustainable economic activities.

Many people would like to see the designation extended over a wider area. Surely if Loch Lomond is worthy on the grounds of landscape quality most of the Highlands and Islands of Scotland should also qualify? Perhaps one day this vision of such an extensive national park will become a reality.

MINIMUM IMPACT & OUTDOOR SAFETY

# 3

# THE ENVIRONMENT AND NATURE

*Nature is our medicine.*  **Henry D Thoreau**

The West Highland Way encompasses the Lowlands and Highlands, passing from wooded glen to high mountain and all manner of habitats in between. This abundance of countryside (97% of Scotland has not been built on) with few people living in it (about eight people per square kilometre in the Highlands) has resulted in a rich variety of wildlife. For the walker interested in the natural environment it is a feast for the senses.

It would take a book several times the size of this to list the thousands of species which you could come across on your walk. A brief description of the more common animals and plants you may encounter as well as some of the more special species for which Scotland is well known is given on pp65-78. If you want to know more refer to the field guides listed on p42.

Conservation issues are also explored on the premise that to really learn about a place you need to know more than the names of all the plants and animals in it. It is just as important to understand the interactions going on between them and man's relationship with this ecological balance.

## Conserving Scotland's nature

*[Since 1945] the normal landscape dynamics of human adaptation and natural alteration had been replaced by simple destruction. The commonest cause was destruction by modern agriculture; the second, destruction by modern forestry.*
**Oliver Rackham**  *The Illustrated History of the Countryside*

The statistics of how the Scottish land has been treated over the last 70 years do not make comfortable reading. More than half of the hedgerows which existed at the end of the Second World War have been pulled up; a quarter of the broadleaved woods have disappeared; a third of heather moorland has been destroyed; half the lowland peat mires have been lost. These are all important habitats for a diverse range of wildlife species. When they are replaced by monocultural conifer plantations or sheep grassland the rich web of plant and animal life also disappears leaving behind a poor substitute for nature's bounty. The stark results of this destruction are highlighted by the decline in Scotland's farmland birds over the last 35 years. The numbers of sky-lark, bullfinch and linnet for example have diminished by almost two-thirds, while partridge numbers are down by three-quarters. Species of all kinds have suffered similar fates as habitats continue to be destroyed.

Nature conservation arose tentatively in the middle of the nineteenth century out of concern for wild birds which were being slaughtered to provide feathers for the fashion industry. As commercial exploitation of land has increased over the intervening century so too has the conservation movement. It now has a wide sphere of influence throughout the world and its ethos is upheld by international legislation, government agencies and voluntary organisations.

## NATURESCOT

Formerly known as Scottish Natural Heritage, this is the main government body concerned with the preservation of wildlife and landscape in Scotland. They manage the 43 **National Nature Reserves** (NNRs), of which Loch Lomond is a prime example, to conserve some of the best examples of Scotland's varied habitats. Along with the land owned and managed by voluntary conservation groups there are some 75 local nature reserves across Scotland creating refuges for many endangered species.

However, about 94% of Scottish land is in the hands of foresters and farmers who generally put economic returns above concern for habitat and wildlife. NatureScot has the difficult job of protecting this land from the grossest forms of damage using a complex array of land designations and statutory mechanisms, all shortened to mind-boggling acronyms.

One of the most important designations and one that covers 12.6% of Scotland is **Site of Special Scientific Interest** (SSSI; there were 1422 in Scotland at the time of writing). These range in size from those of just a few acres protecting natural treasures such as wild-flower meadows, important nesting sites or a notable geological feature, to vast swathes of upland, moorland and wetland. Owners and occupiers of 'triple-SIs', as they are often known, have to abide by strict guidelines and must notify NatureScot of any proposed actions which would affect the land.

❏ STATUTORY BODIES
● **NatureScot** (🖳 nature.scot) Public body responsible for advising the Scottish government on the conservation and enhancement of Scotland's natural heritage.
● **Forestry & Land Scotland** (🖳 https://forestryandland.gov.scot) Government department that looks after Scotland's national forests for a variety of uses, established following changes in structure to the UK's Forestry Commission in April 2019.
● **Loch Lomond and The Trossachs National Park Authority** (🖳 lochlomond-trossachs.org) Oversees one of Scotland's two national parks, and the one with most relevance to the West Highland Way.
● **Cairngorms National Park Authority** (🖳 cairngorms.co.uk). Body charged with looking after Scotland's – and indeed the UK's – largest national park.

There are 40 areas in Scotland designated as a **National Scenic Area** (NSA). This has provided some recognition for outstanding landscapes such as Ben Nevis and Glen Coe, through which the West Highland Way passes. Along with these designations Scotland finally has two **national parks** (see box p61) to call its own in the shape of Loch Lomond and the Trossachs, and the Cairngorms.

These are all encouraging steps but on their own will never provide complete protection. New developments such as roads and housing still get pushed through in so-called protected areas under the guise of being in the public interest and some landowners ignore the designations, and suffer the rather insignificant penalties when it is in their interest to do so. There is still a long way to go before all our land is treated as something more than just an economic resource to be exploited.

## CAMPAIGNING AND CONSERVATION ORGANISATIONS

These voluntary organisations started the conservation movement back in the mid-1800s and they are still at the forefront of developments. Independent of government and reliant on public support, they can concentrate their resources either on acquiring land which can then be managed purely for conservation purposes, or on influencing political decision-makers by lobbying and campaigning.

Managers and owners of land include: the **Royal Society for the Protection of Birds** (RSPB, 🖳 www.rspb.org.uk/about-the-rspb/at-home-and-abroad/scotland), which manages 200 nature reserves, 77 of which are in Scotland, and is the largest voluntary conservation body in Europe with over a million members; and the **National Trust for Scotland** (🖳 nts.org.uk) which, with about 300,000 members, is Scotland's largest conservation charity. It protects, through ownership, both countryside and historic buildings.

Lesser known but equally important groups include: the **John Muir Trust** (🖳 www.johnmuirtrust.org) which is dedicated to safeguarding and conserving wild places (the trust owns and manages about 60,500 acres (just under 25,000 hectares) in places such as Skye, Knoydart, Sutherland, Perthshire and Lochaber, including Ben Nevis); **Trees for Life** (🖳 treesforlife.org.uk), a group committed to the regeneration of the Caledonian Forest (see p71) in the Highlands; **Woodland Trust** (🖳 woodlandtrust.org.uk); **Scottish Wildlife Trust** (🖳 scottishwildlifetrust.org.uk) which covers all aspects of conservation across Scotland through a network of local groups; and the Scottish branch of **Butterfly Conservation** (🖳 butterfly-conservation.org/in-your-area/scottish-office).

### (Photos opposite)
● **Top – Left**: You'll pass numerous isolated patches of Caledonian pine (see p69), such as this one in Glen Falloch (© BT). **Right**: Ptarmigan (see p78) on the slopes of Ben Nevis (© BT) and (**below**) young red deer stag by Kings House Hotel. (Don't try to feed the deer here; recently a tourist was charged by a stag when he offered it a chocolate digestive biscuit).
● **Centre**: Red deer are quite common in Scotland (see p72; photo © Joel Newton).
● **Bottom – Left**: One of Britain's more unusual species of flora, the carnivorous sundew plant (see p166). Another carnivorous plant you may see on the northern section of the walk is the butterwort (photo opposite p65). **Middle**: Feral goat (see p73), Loch Lomond. **Right**: The hardy blackface sheep is the main breed you'll see on your walk.

THE ENVIRONMENT & NATURE

Common Dog Violet
*Viola riviniana*

Honeysuckle
*Lonicera periclymemum*

Dog Rose
*Rosa canina*

Self-heal
*Prunella vulgaris*

Germander Speedwell
*Veronica chamaedrys*

Herb-Robert
*Geranium robertianum*

Lousewort
*Pedicularis sylvatica*

Rowan (tree)
*Sorbus aucuparia*

Yellow Rattle
*Rhinanthus minor*

Common Knapweed
*Centaurea nigra*

Ramsons (Wild Garlic)
*Allium ursinum*

British Bluebell
*Hyacinthoides non-scripta*

dry peaty soils and **cross-leaved heath** (*Erica tetralix*) prefers wetter boggier ground. Other members of the heather family include **blaeberry** (*Vaccinium myrtilis*, called bilberry in England), **bog bilberry** (*V. uliginosum*) and **cowberry** (*V. vitis-idaea*) which all have edible berries.

In boggy areas such as Rannoch Moor look for **bog myrtle** (*Myrica gale*), **common** and **harestail cottongrass** (*Eriophorum angustifolium* and *E. vaginatum*) and the incredible carnivorous **round-leaved sundew** (*Drosera rotundifolia*) which traps and digests small insects. On drier heaths you can't miss the prickly **whin** (*Ulex europaeus*) bushes, called gorse in England, with their yellow flowers and the similar but spineless bushes of **broom** (*Cytisus scoparius*).

## Mountain

If you explore some of the mountains along the way you may come across alpine plants, in particular **starry**, **purple**, **yellow** and **mossy saxifrage** (*Saxifraga stellaris*, *S. oppositifolia*, *S. aizoides* and *S. hypnoides*) whose dramatic name means 'rock-breaker'. Other flowers to look out for are **alpine lady's-mantle** (*Alchemilla alpina*), **trailing azalea** (*Loiseleuria procumbens*) and **northern bedstraw** (*Galium boreale*).

THE ENVIRONMENT & NATURE

---

❏ **MOORLAND AND HEATHER**
*To a fool who cries 'Nothing but heather!' where in September another*
*Sitting there and resting and gazing around*
*Sees not only the heather but blaeberries*
*With bright green leaves and leaves already turned scarlet,*
*Hiding ripe blue berries; and amongst the sage-green leaves*
*Of the bog-myrtle the golden flowers of tormentil shining;*
*And on the small bare places, where the little Blackface sheep*
*Found grazing, milkworts blue as summer skies;*
*And down in neglected peat-hags, not worked*
*Within living memory, sphagnum moss in pastel shades*
*Of yellow, green and pink; sundew and butterwort*
*Waiting with wide-open sticky leaves for their tiny winged prey;*
*And nodding harebells vying in their colour*
*With the blue butterflies that poise themselves delicately upon them,*
*And stunted rowan with harsh dry leaves of glorious colour.*
*'Nothing but heather!' – How marvellously descriptive! And incomplete!*
**Hugh MacDiarmid** *Lucky Poet*

Heather is an incredibly versatile plant which is put to many uses. It provides fodder for livestock, fuel for fires, an orange dye and material for bedding, thatching roofs, basketwork and brooms. It is still used in place of hops to flavour beer and the flower heads can be brewed to make a good tea. It is said that Robert Burns used to drink such a 'moorland tea' made from heather tops and the dried leaves of blackberry, speedwell, bilberry, thyme and wild strawberry.

Bees are also responsible for heather honey, widely acclaimed the world over. In high summer the heather moorlands are in bloom and the bees will collect pollen exclusively from this source. The result is a much sought-after dark amber honey full of flavour.

## TREES

*In the past 500 years we have destroyed over 99
per cent of our equivalent of the rainforests.*
**David Minns** *The Nature of Scotland*

### The woods of Caledon

When the Romans arrived in Scotland almost 2000 years ago they named it Caledonia or 'wooded heights'. By the time Samuel Johnson and James Boswell toured the country in 1773 it was possible to remark, 'A tree might be a show in Scotland as a horse in Venice'. The tree cover which so amazed the Romans consisted of oak in the low-

**Hazel (with flowers)** lands with Scots, or Caledonian, pine in the Highlands. This is still Scotland's natural pattern of woodland and it has existed for 7000 years, since the end of the last Ice Age. However, today less than 1% of the original woods remain.

Before the Romans tree cover had already been much reduced by Neolithic peoples. As the population expanded over the following centuries so the forests continued to shrink as land was converted to agriculture. In more recent times large areas of timber were felled for industry and warfare. However, from the 18th century onwards it was the more subtle processes of sheep grazing and the management of land for field sports that ensured that once the trees were gone they would never return. Overgrazing the land with sheep and deer (which eat young trees) and the burning of heather to maintain the grouse moors have meant that new trees never get established.

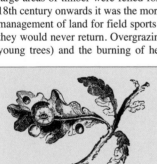

❏ **OAK LEAVES WITH GALLS**
Oak trees support more kinds of insects than any other tree in Britain and some affect the oak in unusual ways. The eggs of gall-flies cause growths known as galls on the leaves. Each of these contains a single insect. Other kinds of gall-flies lay eggs in stalks or flowers, leading to flower galls, growths the size of currants.

### Indigenous trees on the Way

There are some glorious examples of **oak woodland** on the southern half of the Way, in particular along Loch Lomond. The two native species of oak, the common or pedunculate (*Quercus robur*) and the sessile (*Q. petraea*), grow here along with many hybrids. These woods can't strictly be described as natural as most were planted in the early 19th century but they provide a wonderful home for a wide range of species and offer beautiful walking. Some of the islands in the Loch support semi-natural oak woods with a more random planting pattern, wider age range of trees and conse-

THE ENVIRONMENT & NATURE

❏ **ASH DIEBACK**
Described by The Tree Council as 'the most damaging tree disease since Dutch elm', Chalara ash dieback appears to have originated in Denmark and was first identified in England in 2012. It has spread rapidly and in recent years symptoms of the disease have become increasingly visible in Scotland. Current evidence suggests that at least 50-75% of Scotland's 11 million mature ash trees may die over the next two decades. See 🖳 tree council.org.uk for more information about the action plan, known as the Ash Dieback Toolkit, to deal with the problem.

quently more natural diversity. The oak woods are far more diverse than their single species name would suggest. **Elm** (*Ulmus glabra*), **hazel** (*Corylus avellana*) and **ash** (*Fraxinus excelsior*) intermingle with the oaks on good soil while pioneer species such as **rowan** (*Sorbus aucuparia*), **silver birch** (*Betula pendula*) and **downy birch** (*B. pubescens*) and the much-rarer **aspen** (*Populus tremula*) congregate on poorer soils along with **holly** (*Ilex aquifolium*).

**Ash (with seeds)**

Pioneer species play the vital role in a forest ecosystem of improving the soil. In a natural system unaffected by man they would gradually be succeeded by longer-lived species such as oak and Scots pine. Being hardy, brave lone rowans and birches are often to be seen growing in inaccessible ravines or high up on crags where they are safe from sheep and deer. In wet marshy areas and along rivers and streams you will find **alder** (*Alnus glutinosa*).

Sadly there is little left of the once-majestic **Caledonian pine** (*Pinus sylvestris*) forests which would have covered so much of Scotland in the distant past. Walkers on the Way will pass numerous isolated patches of these beautiful old trees but nothing that could be described as a forest. Some of the oldest Scots pines in Scotland are over 500 years old, they can grow up to 120ft (36m) high and can have a girth

**Alder (with flowers)**

**Birch (with flowers)**

THE ENVIRONMENT & NATURE

of 12ft (3.6m). They are easily identified by their reddish brown upper trunk and pairs of blue-green needles about 2 inches (5cm) long.

The so-called pinewoods also support **juniper** (*Juniperus communis*), **birch** (*Betula pendula* and *B. pubescens*) and **willow** (*Salix spp.*).

### Conifer plantations

On the face of it the 20th century was a boom time for trees in Scotland. Tree cover leapt from a disastrous 4% at the start of the 20th century to 14% by the end (and around 18.5% now, although still rather poor when compared with the EU average of 38%). What these figures disguise is that over 90% of this planting was in conifer plantations; certainly no substitute for oak and Scots pine, and in terms of land use and ecology, about as far removed from the native forests as it is possible to get while still growing trees.

**Juniper (with berries)**

The mass planting of the uplands with conifers was fuelled by the need for a strategic reserve of timber after two world wars. The low quality land in the hills supported marginal sheep farming and was of little value to agriculture. Why not utilise it for growing timber? The Forestry Commission, a government funded by the taxpayer, needed a tree which grew fast with little management and at low cost. The **Sitka spruce** (*Picea sitchensis*), a native of North America, fitted the bill. Industrial methods of cultivation totally inappropriate to remote parts of the British uplands could be used and soon gangs of contract workers were ploughing up the land behind caterpillar tractors.

The 2000 square miles (3000 sq km) made into forest by the Forestry Commission was substantially expanded during the 1970s and '80s when tax arrangements allowed many wealthy private investors to use forestry as a way to shelter their earnings. These short-sighted policies produced the eye-sores accurately described as 'blanket forestry'; same-age trees planted close together in neat regimented rows enclosed by miles of straight-running deer-proof fencing. By the time you reach Fort William you will be familiar with these as parts of the Way follow forest rides through such plantations.

---

### ❏ THE VALUE OF TOURISM

In the past land was valued only for the produce or resources which could be taken from it; today a figure can be put on the economic value of the Scottish scenery itself. Tourism generates around £12 billion every year for the Scottish economy and the number one reason given for visiting is 'the scenery'. In a world which increasingly values nothing unless it can be given a monetary figure it is good to know that even the humble walker is playing a part in protecting the landscape by simply being there.

The visual impact is almost inconsequential when compared to their **ecological impact**. Thousands of acres of species-rich moorland have been ploughed up and replaced by a monoculture of conifers. With it go birds such as the merlin and golden plover. Once mature the plantations cannot support much wildlife as the close canopy allows little light to penetrate to the forest floor. Nothing else can grow and as a consequence few animals venture into this sterile environment.

As with all monocultures pests easily build up and have to be controlled with chemicals. The deep ploughing and use of heavy machinery damages soil structure and also leads to a higher incidence of flash-floods as drainage patterns are altered. It has also been found that acid rain gets trapped in the trees and is released into the streams during a downpour killing young fish and invertebrates. What's more, the end product from this environmentally damaging land-use is a low-grade timber used mainly for paper, a hideous waste of a valuable raw material. Perversely and misleadingly this is often advertised as 'paper from sustainable forestry'.

---

### ❏ GROUND-BREAKING ECOLOGICAL RESTORATION

Forestry and Land Scotland has learnt a few lessons from the past and now has a wider remit to balance timber production alongside environmental and social concerns. Where mature conifers are felled the area is replanted with a wider range of species. This will in time produce more varied habitats for wildlife, be more sympathetic to the landscape and encourage the use of forests for recreation. Good examples of these new-look plantations are the Forest Enterprise managed forests in **Glen Nevis** at the northern end of the trail.

While these new plantations are a slight improvement on what went before they do little to regenerate Scotland's damaged ecosystems. Far more encouraging is the rising interest in a new field of scientific research; that of ecological restoration. If we are to improve the life-carrying capacity of the earth large parts of land which have been severely degraded by man must be restored to their former vitality and diversity. Walkers will see work already underway along the eastern shore of **Loch Lomond** to regenerate the indigenous woodlands. Cashel Forest (see box p122) was just one of over 80 projects throughout the country under the umbrella of the Millennium Forest for Scotland. Funded largely by the lottery, the project aims to curb the decline of native woodland which at present covers only 1% of Scotland's land area.

In the north of Scotland another ambitious project is being co-ordinated by Trees for Life (🖳 treesforlife.org.uk); their vision is to restore the **Caledonian pine forest** to a 600-square-mile area west of Inverness, between Glen Carron and Glen Moriston. Since 1989 Trees for Life staff and volunteers, with assistance from Forest Enterprise and the National Trust for Scotland, have planted over half a million Scots pine trees in this area. If you would like to get involved with this commendable scheme see p64 for their contact details.

This really is ground-breaking work. Unlike most other projects which have some utilitarian purpose, this is being conducted purely for the sake of restoring the wild forest as a home for wildlife and to perform its true ecological function for the Earth. Although several groups are working to restore the Scots pine forests this is the only one to do so over such a large area. Ultimately restoring such large ecosystems as the Caledonian Forest is the only way to start to reverse man's impact on the planet.

Thankfully, in the 21st century even big business is beginning to recognise the importance of conservation and environmentally friendly practices. While there are still many stands of tightly packed sitka spruce across Scotland, Forestry & Land Scotland does now have an active conservation programme (see box p71) through which they plant native species and leave clear areas, particularly around streams and rivers, to encourage wildlife.

## MAMMALS

The animal most frequently associated with the Scottish Highlands is the **red deer** (*Cervus elaphus*), justifiably referred to as 'the monarch of the glen'. This is Britain's largest land mammal and one that most walkers will have a good chance of seeing. They can be found either in their preferred habitat of natural woodland, like that along Loch Lomond, or out on the open hills, a harsh environment to which the red deer has had to adapt since the demise of deciduous woods. Although traditionally a forest dweller you will rarely see deer in the sterile environment of mature conifer plantations. In summer they often move onto windy high ground to avoid midges while in winter they come down into the valley bottoms to find better food.

Male deer (stags) grow beautiful antlers every year. They are discarded in April or May and will be fully regrown by July or August ready for the rut in late September. At this time of year you may hear stags roaring at each other across the glens, the beginning of the competition for mating rights with a harem of hinds (females). If a stag is out-roared he will usually back down and concede his harem to the challenger. Occasionally the competition will move on to the next stage where the stags lock antlers in a battle of strength until one of them submits. Calves are usually born the following June and can live for up to 15 years.

Population estimates vary between 360,000 and 400,000; even if the lower figure is the correct one this still represents the highest it's ever been and is felt by many to be jeopardising the ecology of the Highlands. In particular, such high numbers prevent the natural regeneration of many important trees and flowers. This imbalance was caused by man through the eradication of their natural predators, the wolf (the last wolf was killed in 1743), lynx and brown bear, and by maintaining high deer numbers for stalking on sporting estates (see p55). Today's marksmen are trying harder to emulate natural predators by weeding out the old, weak and young and by culling more hinds (as opposed to the traditional target of large healthy stags for trophies) in an attempt to redress the balance.

Scotland's other native deer is the smaller **roe deer** (*Capreolus capreolus*), mainly to be seen in woodland and they can sometimes be identified by their loud bark made when running away.

The red deer is most likely to be confused with the non-native **fallow deer** (*Cervus dama*). Found mainly in deciduous woodland, it is smaller, less common and distinguished by prominent white spots on its reddish brown coat and a black stripe running down its tail. The males have impressive spade-like antlers. The other non-native is the **sika** deer, originally from East Asia. Of a medium-size, they have a smaller head in comparison to their body, an all-white tail, pointed antlers and a distinctive, 'furrowed brow' that makes them appear almost angry. Conservationists have expressed concern that sika deer have been known to breed with red deer, thereby producing hybrids of the two that could, in time, negatively impact the population of pure red deer.

Other common and familiar mammals include **foxes** (*Vulpes vulpes*), **badgers** (*Meles meles*), **mountain hares** (*Lepus timidus*), **stoats** (*Mustela erminea*) and their smaller relation, the **weasel** (*Mustela nivalis*), **hedgehogs** (*Erinaceus europaeus*), **voles**, **mice** and **shrews**. More unusual are the **feral goats** (*Capra hircus*) living in the caves and woods north of Rowardennan on the eastern shore of Loch Lomond. These are descendants of goats which escaped during the Highland clearances (see box below) in the 18th and 19th centuries.

The Highlands, being relatively unpopulated, are a vital refuge for some key British species which elsewhere have either disappeared altogether or are nearing extinction. The woods and forests, for example, are the last stronghold of Britain's only native squirrel, the **red squirrel** (*Sciurus vulgaris*). Their numbers have fluctuated dramatically over the years, disappearing almost entirely by the mid 1700s due to the clearing of ancient pine forests and epidemics of disease, and then establishing themselves once again in the new conifer plantations. Here this delightful creature exists in moderate numbers and has so far avoided the recent catastrophic decline experienced in much of England. The introduction of the American **grey squirrel** (*Sciurus carolinensis*) at the end of the 19th century is blamed for this demise south of the border and it is only by keeping this species out of Scotland's red squirrel habitats that a similar fate can be avoided.

## ❏ SHEEP

Sheep have played an important role in shaping the Highlands. Medieval peasant farmers kept them in small numbers alongside goats and black cattle as part of a mixed, semi-communal system of farming. In summer some of the villagers moved the livestock from the low-lying villages up to the higher *shielings* to make the most of the new hill grass. In autumn they returned to harvest the oats in the glen, an annual cycle that existed for centuries.

Things began to change dramatically in the 18th century with the increased commercialisation of farming. New methods of sheep husbandry were developing in the Scottish Borders and prices for wool and mutton were increasing because of the swelling urban population. Lowland shepherds looked to the Highlands for grazing their **Cheviot** and **Blackface** sheep and Highland landlords, eager to make a profit, were happy to rent out the shielings. The peasant farmers were 'encouraged' to move by increased rents and occasionally by force and were given poor land on the coast, called *crofts*, as compensation. When crofting failed to give the expected returns from fishing, seaweed harvesting and marginal farming, thousands of Highlanders emigrated to the cities and to the New World, thus completing the so-called Clearances of the Highlands.

Little has changed today. The Highlands are still sparsely populated and Blackface sheep are the predominant stock on the high moorland. By their selective grazing they have created the vegetation synonymous with the area, encouraging the growth of bracken and coarse grasses and preventing the regeneration of trees. Sheep farming along with tourism is how most people now make a living in the Highlands.

It is one of those conservation paradoxes that the commendable attempts to increase the amount of deciduous woodland in the Highlands may also be aiding the spread of the grey squirrel. Coniferous forests are now having to be managed specifically for red squirrels in order to keep this alien invader out.

The **pine marten** (*Martes martes*) is another rare woodland species which has all-but disappeared from England and Wales but is making a comeback in Scotland. In the 19th and early 20th centuries it suffered relentless persecution from gamekeepers which along with habitat loss and the demise of its favourite food, the red squirrel, took it to the brink of extinction. With more enlightened management on sporting estates and the increased spread of woodland this protected species is now able to re-colonise some of its former territory, such as the wooded banks of Loch Lomond. However, you would be very lucky indeed to catch a glimpse of this elusive creature.

An equally shy and similarly persecuted animal is the **wildcat** (*Felis silvestris*), which is similar in appearance to its domestic cousin. It became extinct from southern England as far back as the 16th century and nearly disappeared altogether from Britain in the early 1900s. Reduced harassment from gamekeepers and increased forestry have allowed it to re-colonise much of Scotland north of the central industrial belt.

The **otter** (*Lutra lutra*), that great symbol of clean water and a healthy environment, is also now thriving in the Western Highlands after a sudden decline in the 1950s and '60s which was caused by a combination of water pollution (in particular by organochlorine pesticides), loss of well-vegetated river banks and hunting by otter hounds. In the Highlands they inhabit river banks and sea lochs as fish are their primary food.

### Highland cattle

These domesticated wild-looking shaggy beasts fit perfectly into the dramatic scenery of the Highlands and are uniquely native to Scotland. They are descended from the wild ox, which was living in Scotland before humans, and from the Celtic Shorthorn which was brought to Britain about 5000 years ago. As a result they are well suited to the harsh environment and meagre grazing of the hills. The wealth of the Highlands was based on these cattle until the 17th century. At that time they would have been predominantly black in colour; today the toffee-coloured coat is preferred. You can tell the difference between cows and bulls by the horns: cows' horns are upturned while bulls' turn downwards.

### REPTILES

The **adder** (*Vipera berus*) is the only common snake in Scotland and, of the three species which exist in Britain, the only poisonous one. They pose very little risk to walkers and will not bite unless provoked, doing their best to hide. Their venom is designed to kill small mammals such as mice, voles and shrews so deaths in humans are very rare, but a bite can be extremely unpleasant and occasionally dangerous particularly to children and the elderly. You are most likely to encounter them in spring when they come out of hibernation and during the summer when pregnant females warm themselves in the sun. They are easily identified by the striking zigzag pattern on their back. Should you be lucky enough to encounter one of these beautiful creatures enjoy it and leave it undisturbed. See also p60.

## BUTTERFLIES

With around 33% of the UK's land but only 8.2% of the human population, Scotland is ideal country for Britain's butterfly and moth population. A lepidopterist could spend many a happy hour here finding and identifying such seldom-seen species as the **pearl-bordered fritillary**, which is threatened by habitat loss elsewhere in the UK. Other species prevalent in the highlands include the **large heath butterfly**, **mountain ringlet** and **mountain burnet**. The butterfly that is most conspicuous, however, at least in July, is the **Scotch argus**, which flutters around the path as you stroll through. With brown wings outlined with a row of orange spots, it is very similar to the much rarer **mountain ringlet**, though the latter lacks white dots at the centre of its orange spots.

Despite the wide range of species, Scotland's butterflies are still under pressure from habitat loss and the intensive use of farmland. Thankfully, bodies such as **Butterfly Conservation Scotland** (🖥 butterfly-conservation.org/in-your-area/scottish-office) work to preserve habitats for butterflies, moths and other species. To find out more about their work, visit their website where you can also learn how to help with their conservation efforts: they often run surveys on certain species, asking for reports of sightings.

## BIRDS

### Streams, rivers and lochs
In 2021 much excitement was generated by the first sighting of a **white-tailed eagle**, or **sea eagle**, over Loch Lomond for the first time in over a century. The pair spotted at Loch Lomond were said to be nest prospecting – looking for a suitable place to build a nest – in June, having first been sighted in March 2021. It's worth noting that, despite the top billing given to the golden eagle, the sea eagle can have an even wider wing span: of up to 240cm.

Along lochs and wooded rivers look out for the striking **goosander** (*Mergus merganser*), a sawbill duck which hunts for fish, and the well-known **mallard** (*Anas platyrhynchos*), the ancestor of the farmyard duck. If you are walking in autumn you may catch the evocative sight of **white-fronted** (*Anser albifrons*) and **greylag** (*Anser anser*) **geese** flying in from Greenland to over-winter on Loch Lomond. The white-fronted goose is distinguished by the white on the front of its head at the base of the bill. They return north again at the start of spring.

The **grey wagtail** (*Motacilla cinerea*) and the **dipper** (*Cinclus cinclus*) are two delightful birds which can be seen year-round bobbing up and down on boulders along loch shores or in the middle of fast-flowing streams. With its blue-grey head and back and bright-yellow underparts the grey wagtail is the most striking of all the wagtails. The dipper is unmistakable with its dinner-jacket plumage (black back and white bib) and can perform the amazing feat of walking underwater along streambeds. They are joined in summer by **common sandpipers** (*Tringa hypoleucos*), a tame long-legged, long-billed wader easily identified by its wagtail-like dipping action.

## Woodland

The familiar woodland residents of chaffinches, robins, tits, songthrushes, blackbirds and tawny owls are joined by spring and summer visitors. Tropically bright **redstarts** (*Phoenicurus phoenicurus*), relatives of the robin, spend a lot of time on the ground looking for food, often motionless before suddenly pouncing on insects or worms; acrobatic **pied flycatchers** (*Ficedula hypoleuca*) dart after insects in mid air; rather nondescript brown **tree pipits** (*Anthus trivialis*) perform song flights while darting from one high perch to another; yellow and green **wood warblers**

BLACK GROUSE
L: 580mm/23"

(*Phylloscopus sibilatrix*) restlessly flit around in the woodland canopy along with tiny **willow warblers** (*Phylloscopus trochilus*), those miracles of bird migration that travel 2000 miles at a never faltering speed of 25mph to spend the winter in central Africa.

In hilly woodland these species may be joined by the increasingly rare **black grouse** (*Lyrurus tetrix*). The male blackcock is unmistakable with his blue-black plumage but the female could be confused with the red grouse, though they rarely share the same habitat.

In **pine forests** you will find seed-eating finches such as **siskins** (*Serinus serinus*), **red crossbills** (*Loxia curvirostra*) and **Scottish crossbills** (*Loxia scotica*). The latter is very special indeed as it is found nowhere else but Scotland, the only bird with this distinction. This canary-like bird uses its powerful crossover bill to prise open the tough cones of the Scots pine to extract the seed, its principal food.

The **capercaillie** (*Tetrao urogallus*), the largest game-bird in Britain, is another casualty of scant pinewood habitat. The capercaillie is regarded as an accurate indicator species, its low numbers alerting us to the decline of mature, varied forests. Some forward-thinking people are well aware of this bleak situation and are already working to restore Scotland's beautiful pinewoods. This should bring a brighter future not only for these birds but also for the whole ecology of the Highlands.

## Open hillside and moorland

**Golden plovers** (*Pluvialis apricaria*), **meadow pipits** (*Anthus pratensis*) and **stonechats** (*Saxicola torquata*) are joined in summer by **whinchats** (*Saxicola* *rubetra*) and **wheatears** (*Oenanthe oenanthe*) out on the open hills. In autumn huge flocks of **redwings** (*Turdus iliacus*) and **fieldfares** (*Turdus pilaris*) fly over from Scandinavia to feed on ripe berries.

**STONECHAT**
L: 135MM/5.25"

Walkers on heather moorland often put up a covey of **red grouse** (*Lagopus lagopus*) which will speed downwind gliding and whirring just above the ground. This plump copper-coloured bird is highly valued for its sporting potential and is probably best known for its association with the 'Glorious Twelfth', the start of the grouse-shooting season in August, one of those over-hyped British rituals. There is no doubt, however, that if it weren't for grouse shooting we wouldn't have the magnificent upland moors we have today. They would almost certainly have been given over to the green deserts of conifer forests and sheep-grazing.

Birds of prey likely to be seen on moorland include **kestrels** (*Falco tinnunculus*), a small falcon often seen hovering in search of beetles or mice, the much less common **merlin** (*Falco columbarius*), the smallest falcon, which swoops low over the moors twisting and banking as it flies after meadow pipits, and **buzzards** (*Buteo buteo*) which fly in slow wide circles looking for small mammals. Although a large bird, the buzzard is significantly smaller than a golden eagle and can be distinguished by its drawn-out mewing cry.

---

### ❑ SCOTLAND'S ENDANGERED BIRDS

In December 2021 the British Trust for Ornithology (🖳 bto.org) released its latest 'Birds of Conservation Concern', more commonly known as its 'Red list for birds'. This list, compiled by experts, looks at 245 species with breeding, passage or wintering populations in the UK, and sorts each species into one of three lists: green, amber and red. This 'traffic-light' system provides us with a snapshot of how each species is faring, with those birds on the red list being considered to have the highest level of conservation concern. In other words, those most vulnerable and at threat of extinction – and thus most urgently in need of our help.

As you'd probably expect, the list makes for fairly depressing reading. The red list has grown from 67 to 70 species since the last update in 2015.

Of particular concern to Scotland's ornithologists, the **ptarmigan** (see p78) jumped straight from the green to the red list. The species' sensitivity to climate change and a reduction in its mountain habitat were among the reasons cited for this sudden drop in fortunes. The **capercaillie**, too, remains on the red list as it has for several years now. Indeed, it is thought that there are only around 1000 capercaillie left in Scotland. This is not the first time this species has come under attack. In the 18th century the bird was hunted to extinction and those seen in Scotland today originate from Swedish capercaillie used to reintroduce the species in 1837.

On a happier note, the **Scottish crossbill** population has increased to 6800 pairs, thus moving it from the red list down to amber. The **sea eagle**, too, which was hunted to extinction in the early years of the 20th century, have been the subject of a reintroduction programme over the past decade and a small population is now established on Scotland's east coast.

THE ENVIRONMENT & NATURE

## High mountain

The **golden eagle** (*Aquila chrysaetos*), Britain's largest and most majestic bird of prey, is synonymous with Scotland's mountains and touches the essence of wilderness. Populations are at last rising

**GOLDEN EAGLE (SILHOUETTE)**

now and currently all 400 of Britain's breeding pairs of golden eagle live in Scotland. Spiralling upwards on the thermals this huge bird with its seven-foot (2m) wingspan and long open primary feathers couldn't be confused with any other. It feeds mainly on grouse, ptarmigan and mountain hares but won't turn down dead sheep and other carrion.

**GOLDEN EAGLE**
L: 910MM/36"

As thrilling a sight as the golden eagle is the **peregrine falcon** (*Falco peregrinus*) in flight. This king of the air can reach speeds of 50mph (80km/h) in level flight with swift shallow beats of its long pointed wings interspersed by long glides. But it shows off its true talents when diving after pigeon or grouse, its principal prey, sometimes reaching an incredible 180mph (290km/h). In the 1950s the population of peregrines dropped suddenly and disastrously. During this crisis Scotland held the only healthy population of peregrines in the world. The species was probably saved by the RSPB's and British Trust for Ornithology's painstaking research which linked the decline to the use of pesticides, in particular dieldrin and DDT. These chemicals were being used by farmers to treat their grain which was then ingested by seed-eating birds who in turn were eaten by peregrines. The revival of the species is one of the great success stories of modern conservation.

Above 2000ft (600m) you might see fearless **ptarmigan** (*Lagopus muta*), a cousin of the red grouse, scurrying across the ground in front of you. In winter its grey speckled plumage turns to pure white except for a black tail. **Snow buntings** (*Plectrophenax nivalis*), looking like pale sparrows, occasionally nest in the high mountains but most arrive in the winter migration from the Arctic.

**RAVEN**
L: 650MM/25"

Also haunting these heights are jet black **ravens** (*Corvus corax*), a massive crow with a powerful beak which soars at great speed across the sky occasionally rolling onto its back with half-folded wings as if to prove its mastery of flight.

# GLASGOW

## City guide

Everyone walking the West Highland Way really should take a few days at the beginning or end of their walk to spend some time in this the best of all Scottish cities, once known as the 'Second City of the Empire'. The economic downturn in the latter half of the 20th century was tough for Glasgow and its people but there's been a dramatic transformation since then, despite the recessions.

Glasgow's a fascinating and lively place, populated by some of the friendliest people in the country. You'll find some of the top museums and art galleries in Britain including the inspiring **Riverside Museum**, designed by Zaha Hadid; numerous shrines to the world-famous architect and designer, **Charles Rennie Mackintosh**; interesting museums such as **The Tenement House**, an early 20th-century time capsule, and the award-winning **St Mungo's Museum of Religious Life & Art**; the gothic **Glasgow Cathedral**; top-class **restaurants**, vibrant **nightlife** and one of the liveliest **arts scenes** in Europe.

En route to or from the West Highland Way you'll be coming through the city anyway but ideally you should plan your holiday so that you have time both to spend a few days here and to do the half-day walk from Glasgow to Milngavie, rather than simply take the train (or a bus) to the start of the West Highland Way.

### ORIENTATION

The centre of the city is on the north side of the River Clyde, with the M8 motorway sweeping across the north and through the west. The two main railway stations and bus station are in the centre. The two main accommodation areas we've given details about are just north of the main shopping street, Sauchiehall, and west of the M8 in the Kelvingrove area. The main commercial area is Merchant City and around George Square. Milngavie (see p101) and the start of the West Highland Way are 10 miles north-west of the centre.

### ARRIVAL AND DEPARTURE

**Glasgow Airport** (🖳 glasgowairport.com) is nine miles west of the city. The Airport Express bus service (🖳 firstbus.co.uk/greater-glas

gow) No 500 leaves (daily approx 5am-11pm; 2-4/hr; 15-25 mins; £8.50/14
sgl/rtn) from outside the main terminal building for the city centre and rail-
way/bus stations. A taxi will cost from £45, depending on the time of day.

Most airlines now use Glasgow Airport but some Ryanair flights from
Europe use **Prestwick Airport** (🖳 glasgowprestwick.com), 29 miles to the
west of the city. There are trains from here to Glasgow Central (Mon-Sat 4/hr,
Sun 2/hr; 40-50 mins) as well as a Glasgow to Ayr bus service (Stagecoach's
X77; 1-3/hr; approx 50 mins) to **Buchanan bus station**, two blocks north of
Queen Street station, which is the terminus for both local and national bus and
coach services.

There are two main railway stations: **Central** for services on the West Coast
Main Line from London Euston Milngavie and to south Scotland, and **Queen
Street** for Milngavie and for north and east Scotland. Glasgow City's 398
Station Link bus (daily 8am-8pm 1-5/hr) operates between the two (they tell
you to allow 30 mins for connections between the two stations) and continues
to Buchanan bus station; if you have a connecting rail ticket there's no charge
to use it. It takes only about 15 minutes to walk, though.

See pp46-9 for national public transport information.

## GETTING AROUND – AND TO MILNGAVIE

For information on public transport use Traveline Scotland's excellent journey-
planning website (🖳 travelinescotland.com) or look at Strathclyde Public
Transport's website (🖳 spt.co.uk).

### Subway

The Glasgow Subway (🖳 spt.co.uk/subway), otherwise known as the
Clockwork Orange, operates a circular route around the city. A **single/return**
paper ticket costs £1.75/3.30; an **all day ticket** (£4.20) gives unlimited travel on
the system for a day. Note that fares are cheaper (£1.55/3 for single/return, £3
for all day tickets) if you go online and register for one of their **smartcards**.

### Bus

There's a good bus service around the city; tickets for journeys in the city centre cost £1.70. Pay the driver as you board.

### Taxi

If you're in a small group it may be worth taking a taxi (☎ 0141-429 7070, 🖳
glasgowtaxis.co.uk). From Central station it should cost approximately £10-12
to Glasgow Youth Hostel and about £25 to Milngavie.

### To and from Milngavie                              (see also pp46-9)

● **By train**  The quickest way to Milngavie is by train. There are direct services **from Queen Street station** (£3.90; daily 2/hr) taking 23-30 mins, between
about 7.40am and 8.40pm, Monday to Saturday, and on Sunday between about
9.30am and 9.30pm. You can also take a train **from Glasgow Central** but this
requires a change, usually at either Partick or Hyndland.

● **By bus** Most services start at Stockwell Place, passing Central station on Hope St then crossing Sauchiehall St, including First Glasgow's **No 60A** bus (Mon-Sat 1-3/hr, Sun 1-2/hr) to Milngavie which takes around 45 minutes.

You can also jump on First Scotland East's bus **No X10/X10A**: the first service leaves Buchanan bus station at 6.30am (Mon-Fri), 9.10am (Sat) or 11am (Sun). Services go to Milngavie Station.

## SERVICES

### Tourist information
**Glasgow iCentre** (☎ 0141-566 4083, 🖳 visitscotland.com; Mon-Sat 9am-5pm, Sun 10am-4pm), is at 156a/158 Buchanan St. It has information on all parts of Scotland as well as the city.

### Post office
Glasgow's main post office (Mon-Sat 9am-5.30pm, Tue from 9.30am) is at 136 West Nile St but there are a number of others centrally too.

### Supermarkets
For supermarkets you have several choices, including the three marked on the map on pp82-3. They are: **Waitrose** on Byres Road near the Botanic Gardens (Mon-Fri 81m-10pm, Sat to 9pm, Sun 9am-8pm); and both **Tesco** (daily 7am-11pm) and **Aldi** (Mon-Sat 7am-10pm, Sun 9am-8pm) across town on the High Street. There are several others dotted around the centre too.

### Internet access
Most restaurants and coffee shops have wi-fi, as do B&Bs and hotels, which is free unless otherwise stated. If you need a computer head to one of the many **libraries** in the city (🖳 glasgowlife.org.uk/libraries; phone booking required for computer terminal; free).

### Left luggage
Left-luggage facilities are available at Glasgow Central station (🖳 left-bag gage.co.uk) – really useful if you've time to kill in Glasgow but aren't staying overnight. The charge is £7.50 for 3 hours or £12.50 for 24 hours.

### Outdoor equipment shops
There are several outdoor equipment shops for any last-minute purchases you need to make before setting off into the wilds. The most exciting is **Tiso Glasgow Outdoor Experience** (☎ 0141-559 5450, 🖳 tiso.com/shops/glasgow-outdoor-experience; Mon-Sat 9am-5pm, Sun from 10am), north-east of Buchanan bus station on Couper St, just off Kyle St. This is a mountain-sports superstore like no other complete with 40ft climbing wall, a good *café* and a 300ft simulated mountain footpath! In the city centre **Tiso** have a more conventional store on Buchanan St. **Nevisport** is at 261 Sauchiehall St.

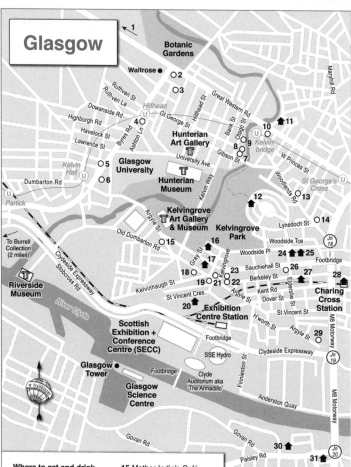

**Where to eat and drink**

2 Òran Mór
3 Crabshakk Botanics
4 The Ubiquitous Chip
5 University Café
6 Number 16
7 Stravaigin
8 Tiffney's Steakhouse
9 Tchai-Ovna House of Tea
& Vegetarian Restaurant
10 Byblos Café
13 Chillies Westend
14 Balti Club

15 Mother India's Café
18 Thai Siam
19 Ben Nevis Bar
21 Crabshakk Finnieston
22 Fanny Trollope's
23 Mother India
26 Mister Singh's
29 Two Fat Ladies at the Buttery
34 Nice 'n' Sleazy
35 Mini Grill Glasgow
38 King Tut's Wah Wah Hut
39 The Bunker Bar
40 Two Fat Ladies City Centre

41 Mackintosh at the Willow
46 The Pot Still
47 Café Wander
48 Halloumi
49 Gamba
53 Thai Orchid
54 Café Fame
55 The Horse Shoe
56 Willow Tea Rooms
58 Ichiban City Centre
62 Cossachok

**Where to stay**
1 To Hotel du Vin Glasgow
  (¾ mile off map)
11 Albion Hotel
12 Glasgow Youth Hostel
16 Alamo Guest House
17 Argyll Guest House
20 The Flower House
24 Acorn Hotel
25 15 Glasgow
27 Clyde Hostel
28 Premier Inn Charing Cross

30 Ibis Budget Glasgow
31 Travelodge Paisley Road
32 McLays
33 Rennie Mackintosh
   Art School Hotel
36 Ibis Glasgow City Centre
37 Malmaison
42 Travelodge Glasgow Central
43 easyHotel Glasgow
44 citizenM
45 Premier Inn
   Buchanan Galleries

50 Ibis Styles Glasgow
   Centre West
51 Hotel Indigo Glasgow
52 Premier Inn
   Argyle Street
57 Euro Hostel
59 Travelodge Glasgow
   Queen St
60 Ibis Styles Glasgow
   George Square
61 Premier Inn
   George Square

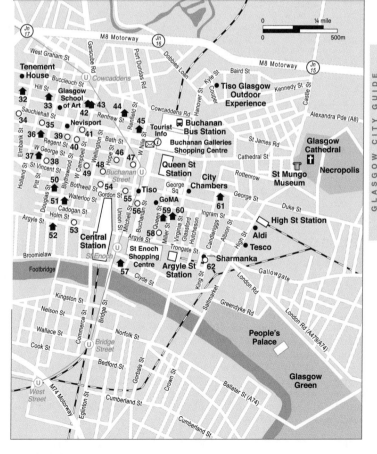

GLASGOW CITY GUIDE

❏ **A BRIEF HISTORY OF GLASGOW**
Glasgow dates back to the founding of the first cathedral and shrine to St Mungo in about 1125. The cathedral was constructed on the spot where Mungo was said to have built a wooden church in the 6th century.

Glasgow grew first as a place of pilgrimage to St Mungo but by the 18th century it had become a major centre for international commerce, handling much of the tobacco trade between Europe and America. This trade helped to finance the growth of local industries including textiles, shipbuilding, ironworks and coal-mining. In the mid-19th century there were 140 cotton mills in the Glasgow area and the shipyards accounted for more than 80% of all vessels built in Britain. The city's heyday came in the second half of the 19th century when many of the grand Victorian buildings you can see today were constructed. By the mid-20th century these industries were in decline and there was widespread unemployment.

In the ensuing decades Glasgow coped remarkably well with the loss of its heavy industries, many jobs having been created in service industries. Parts of the city and suburbs, however, are still depressed and were not helped by the recent recession. The Commonwealth Games in 2014 gave a welcome investment boost and tourism is now an important revenue earner; Glasgow is one of the most-visited cities in Britain.

## FESTIVALS & EVENTS

The main festivals include: **Glasgow Film Festival** (🖳 glasgowfilm.org/glasgow-film-festival), in February or March; **Glasgow Music Festival** (🖳 glasgowmusicfestival.org), in March; **Glasgow International Comedy Festival** (🖳 glasgowcomedyfestival.com) in the same month; the Notting-Hill-Festival-like **West End Festival** (🖳 westendfestival.co.uk) in June; and a **jazz festival** (🖳 jazzfest.co.uk), usually in late June.

Accommodation may be a little hard to come by during these periods so make sure you book well in advance – or avoid these weekends altogether.

## WHERE TO STAY

### Budget accommodation

Glasgow has an excellent choice of budget accommodation. For 18-35 year olds only, *Clyde Hostel* (☎ 0141-221 1710, 🖳 clydehostel.co.uk, 65 Berkeley St; 46 beds plus 30 beds in annex) is a well-located self-catering backpackers' hostel. It's a scruffy but friendly place with private rooms sleeping 2-3 (from £12pp) and 4-14 beds per dorm (£10-25pp). Rates include free internet access. It's a popular place so you need to book well in advance. They claim there are 50 pubs, clubs and restaurants within a five-minute walk of the hostel.

If you're only in Glasgow overnight the soulless *Euro Hostel* (☎ 08455-399 956, 🖳 eurohostels.co.uk, 318 Clyde St; 452 beds; all en suite), in a high-rise building overlooking the River Clyde, is very convenient for the rail and bus stations. Their dorms are modern with up to 14 beds (£10-30pp) and they have single rooms (from £20) and twin rooms (£12-24pp).

❏ PRICES AND ROOM TYPES
The number and type of rooms are given after the address of each entry: S = single room, T = twin room (two beds), D = double room (one double bed), F = family room (sleeps at least three people). Rates quoted are either per person (pp) or per room. Rooms have bathrooms attached (en suite) unless shared facilities are mentioned.

The text also indicates whether the premises have **wi-fi** (WI-FI); if a **bath** (🛁) is available in at least one room; and whether **dogs** (🐕) are welcome.

High up on Park Terrace overlooking the leafy expanse of Kelvingrove Park is the spacious and traditional *Glasgow Youth Hostel* (☎ 0141-332 3004, 🖥 hostellingscotland.org.uk/hostels/glasgow, 8 Park Terrace; 108 beds in rooms sleeping 1-8 people; £15-25pp, sgl rooms from £25-40; 🐕). The hostel is licensed and breakfast is available. If you're staying here consider taking the train to Partick station (on the line to Milngavie) since it is marginally closer to the Youth Hostel than Central station. If you're planning to walk the whole way from Glasgow to Fort William, the route to Milngavie described on pp94-8 begins from Kelvingrove Park – right outside your door if you're staying here.

### Budget chain hotels
The quality of cheaper guesthouses and B&Bs can be very variable making the budget hotel chains a reliable option if you book online far enough in advance to get one of their special deals.

From £24.50 for a room *Premier Inn* (central reservations ☎ 0871-527 9222, 🖥 premierinn.com) is particularly recommended for its comfortable beds and good rooms. They have four central hotels: *Charing Cross* (10 Elmbank Gardens; 🛁), *George Square* (187 George St; 🛁), *Argyle Street* (377 Argyle St; 🛁) and *Buchanan Galleries* (St Andrew House, 141 West Nile St; 🛁). A full cooked breakfast costs £9.50 (from £6.99 for a continental breakfast). Remember that, unlike their closest rivals Travelodge, they do not allow dogs.

Offering equally attractive online deals (from £29 for a room), *Travelodge* (🖥 travelodge.co.uk – reserve online rather than phoning the expensive numbers) has three hotels in central Glasgow: *Glasgow Central* (☎ 0871-984 6141, 5 Hill St; 95D or F; 🛁; 🐕), *Glasgow Queen Street* (☎ 0871-559 1872, 78 Queen St) and *Glasgow Paisley Road* (☎ 0871-984 6142, 251 Paisley Rd; 75D or F; 🛁; WI-FI; 🐕) is just south of the river, half a mile from Central railway station. Travelodge 'unlimited' breakfast starts from £8.75pp. They provide 30 minutes of free wi-fi but after that it's £3 for 24 hours.

Another budget chain operator offering well-located accommodation is easyHotel. Their *easyHotel Glasgow* (online reservations only: 🖥 easyhotel .com, 1 Hill St; 83D/35T) has functional rooms from £22.50. As with easyJet, it's those extras that add up – a TV is £5, WI-FI costs from £3 (though it's free if you join their free clubBedzzz) and if you check out after 10am they may bill you for another night. If you want a room with a window that's extra too.

Another chain offering reliable accommodation – though not always very cheap – is Ibis, part of the **Accor Hotels group** (central reservations ⌨ all .accor.com). Again, to get good prices you must book online well in advance and avoid weekends. *Ibis Glasgow City Centre* (☎ 0141-619 9000; 220 West Regent St; 141D or T; 🐾) has rooms from £45 to over £120; breakfast costs extra. *Ibis Styles Glasgow Centre George Square* (☎ 0141-428 3400; 74 Miller St; 101D or T; 🐾) has rooms from £52 to over £150; breakfast included. South of the river and with rooms from £36, *Ibis Budget Hotel Glasgow* (☎ 0141-429 8013, 2a Springfield Quay; 165D, T or F; WI-FI free in lobby/café; 🐾) is clean and functional with a range of rooms, some including doubles with a bunk bed. The fourth property on their city roster is *Ibis Styles Glasgow Centre West* (☎ 0141-428 4477; 116 Waterloo St; 137D, T or F).

### B&Bs and mid-range hotels

Worth listing for its size and range of rooms, *McLays* (☎ 0141-332 4796, ⌨ mclays.com, 260-76 Renfrew St; 21S/61D, T or F; some share facilities; 🍴; from £30pp, sgl from £27, room only) is a large, rambling place that's very well located. It could do with a tidy but it's fine and very reasonably priced.

On the same street is the more upmarket *Rennie Mackintosh Art School Hotel* (☎ 0141-333 9992, ⌨ renniemackintoshartschoolhotel.co.uk, 218-20 Renfrew St; 11S/9T/3D/1F; £40pp, sgl £35-50) which uses the obvious Glasgow theme but the effect is pleasing. Nearby is *Albion Hotel* (☎ 0141-339 8620, ⌨ albion-hotel.net, 405 North Woodside Rd; 6S/11D, T or F; WI-FI; £22.50-52.50pp, sgl £38-69; breakfast £9pp).

You could also try *Argyll Guest House* (☎ 0141-357 5155, ⌨ argyllguest houseglasgow.co.uk, 970 Sauchiehall St; 3S/17D, T or F; 🍴; from £25pp, sgl from £45, breakfast £8.50pp extra).

*Alamo Guest House* (☎ 0141-339 2395, ⌨ alamoguesthouse.com, 46 Gray St; 4D or T/6D en suite or private facilities; 🍴; WI-FI; from £29.50pp, sgl occ full room rate; min 3 nights in peak season) has two suites. Not far away is *Acorn Hotel* (☎ 0141-332 6556, ⌨ acorn-hotel.com, 140 Elderslie St; 5S/2T/11D; £35-51.50pp, sgl £44-70).

*The Flower House* (☎ 0141-204 2846, ⌨ theflowerhouse.net, 33 St Vincent Crescent; 1S/1T/2D; 🍴; £30-50pp, sgl £40-45) is also recommended, not least for the stunning floral displays around the main entrance.

### Upmarket and boutique hotels

*15 Glasgow* (☎ 0141-332 1263, ⌨ 15glasgow.com, 15 Woodside Place; 3D/1D or T/1D, Tr or Qd; 🍴; £75-160 per room/suite plus £20 supplement for one night stays) is a luxurious boutique B&B with super king-sized beds and monsoon showers, close to Kelvingrove Park. At the weekends there is a two-night stay policy. *Hotel Indigo Glasgow* (☎ 0141-2267700, ⌨ hinglasgow.co.uk, 75 Waterloo St; 94D or T; 🍴; WI-FI; from £86 per room) is a clever conversion of the beautiful old power station, perfectly located in the centre of the city. They have a wide range of packages.

*citizenM* (online booking only: 🖳 citizenm.com, 60 Renfrew St; 198D; WI-FI; £60-170 per room) claims to be the trendiest hotel in Glasgow and probably is. The rooms have large comfortable beds, mood lighting, rain showers and free movies on demand. Stylish *Malmaison* (☎ 0141-572 1000, 🖳 malmaison.com/locations/glasgow, 278 West George St; 10T/62D; ☛; 🐾; from about £70 per room) is housed in a former Episcopal church. At times they have special offers so it is worth checking with them.

Five-star *Hotel du Vin Glasgow* (☎ 0141-378 0385, 🖳 hotelduvin.com/locations/glasgow; 8D or T/32D/9D or F; ☛; 🐾; £100-475 per room), at 1 Devonshire Gardens, occupies five townhouses.

## WHERE TO EAT AND DRINK

There's no shortage of places to eat in Glasgow, everything from the usual chain restaurants to more exciting culinary ventures., **fb**;

### Scottish cuisine

You'll find haggis, tatties and neeps on almost every menu but modern Scottish cuisine goes far beyond that.

*Stravaigin* (☎ 0141-334 2665, 🖳 stravaigin.co.uk, **fb**; 28 Gibson St; café-bar food served Mon-Fri 11am-10pm, Sat & Sun 9am-10pm, restaurant daily 5-11pm, also Sat noon-5pm, Sun 12.30-4pm) produces top-notch fare that's probably best described as Scottish fusion food and the T-shirts and signs proclaim 'Think global, eat local'. Stravaigin's own haggis, neeps 'n' tatties (£15) is, of course, an option, as are vegetarian haggis (£15) and West Coast mussels (£17). Their popular Sunday Brunch (11am-5pm) includes their full Scottish breakfast (£11) and a vegan breakfast (£10). All washed down with a Bloody Mary (£8), of course!

*Number 16* (☎ 0141-339 2544, 🖳 number16.co.uk, **fb**; 16 Byres Rd; Mon-Sat noon-2.30pm & 5.30-9pm, Sun 1-2.30pm & 5.30-8.30pm) is a small restaurant with a large reputation. They offer a 2/3-course lunch menu (£20/25; Mon-Sat) and a la carte options (main from £19.50) in the evenings.

*The Ubiquitous Chip* (☎ 0141-334 5007, 🖳 ubiquitouschip.co.uk, **fb**; 12 Ashton Lane; open daily noon-midnight; food Wed & Thur 5pm-midnight, Fri-Sun noon-midnight) is just off Byres Rd and is a Glasgow institution, open for more than 45 years. You can eat in the restaurant, the brasserie (each has its own menu) or on the roof terrace. How does Argyll venison cooked with coffee, merguez, burnt aubergine and fermented grains sound? Main dishes cost around £18-25 (their steak is £30-35). And if it's just drinks you're after you can choose from one of their three bars, including the Wee Whisky Bar, which they reckon serves 'more whiskies per square foot than any other bar in Scotland'.

### Fish

*Crabshakk* (🖳 crabshakk.com, **fb**) now has two branches. The original *Crabshakk Finnieston* (1114 Argyll St; daily noon-midnight) is tiny but excellent and you'll need to book. The second branch is *Crabshakk Botanics* (18

GLASGOW CITY GUIDE

Vinicombe St; see website for opening hours). Choices include shellfish chowder (£9.95), fish & chips (£14.95) and whole brown crab (£19.95). Oysters are £2.35 each and a whole or half a lobster costs what the market dictates!

For a celebratory dinner it would be hard to beat *Two Fat Ladies at the Buttery* (☎ 0141-221 8188, 🖳 twofatladiesrestaurant.com, **fb**; 652 Argyle St; Tue-Sun noon-10pm), though you might not think it from the location near the M8. Two/three courses cost £25/32 at lunch and pre/post theatre; main dishes in the evening are £19-34. *Two Fat Ladies City Centre* (118A Blythswood St) was temporarily closed at the time of research – check the website for details of reopening.

*Gamba* (☎ 0141-572 0899, 🖳 gamba.co.uk, **fb**; 225A West George St; Wed-Fri 5-10.30pm, Sat noon-10.30pm) is another top-class fish restaurant. Main dishes cost from £25 for the whole blackened sea bream, rising to £49 for the surf-n-turf.

## World cuisines

*Fanny Trollope's* (☎ 0141-564 6464, 🖳 fannytrollopes.co.uk, **fb**; 1066 Argyle St; Tue-Thur 5-9pm, Fri & Sat noon-midnight, Sun 1-8.30pm) is a popular bistro serving seasonal food imaginatively cooked. Monkfish cheeks, king prawn, spinach satay with crispy onions & coconut rice is £16.50.

*Ichiban City Centre* (☎ 0141-204 4200, 🖳 ichiban.co.uk, **fb**; Mon-Thur noon-9pm, Fri-Sun to 10pm) is in the heart of the city at 50 Queen St. The menu is excellent value (approx £9-10 per meal). There's a range of noodles (soba, udon or ramen) as well as tempura and sushi. Takeaway is available.

*Tiffney's Steakhouse* (☎ 0141-328 9557, 🖳 tiffneys.com, **fb**; 61 Otago St; Mon & Wed-Thur 4-9.30pm, Fri-Sat 4-10pm, Sun 4-9pm) serves prime dry-aged Highland beef steaks – from a 300g rib-eye (£34) to a 500g T-bone (£42). For something a little cheaper but still very good, there's *Mini Grill Glasgow* (☎ 0141-332 2732, 🖳 minigrillglasgow.co.uk; **fb**; 244 Bath St; Mon-Thur noon-10pm, Fri & Sat to 11.30pm, Sun to 9pm) where there's steak or venison from £22.

There's excellent borscht (£3.50) at *Cossachok* (☎ 0141-553 0733, 🖳 cafe cossachok.com; 10 King St; Wed-Sun noon-11pm), the Russian café-gallery near Sharmanka (see p92), and you can follow this with blinis, an Uzbek lamb pilaf or beef Stroganoff. The Moscow Blintzes (thin pancakes, £11.95) are recommended. Main dishes are £8.45-14.95 and there's a tempting range of vodkas.

For good Thai food, *Thai Siam* (☎ 0141-229 1191, 🖳 thaisiam glasgow.com, 1191 Argyle St; Tue-Sat noon-2.30pm & 5-9.30pm, Sun 5.30pm-9.30) is popular. Nearer the station end of Argyle St is another good place, *Thai Orchid* (☎ 0141-847 0315, 🖳 thai-orchid.net, **fb**; 346 Argyle St; Tue-Thur 4-10pm, Fri noon-2pm & 5.30-10pm, Sat 1-10pm).

For Greek food, *Halloumi* (☎ 0141-204 1616, 🖳 www.halloumiglas gow.co.uk, **fb**; Sun-Thur noon-10pm, Fri & Sat to 10.30pm) at 161 Hope St is a smart but relaxed mezze restaurant with dishes from £5.90 to £7.90 (they recommend three per person) including such favourites as lamb dolmades (minced lamb and rice in vine leaves) and vegetable moussaka (£6.50).

There are numerous Indian restaurants. *Mother India* (☎ 0141-221 1663, 💻 motherindia.co.uk, **fb**; 28 Westminster Tce; Mon-Thur 5-9.45pm, Fri & Sat 1-10pm, Sun 1-9.45pm) is probably the best. It's a large place with a variety of dining options and good vegetarian choices. Main dishes range from vegetable karahi at £9.50 to king prawn and monkfish served with ginger and dill (£16.50). In the same family is *Mother India's Café* (☎ 0141-339 9145, 💻 motherindia.co.uk, 1355 Argyle St; Sun-Thur noon-10pm, Fri & Sat noon-10.30pm) which is based on a clever concept – it's an Indian tapas bar. Dishes are approximately £5-8. You can't book but service is rapid and the food excellent. Both branches also offer takeaway.

Stiff competition is provided by *Mister Singh's* (☎ 0141-221 1452, 💻 mistersinghsindia.com, **fb**; Tue-Thur 4-10pm, Fri & Sat 1-11pm, Sun 3-10.30pm, last table 8.30/9pm) at 149 Elderslie Street. The uniform of the waiters here – kilt and turban – is reflected in the food, which offers a few Scottish twists to the usual Indian fare such as haggis, neeps and tatties samosas for starters (£5.75).

Subcontinental rivals include *Chillies Westend* (☎ 0141-331 0494, 💻 chilliieswestend.com, 176 Woodlands Rd; daily 4-11pm), which is good value and you can BYOB with no corkage charge.

Open almost until dawn, *Balti Club* (☎ 0141-332 5495, 💻 balticlub.co.uk, 66 Woodlands Rd; daily 5pm-3.30am) is a take-away that does everything from chicken biriyani (£7.60) to burgers (from £2.95) and has been running for years.

### Cafés

*University Café* (☎ 0141-339 5217, **fb**; 87 Byres Rd; daily 10am-8pm) has been a Glasgow institution since 1918. It's very popular, serving incredibly cheap traditional café fare such as burgers and has an adjoining chip shop. Don't miss the wonderful ice-cream made by the Italian family who run the café.

In the heart of the action *Café Wander* (☎ 0141-353 3968, **fb**; Mon-Fri

---

❏ **TEAROOMS**

The Mackintosh connection means that a visit to a tearoom seems an integral part of a visit to Glasgow. In 1878 Kate Cranston opened the first of what was to become a little chain of city tearooms. She employed local artists and architects such as George Walton and Charles Rennie Mackintosh to design some of them. Most famous is the Willow Tea Rooms, now rebranded as *Mackintosh at the Willow* (☎ 0141-204 1903, 💻 www.mackintoshatthewillow.com, 215-217 Sauchiehall St; daily 11am-5pm); though closed in 1928 it has been faithfully recreated and reopened – complete with those uncomfortable high-backed Mackintosh chairs. It's a popular place; queues can be long despite the prices (afternoon tea from £27).

If the queues are too long or the prices too high, there's **another** Mackintosh-designed tearoom, the *Willow Tearoom*, at 97 Buchanan St (☎ 0141-204 5242, 💻 willowtearooms.co.uk; Mon-Fri 9am-5pm, Sat to 6.30pm, Sun 10am-5.30pm), with afternoon tea a more reasonable £15.50.

8am-5pm, Sat 9am-5pm), at 110 West George St, serves an imaginative variety of dishes from delicious smoothies (from £3.35) to scrumptious porridge with raisins and cinnamon (£4).

Bohemian *Tchai-Ovna House of Tea & Vegetarian Restaurant* (☎ 0141-357 4524, 🖥 tchaiovna.com, **fb**; Tue-Sun 11am-10pm; 42 Otago Lane off Otago St) serves 100 varieties of tea and great veg food in its rustic cabin.

There's a great range of delicious and authentic Lebanese dishes at *Byblos Café* (☎ 0141-339 7980, 🖥 bybloscafe.weebly.com, **fb**; 6 Park Rd; Mon-Sat noon-8pm). Fattouch salad is £5.95, shawarma chicken pizza £9.50, best washed down with some strong Lebanese coffee.

On Hope St at No 127, *Café Fame* (☎ 0141-258 3838, **fb**; Mon-Fri 9am-4pm, Sat from 9.30am) has comfortable seating with cushions galore and some fine Italian coffee and cake, all served in a lovely bright Art Deco space.

### Bars, pubs and pub food

The former Kelvinside parish church has undergone an astonishing transformation into a very popular entertainment venue known as *Òran Mór* (☎ 0141-357 6200, 🖥 oran-mor.co.uk, **fb**; top of Byres Rd/Great Western Rd; daily 9am to at least 2am) with a range of bars, restaurants, music and theatre venues.

A more traditional drinking place is *The Pot Still* (🖥 thepotstill.co.uk, **fb**; 154 Hope St; daily 11am-midnight), which boasts several hundred single malts. Near Central Station, *The Horse Shoe* (🖥 thehorseshoebarglasgow.co.uk) is famous as the place to go for a pie and a pint at lunchtime. Opposite Crabshakk at 1147 Argyle St, the *Ben Nevis Bar* (**fb**; Mon-Sat 11.30am-midnight, Sun from 12.30pm), is a very pleasant place for a wee dram.

While there are fewer traditional pubs around than there once were, there's no shortage of stylish bars, particularly along Hope St, Bath St, Sauchiehall St and Byres Rd. *The Bunker Bar* (🖥 thebunkerbar.com, **fb**; Tue-Thur & Sun 5pm-1am, Fri & Sat 1pm-3am), on Bath St, has a menu serving burgers and pizzas. It can get raucous by night.

*Nice 'n' Sleazy* (🖥 nicensleazy.com, **fb**; 421 Sauchiehall St; daily 2pm-3am) has a great juke box, good-value burgers and is the place to plug into Glasgow's alternative music scene.

There's also a good selection of bar food (Mon-Fri noon-2.30pm and daily from 6pm) at long-running *King Tut's Wah Wah Hut* (☎ 0141-221 5279, 🖥 kingtuts.co.uk, 272a St Vincent St; Mon-Fri noon-1am, Sat 4pm-1am, Sun 3pm-1am); it is still a great place for live rock music. Britpop pioneers Oasis were discovered here.

## WHAT TO SEE AND DO

### Glasgow Cathedral

(🖥 glasgowcathedral.org.uk; summer Mon-Sat 10am-noon and 1-5pm, Sun 1-5pm; services Sun 11am & 4pm; free but donation appreciated) This is the only medieval cathedral on the Scottish mainland to have survived the Reformation and it's an excellent example of the Gothic style. Much of the current building dates from the 13th century; the original cathedral was built in about 1125 as a shrine to Mungo, the 6th-century priest who later became the city's patron saint. His remains still lie here; in the Middle Ages they were the focus of thousands of pilgrims each year.

When money became available in the 1990s for renovations the bishop sensibly spent it not on sandblasting the smoke-stained exterior but on a new cen-

## ❏ GLASGOW LIFE MUSEUMS

Glasgow Life is a charity that delivers cultural, sporting and learning activities on behalf of Glasgow City Council. Under the Glasgow Life umbrella, Glasgow Museums is the largest museum service in the UK outside London, and operates 10 venues across the city, with a collection totalling over one million objects.

For further details of all 10 museums and galleries, including the latest opening times and ticket booking requirements, see 🖥 glasgowlife.org.uk/museums. Here is a summary of the most popular ones, all of which have **free admission** and operate the same **opening hours** (Mon-Thur & Sat 10am-5pm, Fri & Sun 11am-5pm).

**St Mungo Museum of Religious Life & Art** (☎ 0141-276 1625, 2 Castle St; temporarily closed at the time of research, check website for reopening plans) Right opposite the cathedral and an attraction you should not miss, this museum was opened in the early 1990s. In addition to the galleries devoted to Religious Life and Religious Art (covering the world's main religions), there is one outlining the history of religion in Scotland, as well as a Zen garden.

**Riverside Museum** (☎ 0141-287 2720; Clydeside Expressway) This wonderful modern building was designed by Zaha Hadid and opened in 2011. The fact that it is a museum of transport should not put you off if cars and trains aren't your thing, as the exhibits are cleverly displayed and the building itself is spectacular. Glasgow has a long and distinguished history of building ships and trains and a rather less distinguished history of building cars (the Albion and the Hillman Imp, for example).

**People's Palace** (☎ 0141-276 0788; Glasgow Green) Set in a park, this museum tells the story of Glasgow and its impact on the world as the 'Second City of the Empire'. It's attached to the Winter Gardens (daily 10am-5pm), a vast Victorian glasshouse filled with tropical plants and a convenient tea garden.

**Gallery of Modern Art (GoMA)** (☎ 0141-287 3050; Royal Exchange Sq) Housed in a beautiful former library, it is well worth a visit with pieces from Turner nominees and changing exhibitions.

**Kelvingrove Art Gallery & Museum** (☎ 0141-276 9599; Argyle St) This is one of the most popular free tourist attractions in the country, bringing in over 1.3 million people a year. The art gallery is strong on 19th- and 20th-century works, particularly those by Scottish artists. One of the benefits of the gallery's massive restoration was that it can now display about 8000 items. However, there are about 200,000 historical objects in the building.

Riverside Museum

*Nikodym (the Co-operation of the Genders), one of the fascinating kinemats you can see at Sharmanka.*

tral heating system. The immense blackened mass of the cathedral with the grand memorials of the **Necropolis** rising up on the hill behind only add to the wonderful Gothic effect. The best view of this is from the top floor of nearby St Mungo's Museum.

### Sharmanka
(☎ 0141-552 7080, 🖳 sharmanka.com, Trongate 103; three different shows; tickets from £8; see website for times and to book)   This unforgettable performance of Russian mechanical carved figures (*kinemats*) is, quite simply, unique. It was created by Eduard Bersudsky and Tatyana Jakovskaya who moved to Glasgow from St Petersburg in 1996. The themes are very Russian: 'the human spirit struggling against the relentless circles of life and death' and there are literary influences such as Bulgakov's *The Master and Margarita*. A magical 30 (or 60) minutes of jingly-jangly Russian madness.

### Mackintoshiana
The Art Nouveau designs of Charles Rennie Mackintosh are almost a cliché but he is Scotland's most famous architect and designer and many of the buildings he designed are in Glasgow – and well worth seeing. Born in 1868 he studied at Glasgow School of Art and later won a competition to design its new building, a building that is regarded as his greatest achievement.

In 2014 a disastrous fire destroyed a major part of the building, including the jewel in the crown, the exquisite library. Restoration was nearly complete when in June 2018 catastrophe struck again and a second larger fire rampaged through the building, which was still closed at the time of research. See **Glasgow School of Art Visitor Centre** (🖳 www.gsa.ac.uk, 167 Renfrew St) for an update on the current situation.

The **Hunterian Art Gallery** (🖳 gla.ac.uk/hunterian; Tue-Sat 10am-5pm, Sun 11am-4pm; gallery admission free, Mackintosh House £6) has an extensive collection of Mackintosh's work as well as reconstructed rooms from Mackintosh's own house. Follow your visit to the art gallery with sustenance at one of the branches of the **Willow Tea Rooms** (see box p89), which were reconstructed using Mackintosh designs.

### The Tenement House
(☎ 0131-458 0200, 🖳 nts.org.uk/visit/places/the-tenement-house, 145 Buccleuch St; Mar-Dec Thur-Mon 10am-5pm, Jan & Feb Fri-Sun only; £8.50, free to National Trust members)   Don't miss this little time capsule, just a short walk north of Sauchiehall St. Tenements were four- or five-storey buildings arranged around a square that provided a communal space for the flats, some only a room or two, within the buildings. This is how many Glaswegians lived

in the first half of the 20th century. What is fascinating about this rather more upmarket flat that comprised several rooms and even a bathroom, is that the last owner, Agnes Toward, changed little in all the time she was here, from 1911 to 1965. There are still gas lights, snug bed closets by the fireplace and Izal-medicated lavatory paper in the loo.

### Burrell Collection

(☎ 0141-287 2550, 🖳 burrellcollection.com; Pollok Country Park; Mon-Thur & Sat 10am-5pm, Fri & Sun 11am-5pm; free)    One of Britain's top art galleries, it reopened in March 2022 after a major refurbishment and redisplay. It's notable partly because it's a very personal collection: about 8000 objects assembled by Sir William Burrell (1861-1958), the Glasgow shipping magnate; and partly for the way these items are displayed: in a modern, purpose-built gallery that allows the light and views of the surrounding park to stream in.

The Burrell Collection is a ten-minute walk into the park; you can reach the park by train (from Central station to Pollokshaws West). It's also on First's bus routes Nos 34A, 57 and 57A from the city centre.

### Glasgow Science Centre

(☎ 0141-420 5000, 🖳 glasgowsciencecentre.org; Apr-Aug daily 10am-5pm, Sep-Mar Sat & Sun only; £12.50; booking essential) This popular attraction has a Science Mall with interactive displays, a planetarium and an IMAX cinema. Beside it is the 127m, rotating **Glasgow Tower** (☎ 0141-420 5000, 🖳 glasgow sciencecentre.org/discover/our-experiences/glasgow-tower; £6.50), the tallest free-standing structure in Scotland; on a clear day there are superb views over the city and up towards Loch Lomond and the route of the West Highland Way. At the time of research the tower was closed for refurbishment of the glazing panels. It should reopen in 2023 but check the website for an update.

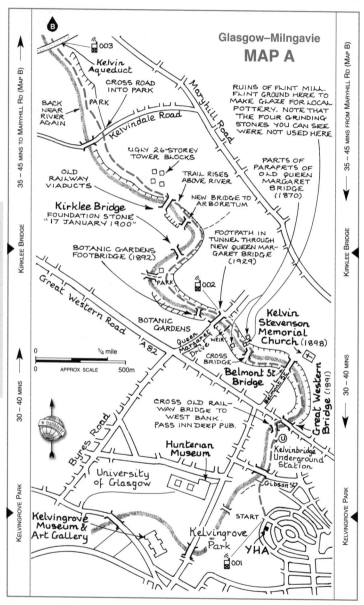

# Walking from Glasgow to Milngavie

Walking from Glasgow to Milngavie is highly recommended for two reasons. First, being only 10 miles (16km) in length and easy walking on the flat – it takes **3¼-4hrs** (walking time only; see box p99) – it's a good way to warm up for the longer days ahead. Second, it's a great walk in its own right: not tramping along busy streets as you might expect but following the River Kelvin through parks before emerging into fields beyond the city. Two miles before Milngavie the Kelvin is joined by another river, Allander Water, which you follow to reach the official start of the West Highland Way. The route is well signposted following two official footpaths, the Kelvin Walkway and the Allander Walkway.

With nowhere right on the route for food and drink you have three options:
● Take a packed lunch;
● Leave the trail on the Kelvingrove Park to Maryhill section and climb up to one of the many bridges you pass beneath to get back into the city, although this would rather detract from the serenity of the walk;
● Set off early and stop at around the 8-mile point where there are two places to eat not far off the trail. Two miles from Milngavie, the ***Tickled Trout*** pub (Map C, p97; ☎ 01360-621968, 🖥 vintageinn.co.uk; 878 Boclair Rd; 🐾; Mon-Sat noon-10.30pm, Sun noon-9.30pm) has lunch options such as hot beef brisket sandwich with fries for £7.95, as well as steaks, burgers and pizza. Beside it is Dobbies Garden Centre (🖥 dobbies.com/milngavie) which has a *café* (daily 9am-5.30pm), food hall and deli.

## ROUTE OVERVIEW

The best place to start is in Kelvingrove Park: the Kelvin Walkway runs right through it. Some of the places to stay in Glasgow are within walking distance of the park; alternatively take the subway to Kelvinbridge Station.

**Kelvingrove Park to Maryhill**          [Map A, opposite, Map B, p96]
This section is just under 3½ miles (5.5km, 1¼-1½hrs) and an easy walk all along the River Kelvin as it winds through the city. For most of the time, however, you won't be aware of the fact that you're in an urban landscape as the city is often high above the river and you're insulated from it by thick tree cover.

In **Kelvingrove Park**, follow the path along the east bank of the river and you'll go under a bridge (Gibson St) as you leave the park. You then reach the site of the former Kelvinbridge Railway Station with the current **Kelvinbridge underground station** nearby. The route now crosses to the west bank of the river for the next half-mile and a very peaceful wooded stretch of walking beside the slow-flowing river with the bustling city 50ft above you. It then returns to the east bank and the ruins of a **flint mill**.

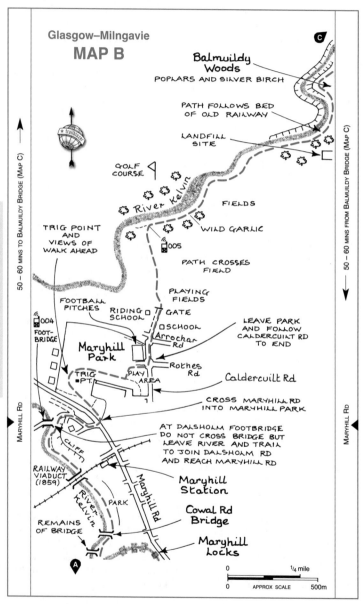

Glasgow–Milngavie
**MAP B**

**C**

Balmuildy Woods
POPLARS AND SILVER BIRCH

PATH FOLLOWS BED
OF OLD RAILWAY

LANDFILL
SITE

GOLF
COURSE

River Kelvin

FIELDS

WILD GARLIC

TRIG POINT
AND
VIEWS OF
WALK AHEAD

005

PATH CROSSES
FIELD

PLAYING
FIELDS

FOOTBALL
PITCHES

RIDING
SCHOOL

GATE

004

FOOT-
BRIDGE

Maryhill
Park

SCHOOL

Arrochar
Rd

LEAVE PARK
AND FOLLOW
CALDERCUILT RD
TO END

TRIG
PT.

PLAY
AREA

Rothes
Rd

Caldercuilt Rd

CROSS MARYHILL RD
INTO MARYHILL PARK

CLIFF

AT DALSHOLM FOOTBRIDGE
DO NOT CROSS BRIDGE BUT
LEAVE RIVER AND TRAIL
TO JOIN DALSHOLM RD
AND REACH MARYHILL RD

RAILWAY
VIADUCT
(1859)

River Kelvin

PARK

Maryhill Rd

Maryhill
Station

REMAINS
OF BRIDGE

Cowal Rd
Bridge

Maryhill
Locks

**A**

MARYHILL RD

MARYHILL RD

50 – 60 MINS TO BALMUILDY BRIDGE (MAP C)

50 – 60 MINS FROM BALMUILDY BRIDGE (MAP C)

GLASGOW TO MILNGAVIE

0        ¼ mile
0                        500m
APPROX SCALE

After a further two miles of walking along the river you leave it along a side road (Dalsholm Rd, Map B) to emerge onto Maryhill Rd and the suburbs of Glasgow. **Maryhill Station** is to the right but you continue ahead, crossing Maryhill Rd and entering Maryhill Park.

**Maryhill to Milngavie [Map B, opposite; Map C, below; Map D, p98]**
This is the countryside section of the walk. It's just over 6½ miles long (10.5km, 2-2½hrs) and also easy walking.

From Maryhill Park there are views of the walk ahead and the last views of Glasgow. Leaving the park and passing through a field you rejoin the path along the River Kelvin. After 1½ miles following the river you reach Balmuildy Bridge and the A879 (Map C). Depending on the time of year, the riverside trail can be fairly overgrown. If this was the case between Maryhill and Balmuildy Bridge you can be sure that the next section will be even more overgrown. If it's also raining you may want to keep your boots and legs dry and take the short-cut along the A879 (20-25 mins) to join Allander Water, which you follow almost all the way into Milngavie.

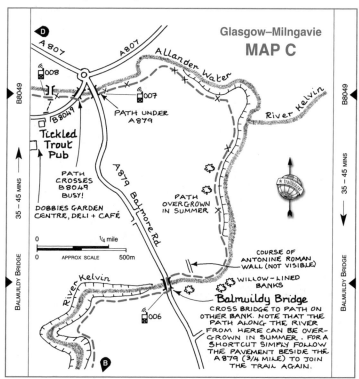

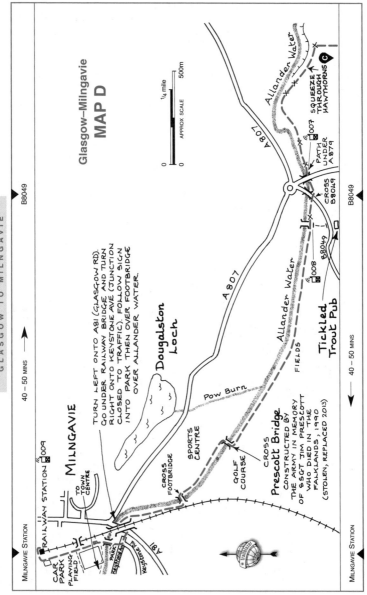

GLASGOW TO MILNGAVIE

MILNGAVIE STATION ◀        40 – 50 MINS ⟶        B8049 ◀

Glasgow–Milngavie
MAP D

¼ mile
0                    500m
0
APPROX SCALE

MILNGAVIE

TO TOWN CENTRE

RAILWAY STATION 🏨 009

CAR PARK

PLAYING FIELD

KEYSTONE RD

A81

CROSS FOOTBRIDGE

SPORTS CENTRE

Pow Burn

Dougalston Loch

A807

Allander Water

CROSS Prescott Bridge
CONSTRUCTED BY THE ARMY IN MEMORY OF SSGT JIM PRESCOTT WHO DIED IN THE FALKLANDS, 1990 (STOLEN, REPLACED 2013)

GOLF COURSE

FIELDS

Tickled Trout Pub

🏨 008    B8049

CROSS B8049

PATH UNDER A879

🏨 007

A807

Allander Water

SQUEEZE THROUGH HAWTHORNS ●C

TURN LEFT ONTO A81 (GLASGOW RD). GO UNDER RAILWAY BRIDGE, AND TURN RIGHT ONTO KEYSTONE AVE (JUNCTION CLOSED TO TRAFFIC). FOLLOW SIGN INTO PARK THEN OVER FOOTBRIDGE OVER ALLANDER WATER.

MILNGAVIE STATION ◀        40 – 50 MINS ⟶        MILNGAVIE STATION ◀

# ROUTE GUIDE & MAPS

## Using this guide

The trail guide and maps have not been divided into rigid daily stages since people walk at different speeds and have different interests. The **route summaries** describe the trail between significant places and are written as if walking the Way from south to north.

To enable you to plan your own itinerary, **practical information** is presented clearly on the trail maps. This includes walking times for both directions, waypoints (see pp195-8 for full list), all places to stay, camp and eat, as well as shops where you can buy supplies. Further service **details** are given in the text under the entry for each place. For **map profiles** see the colour pages at the end of the book. For an overview of this information see 'Itineraries' p33 and the village facilities table on p31. The cumulative **distance chart** is on p200.

### TRAIL MAPS   [see key map inside cover; symbols key p202]

### Scale and walking times

The trail maps are to a scale of 1:20,000 (1cm = 200m; $3^{1}/_{8}$ inches = one mile). Walking times are given along the side of each map and the arrow shows the direction to which the time refers. Black triangles indicate the points between which the times have been taken. **See important note below on walking times**.

The time-bars are a tool and are not there to judge your walking ability; there are so many variables that affect walking speed, from the weather conditions to how many beers you drank the previous evening. After the first hour or two of walking you will be able to see how your speed relates to the timings on the maps.

### Up or down?

On the trail maps in this book, the walking trail is shown as a dashed red line. An arrow across the trail indicates the slope; two arrows

---

☐ **IMPORTANT NOTE – WALKING TIMES**
Unless otherwise specified, **all times in this book refer only to the time spent walking**. You will need to add 20-30% to allow for rests, photography, checking the map, drinking water etc, not to mention time to simply stand and stare. When planning the day's hike count on 5-7 hours' actual walking.

show that it is steep. Note that the arrow points towards the higher part of the trail. If, for example, you are walking from A (at 80m) to B (at 200m) and the trail between the two is short and steep it would be shown thus: A— — — >> — — – B. Reversed arrow heads indicate a downward gradient.

### GPS waypoints

The numbered GPS waypoints refer to the list on pp195-8.

### Other features

Features are marked on the map when pertinent to navigation. In order to avoid cluttering the maps and making them unusable not all features have been marked each time they occur.

## ACCOMMODATION

Apart from in large towns where some selection of places has been necessary, everywhere to stay that is within easy reach of the trail is marked. Where accommodation is scarce, however, some of the places listed are a little further away. If that is the case, many B&B proprietors will offer to collect walkers from the nearest point on the trail and deliver them back again the next morning, if requested in advance. Details of each place are given in the accompanying text.

The number of **rooms** of each type is stated, ie: **S** = Single, **T** = Twin room, **D** = Double room, **Tr** = Triple room and **Qd** = Quad. Note that most of the triple/quad rooms have a double bed and one/two single beds (or bunk beds); thus for a group of three or four, two people would have to share the double bed but it also means the room can be used as a double or twin. See also p21.

**Rates** quoted are **per person (pp) based on two people sharing a room** for a one-night stay; rates are usually discounted for longer stays. Where a **single room (sgl)** is available the rate for that is quoted if different from the rate per person. The rate for **single occupancy (sgl occ)** of a double/twin may be higher, and the per person rate for three/four sharing a triple/quad may be lower. Unless specified, rates are for bed and breakfast. At some places the only option is a **room rate**; this will be the same whether one or more people use the room. Rates are for the summer high season.

Unless otherwise specified, rooms have bathrooms attached (en suite) and most of these have only a shower. In the text (▼) signifies that at least one room has a bathroom with a **bath**, or access to a bath, for those who prefer a relaxed soak at the end of the day. The text also mentions whether the premises have **wi-fi** (WI-FI), if **packed lunches** (Ⓛ) are available and whether **dogs** (🐕– see also pp198-9) are welcome in at least one room. It can be useful to check the **Facebook page** (**fb**) for small or seasonal businesses, as these tend to be kept more up-to-date with changes to opening times than regular websites.

# Milngavie to Fort William

See pp95-8 for the route guide and maps covering the walking route from **Glasgow to Milngavie**.

## MILNGAVIE      see map p102

The West Highland Way officially begins in Milngavie (pronounced 'mullguy'). This middle-class commuter suburb on the northern edge of Glasgow has few attractions to entice the walker to linger. It's a nice enough place to stay if you arrive too late to begin your walk, though.

The small pedestrian centre has plenty of shops and if you've got time to spare **Lillie Art Gallery** (☎ 0141-956 5536; 🖳 edlc.co.uk/heritage-arts/lillie-art-gallery, Tue-Sat 10am-1pm & 2-5pm, admission free) comprises one of Scotland's best collections of home-grown 20th-century art.

## Services

Walking from the station to the start of the West Highland Way you pass through the main shopping precinct. Stock up with cash while you have the chance; several **banks** here have cash machines.

There's a **post office** (Mon-Fri 8.30am-5.30pm, Sat 9am-5.30pm) inside Day-Today Convenience Store (Mon-Sat 5am-6pm, Sun 6am-2pm); a Greggs **bakery** (daily 7am-5pm), with plenty of pies and pasties to set you up for the day's walk, by the bridge, and a Subway **sandwich shop** (Mon-Sat 8am-7pm, Sun to 5pm) opposite.

The Boots **chemist** (Mon-Fri 9am-6pm, Sat 9am-5.30pm) is on the main square.

There are several **supermarkets**: Marks & Spencer Food Hall (Mon-Fri 8am-8pm, Sat 8am-7pm, Sun 9am-6pm) on the main square, Tesco (Mon-Sat 7am-11pm, Sun 8am-10pm) the other side of Woodburn Way and Waitrose (Mon-Fri 8am-9pm, Sat 8am-8pm, Sun 9am-8pm) by the roundabout just south of Milngavie.

## Transport

[See also pp45-9] Scotrail's **train** service between Milngavie Station and Glasgow takes 23-30 minutes with 1-2 trains an hour. For **buses**, First Glasgow's No 60A, Glasgow Citybus 15 and First Scotland East's X10/X10A services run to Glasgow. In the other direction, the X10/X10A operate to Balfron, Strathblane, Killearn & Stirling.

Two local **taxi** firms are Ambassador Taxis (☎ 0141-956 2956, 🖳 ambassadortaxis.co.uk) who have an office at 29 Douglas St, just off the main square, and Station Taxis (☎ 0141-942 4555, 🖳 station taxis.co.uk).

## Where to stay

Campers will need to walk the first ten miles of the Way to Easter Drumquhassle (see p110).

There are two **Premier Inns** (🖳 premierinn.com) here and if you book well in advance you can get a room for as little as £40 (room only; breakfast £9.50pp). However, rates vary daily and depend on demand so, unless you book very early, expect to pay around £80 for a room. *Premier Inn Glasgow (Milngavie)* (☎ 0141-611 7944; 61D; ☛; WI-FI) is at 103 Main St and has a *Beefeater Grill* (☎ 0141-956 7835; Mon-Fri 6.30am-10pm, Sat & Sun 7am-10pm) attached. *Premier Inn Glasgow (Bearsden)* (☎ 0141-931 9100; 61D; ☛; WI-FI) is at 279 Milngavie Rd.

## Where to eat and drink

For something quick and cheap, there's Indian food for takeaway available from *Perfect Pakora* (☎ 0141-955 1888; Mon-Wed noon-7pm, Thur-Sat to 8pm), the Indian delicatessen on Station Rd. If an ice

ROUTE GUIDE AND MAPS

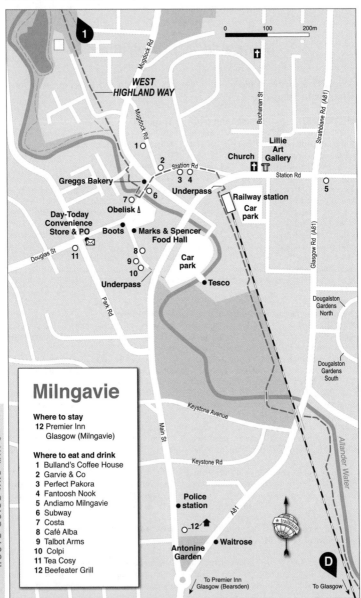

# Milngavie

**Where to stay**
12 Premier Inn
Glasgow (Milngavie)

**Where to eat and drink**
1 Bulland's Coffee House
2 Garvie & Co
3 Perfect Pakora
4 Fantoosh Nook
5 Andiamo Milngavie
6 Subway
7 Costa
8 Café Alba
9 Talbot Arms
10 Colpi
11 Tea Cosy
12 Beefeater Grill

cream is all you're after you can't do better than Scots-Italian *Colpi*, (near Talbot Arms) who've been serving them since 1928.

For a coffee, excellent cakes and light lunches, *Bulland's Coffee House* (☎ 0141-956 6255, **fb**; Mon-Thur 10am-5pm, Fri-Sun from 9am) is highly recommended and it's walker and dog-friendly. *Café Alba* (☎ 0141-956 1163, ☐ cafealba.co.uk, Mon-Sat 9am-4pm, Sun 10am-4pm), 19 Main St, produces fresh, local food and has a good reputation. For those seeking calories before disappearing into the wild, the Alba's Big Breakfast is a bargain (£6.50). Not far away, *Tea Cosy* (☎ 0141-9550121, **fb**; Mon-Sat 9.30am-4.30pm), in a lovely old building is a traditional, charming place where you can pick up a filled roll and a hot drink for less than a fiver.

The *Talbot Arms* (☎ 0141-955 0981, **fb**) is a traditional pub and a great place to start the evening. Other than crisps and nuts, though, they don't do food. *Garvie &*

*Co* (☎ 0141-956 4111, ☐ garvieandco.com, **fb**; Sun-Thur 10am-11pm, Fri & Sat to midnight) is a bistro-style restaurant, bar and bakery on Station Rd. Their steaks (from £14) are good and there are burgers from £11.50.

At 46 Station Rd, fish-themed, *Fantoosh Nook* (☎ 0141-956 6060, takeaway 0778 333 2435, ☐ fantooshnook.co .uk; Thur-Sat noon-4pm & 6.30-10.30pm, takeaway Thur-Sat 4-6pm; WI-FI) offers set-course lunch menus (£16.95/19.95 for 2/3 courses) and has received numerous five-star reviews from both locals and visitors alike. The seafood comes from the local fishmonger across the street who owns the restaurant.

Popular for an evening out is the glitzy *Andiamo Milngavie* (☎ 0141-956 7346; ☐ andiamo-restaurants.com, **fb**; daily noon-10.30pm) at 1 Glasgow Rd. Good quality Italian fare is available on the extensive and reasonably-priced menu.

## MILNGAVIE TO DRYMEN                                        MAPS 1-8

This beginning stage is **12 miles (19.5km)** and takes 3¾-5hrs to walk (walking time only). It neatly splits into three distinctly different sections.

The walk starts officially at the obelisk (see Map 1). The first 6 miles (10km, 1¾-2¼hrs) provide easy and interesting walking along gentle paths through amenity parks and woodland leading you quickly out of the suburbs into genuine countryside. You pass **Craigallian Loch** (Map 2) with its surprise views of the rugged Campsie Fells and then, after crossing the B821, you arrive on an indistinct ridge overlooking Blane Valley. From here there are distant views to the Highlands tantalising you with the splendour of the hills that are to come. A superb descent across open grassland drained by tiny streams takes you round the pretty wooded knoll of **Dumgoyach** to the valley bottom. Here the Way follows the bed of a disused railway (see box p108) for 4 miles (6km, 1½-

---

☐ **MUGDOCK COUNTRY PARK**

A short detour can be made to see the remains of the fortified **Mugdock Castle** dating back to the 14th century and the much newer **Craigend Castle** built as a residence in 1815, now also in ruins. Follow the fingerpost signs in Mugdock Wood (Map 1). These will also lead you to the **Visitor Centre** (☎ 0141-956 6100, ☐ mugdock-country-park.org.uk; daily 9am-5pm). *Stables Tearoom* is open daily 10am-5pm and *Charlie's Coffee Bar*, Tue-Fri 10am-3pm, Sat & Sun to 5pm; there are also several shops.

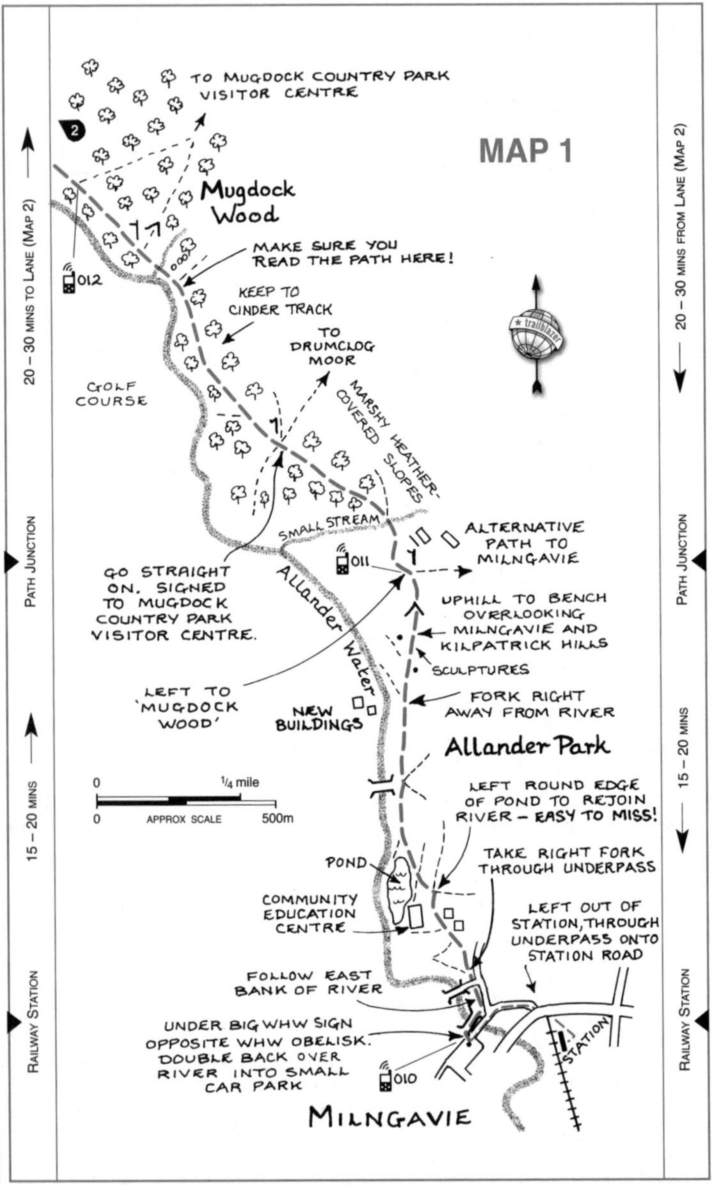

TO MUGDOCK COUNTRY PARK
VISITOR CENTRE

Mugdock Wood

MAP 1

20 – 30 MINS TO LANE (MAP 2)

20 – 30 MINS FROM LANE (MAP 2)

MAKE SURE YOU
READ THE PATH HERE!

KEEP TO
CINDER TRACK

TO
DRUMCLOG
MOOR

012

GOLF
COURSE

MARSHY HEATHER-
COVERED SLOPES

SMALL STREAM

ALTERNATIVE
PATH TO
MILNGAVIE

PATH JUNCTION

PATH JUNCTION

011

Allander Water

GO STRAIGHT
ON, SIGNED
TO MUGDOCK
COUNTRY PARK
VISITOR CENTRE.

UPHILL TO BENCH
OVERLOOKING
MILNGAVIE AND
KILPATRICK HILLS

SCULPTURES

LEFT TO
'MUGDOCK
WOOD'

NEW
BUILDINGS

FORK RIGHT
AWAY FROM RIVER

Allander Park

15 – 20 MINS

15 – 20 MINS

0       ¼ mile
0   APPROX SCALE   500m

LEFT ROUND EDGE
OF POND TO REJOIN
RIVER - EASY TO MISS!

TAKE RIGHT FORK
THROUGH UNDERPASS

POND

COMMUNITY
EDUCATION
CENTRE

LEFT OUT OF
STATION, THROUGH
UNDERPASS ONTO
STATION ROAD

FOLLOW EAST
BANK OF RIVER

STATION

UNDER BIG WHW SIGN
OPPOSITE WHW OBELISK.
DOUBLE BACK OVER
RIVER INTO SMALL
CAR PARK

010

MILNGAVIE

PATH JUNCTION

RAILWAY STATION

RAILWAY STATION

ROUTE GUIDE AND MAPS

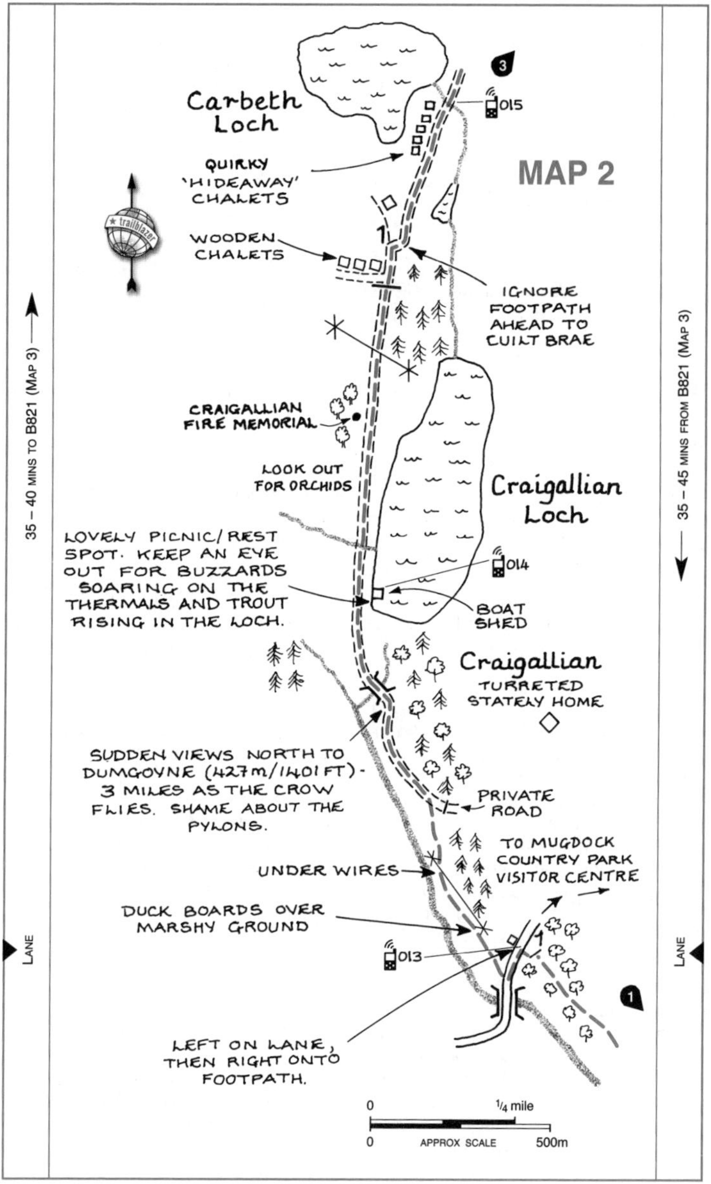

Carbeth
Loch

📶015

3

QUIRKY
'HIDEAWAY'
CHALETS

MAP 2

WOODEN
CHALETS

IGNORE
FOOTPATH
AHEAD TO
CUILT BRAE

35 – 40 MINS TO B821 (MAP 3)

35 – 45 MINS FROM B821 (MAP 3)

CRAIGALLIAN
FIRE MEMORIAL

LOOK OUT
FOR ORCHIDS

Craigallian
Loch

LOVELY PICNIC/REST
SPOT. KEEP AN EYE
OUT FOR BUZZARDS
SOARING ON THE
THERMALS AND TROUT
RISING IN THE LOCH.

📶014

BOAT
SHED

Craigallian
TURRETED
STATELY HOME

SUDDEN VIEWS NORTH TO
DUMGOYNE (427m/1401FT) -
3 MILES AS THE CROW
FLIES. SHAME ABOUT THE
PYLONS.

PRIVATE
ROAD

TO MUGDOCK
COUNTRY PARK
VISITOR CENTRE

UNDER WIRES

DUCK BOARDS OVER
MARSHY GROUND

📶013

1

LANE

LANE

LEFT ON LANE,
THEN RIGHT ONTO
FOOTPATH.

0                    ¼ mile

0                            500m
APPROX SCALE

ROUTE GUIDE AND MAPS

---

❏ CRAIGALLIAN FIRE MEMORIAL SITE
The West Highland Way passes right beside a memorial (see **Map 2, p105**) to an important time in social history. It marks a site that became famous in the 1920s and '30s as an informal meeting place for a range of passers-by that included travellers, climbers and walkers as well as the unemployed escaping the Great Depression in Glasgow and the Clyde. People would stop to sit round the fire that was often started here, drink tea, tell stories and discuss the wider issues of the world. In a time before the internet, coming together with like-minded people was the only way, particularly for poorer people, to share ideas.

A few of the so-called fire-sitters would go on to fight in the Spanish Civil War and others – less romantically but more importantly for walkers such as us – to campaign for greater access to the countryside.

For more information see 🖳 strathblanefield.org.uk then search Craigallian Fire.

---

2hrs). Straight and level, it is easy, if unglamorous, walking through gentle farmland, though the constant background hum from the traffic on the A81 can be intrusive.

Only yards from the trail is **Glengoyne Distillery** (Map 4; ☎ 01360-550254, 🖳 glengoyne.com; daily 10am-5pm). It would be a shame to pass without a quick visit and a revitalising wee dram. There are several tours: the cheapest costs £18 (75 mins; booking essential), which allows you to sample their 18-year-old Highland single malt whisky. Tours start on the hour.

The Way joins a quiet hedge-lined minor road at the pretty sandstone hamlet of **Gartness** (Map 6) and follows it for 2 miles (3km, ½-¾hr) to the outskirts of **Drymen**, a large bustling village where many choose to spend the night.

### BLANEFIELD                    Map 3
This small village lies just over a mile (20-25 mins) east of the trail. **Food** is available, but for somewhere to stay you would need to go to Strathblane. Unless you're starving continue to Drymen.

*Coffee at the Wilsons* (☎ 07761-102903, 🖳 www.coffeeatthewilsons.co.uk; 🐾; Mon-Fri 8.30am-4pm, Sat from 9am, Sun from 10am) has filled rolls, toasties, light meals (£2.50-6.50), breakfasts (£2.50-

6.95). Next door is a small **food shop**, open daily from 10am until at least 7pm, and there is an **ATM** in there. There's also *Chillies Takeaway* (☎ 01360-770727; Mon-Fri 4-10pm, Sat & Sun to 11pm).

First Scotland East's X10/X10A **bus** services stop here; see pp45-9 for details. See p45 for details of the Demand Responsive Transport service.

### STRATHBLANE                  off Map 3
A further 10 minutes' walk east along the A81 takes you to the *Kirkhouse Inn* (☎ 01360-771771, 🖳 kirkhouseinn.com; 3T/12D; 🍺; WI-FI; 🕒; £37.50-42.50pp, sgl occ £75-85). **Food**, including such dishes as haggis rolled in oats, neep purée and tatties, served with a whisky sauce (£13), is

available (daily noon-8.45pm).

First Scotland East's X10/X10A **bus** services stop at Kirkhouse Inn and on Milngavie Rd (stop called Milndavie Rd); see pp46-9 for details.

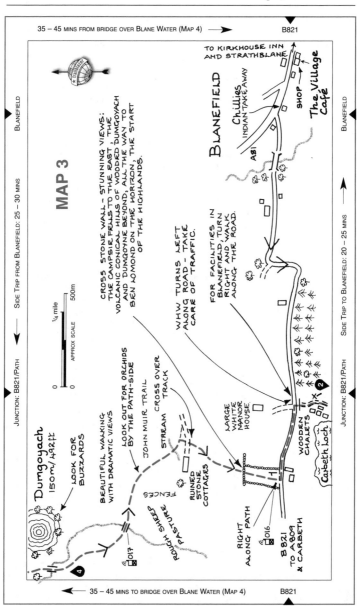

35 – 45 MINS FROM BRIDGE OVER BLANE WATER (MAP 4) →

B821

MAP 3

JUNCTION: B821/PATH    SIDE TRIP FROM BLANEFIELD: 25 – 30 MINS    BLANEFIELD

TO KIRKHOUSE INN
AND STRATHBLANE

BLANEFIELD

Chullies
INDIAN TAKEAWAY

SHOP

The Village Café

A81

CROSS STONE WALL – STUNNING VIEWS:
THE CAMPSIE FELLS TO THE EAST, THE
VOLCANIC CONICAL HILLS OF WOODED DUMGOYACH
AND DUMGOYNE BEYOND, ALL THE WAY TO
BEN LOMOND ON THE HORIZON, THE START
OF THE HIGHLANDS.

WHW TURNS LEFT
ALONG ROAD – TAKE
CARE OF TRAFFIC.

FOR FACILITIES IN
BLANEFIELD, TURN
RIGHT AND WALK
ALONG THE ROAD.

¼ mile

500m

0                    0
APPROX SCALE

LOOK OUT FOR ORCHIDS
BY THE PATH-SIDE

JOHN MUIR TRAIL

STREAM CROSS OVER
TRACK

Dumgoyach
150m/492ft

LOOK FOR BUZZARDS

BEAUTIFUL WALKING
WITH DRAMATIC VIEWS

RUINED STONE
COTTAGES

FENCES

ROUGH SHEEP
PASTURE

017

4

LARGE WHITE MANOR
HOUSE

WOODEN CHALETS

Carbeth Loch

2

RIGHT
ALONG PATH

B821
TO A809
& CARBETH

016

1

JUNCTION: B821/PATH    SIDE TRIP TO BLANEFIELD: 20 – 25 MINS    BLANEFIELD

← 35 – 45 MINS TO BRIDGE OVER BLANE WATER (MAP 4)

B821

ROUTE GUIDE AND MAPS

## DUMGOYNE                     Map 4

The pub, Glengoyne Distillery and a hand-ful of houses comprise the extent of this small hamlet.

The trail goes past the back door (and **water tap**) of *Beech Tree Inn* (☎ 01360-550297, 🖥 thebeechtreeinn.co.uk; **food** Mon-Fri 11am-3pm, Sat & Sun 11am-7pm). The large and varied menu is standard pub-fare but does include deep fried Mars Bars (£4.95).

Just a little further along the Way is a new place and one that we like immensely. *Turnip the Beet* (☎ 07572 095132, 🖥 turnipthebeet.co.uk, **fb**; Wed 9am-6pm, Thur-Sat 10am-6pm, Sun to 4pm) accurately describes itself as a 'World Cuisine deli', conjuring up delicious home-cooked fare, such as a great value curry of the day

(£4.50), wraps and rolls (from £3.50) and all served with a smile. There's an honesty phone box outside filled with goodies for those who are passing when they're not open. They also sell midge repellent and camping gas. Note, however, that, for the moment at least, there are no toilet facilities.

Closer to Dumgoyne than to Killearn, *Oakwood Garden Centre* (Map 5; ☎ 01360-550248) is right by the Way and has a busy café and restaurant serving light lunches and teas daily from 10am to 4pm. There's also a **post office** here (Sun-Fri 9.30am-4.30pm, Sat from 9am).

First Scotland East's X10/X10A **bus** services stop by Glengoyne Distillery; see p46 for details.

---

### 🖥 BLANE VALLEY RAILWAY

Between Dumgoyach Farm (Map 4) and Gartness (Map 6) the Way runs along the route of the former Blane Valley Railway which, between 1882 and 1951, carried passengers from Aberfoyle to Glasgow. The old Dumgoyne Station was by the Beech Tree Inn (see above). The route is now not only used by the West Highland Way but also by a pipeline hidden in the raised embankment carrying water from Loch Lomond to homes and businesses in Central Scotland.

---

## KILLEARN                     Map 5, p111

Killearn is not actually on the West Highland Way; it lies a good 20 minutes' walk east. It is not worth a special detour on its own but some walkers may find its services useful. It's an attractive village overlooking the Campsie Fells and Loch Lomond and is built around the original 18th-century cottages of a planned village. It was here that George Buchanan, a leading historian, scholar and tutor to Mary Queen of Scots and King James VI, was born in 1506. An impressive 31m (103ft) obelisk stands behind Killearn Kirk in memory of him.

There's a **Co-op supermarket** (daily 7am-10pm), a **health centre** (☎ 01360-550339; Mon-Fri 8.30am-6pm) with a **pharmacy** (**-cum-gift-shop**; Mon-Fri 9am-1pm & 2.15-6pm, Sat to 5pm) nearby. There's a **cash machine** in the Co-op. The

**post office** is at the Oakwood Garden Centre (see Dumgoyne, above).

**Food** is available at *Town and Country Designs* (☎ 01360-550830, **fb**; Mon-Fri 9am-4.30/5pm, Sat & Sun from 10am, a traditional establishment with homemade soup, sandwiches, pastries and cakes. The best place for a full meal is *The Old Mill* (☎ 01360-550068, 🖥 theoldmillkillearn.co.uk, **fb**; food Wed-Sun noon-10pm), a delightful old pub-restaurant with exposed ceiling beams and open fires. There's an interesting and varied menu including delicious Scottish scallops (£11-18).

First Scotland East's X10/X10A **bus** service (to Glasgow and Strathblane via Milngavie) calls here regularly throughout the day so it is a convenient place to start or finish a day walk along the West Highland

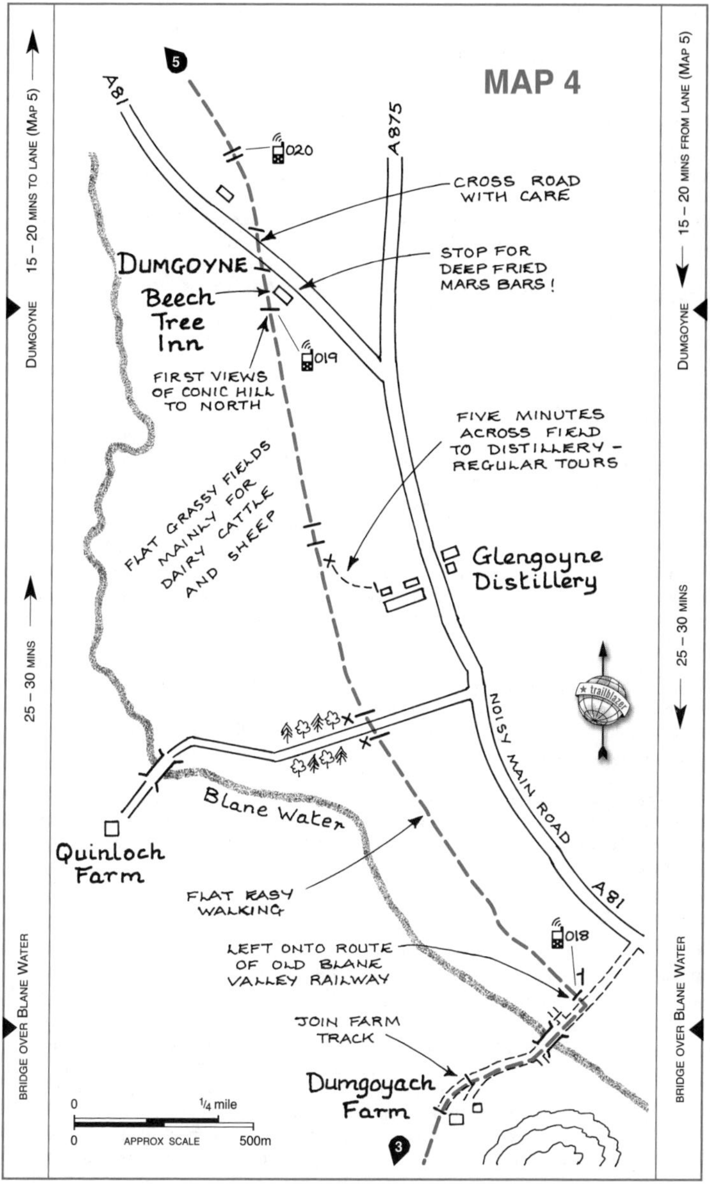

MAP 4

5

A81

020

A875

CROSS ROAD
WITH CARE

STOP FOR
DEEP FRIED
MARS BARS!

DUMGOYNE

Beech
Tree
Inn

019

FIRST VIEWS
OF CONIC HILL
TO NORTH

FIVE MINUTES
ACROSS FIELD
TO DISTILLERY –
REGULAR TOURS

FLAT GRASSY FIELDS
MAINLY FOR DAIRY CATTLE
AND SHEEP

Glengoyne
Distillery

NOISY MAIN ROAD

A81

Blane Water

Quinloch
Farm

FLAT EASY
WALKING

018

LEFT ONTO ROUTE
OF OLD BLANE
VALLEY RAILWAY

1

JOIN FARM
TRACK

Dumgoyach
Farm

3

0                    1/4 mile
0      APPROX SCALE      500m

DUMGOYNE     15 – 20 MINS TO LANE (MAP 5)

BRIDGE OVER BLANE WATER     25 – 30 MINS

15 – 20 MINS FROM LANE (MAP 5)     DUMGOYNE

25 – 30 MINS

BRIDGE OVER BLANE WATER

ROUTE GUIDE AND MAPS

Way; see p46 for details.

Killearn is not in the Demand Responsive Transport scheme (see p45) but it is possible to book a service from here to somewhere in the official DRT area.

## CROFTAMIE                off Map 7, p113

*Croftburn* (☎ 01360-660796, 🖳 croftburn.co.uk; 1T/1D; Easter-Oct; ☎; WI-FI; ⓛ) offers B&B from £38pp (£45 sgl occ). Note that they have a large private car park if you want to leave your car here while walking the Way (phone for information); they also have a secure shed for bicycles. You can easily walk to Croftamie along the Sustrans cycle path which leaves the Way just after Gartness by the bridge over the river. The owners offer free transfers from Drymen; a charge is made for transfers from Rowardennan or Milngavie (£15).

Croftamie is not on a bus route but see p45 for details of the Demand Responsive Transport service.

## EASTER DRUMQUHASSLE
                                  Map 7, p113

Half a mile further on and only 1½ miles (25 mins) short of Drymen is *Drymen Camping* (☎ 07494-144064, 🖳 drymen-camping.co.uk; Apr-Oct, WI-FI; 🐾 £1/night), by Easter Drumquhassle Farm. They charge £10pp which includes the cost of a hot shower and mobile charging. Alternatively, you can hire a **kocoon** (£42 per night, sleeps 2), which is a lined wooden structure with memory foam benches on either side, or a **green pod** (£50 per night, sleeps 2 in a double bed). You'll need your own sleeping bag if you opt to stay in one of these basic structures (or you can rent one).

They also run *Altquhur Byre* (☎ 07980-889790, 🖳 altquhurbyre.co.uk; 1D or T/1D, from £36pp; WI-FI; ⓛ) converted from part of the old barn, with views over the cats, hens and horses of the farmyard. B&B includes a self-service continental breakfast on weekdays with a cooked breakfast at the weekends.

Just before that is *Duncan Family Farm Glamping Pods* (☎ 07749-931144, 🖳 www.duncanfamilyfarms.co.uk; Apr-Oct, WI-FI; ⓛ; 🐾) which resemble shepherds' huts (sleeping 2 adults & 2 children, £120 room rate) but each have their own shower, outside decking area and seating area. They have teamed up with a local supplier to provide evening ready meals that can be heated up in the pods. Breakfast and a packed lunch can also be provided for an extra cost.

Easter Drumquhassle is not on a bus route but see p45 for details of the Demand Responsive Transport service.

## DRYMEN                        Map 8, p115

Pronounced 'drimmen', this is a large attractive village arranged round a neat green. It's a popular first night halt for many walkers on the West Highland Way, even though the trail actually bypasses the village to the east. There is plenty of accommodation both on the outskirts and within the village, several places to eat, a few handy shops and a library.

### Services

The **library** (Mon, Fri 9.30am-1pm & 2-5pm; Tue, Thur 9am-1pm & 2-7pm; Sat 9am-1pm; closed Wed & Sun), has free **internet** access and is open throughout the year. There's a **village shop** (Mon-Fri 9am-3.30pm, Sat 9am-5pm, Sun 9.30am-1.30pm). If you're camping stock up on food in the *Drymen Bakery & Deli* (☎

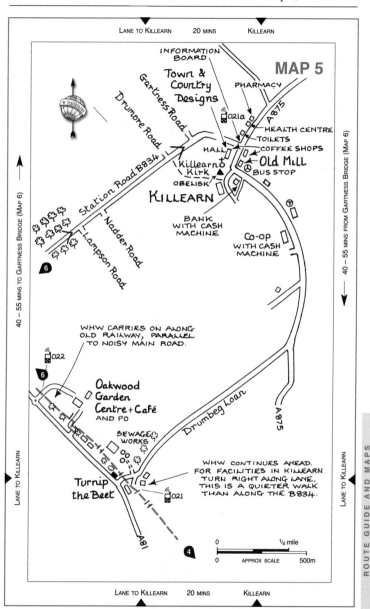

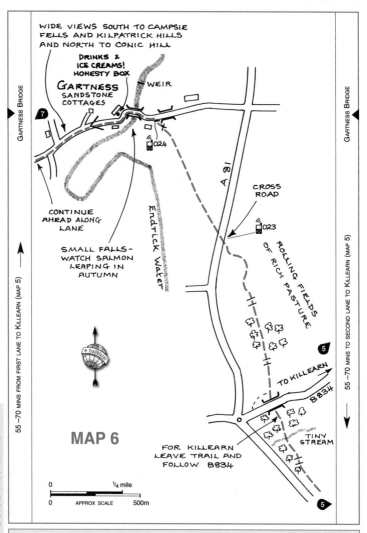

MAP 6

01360-660070, **fb**; daily 7.30am-5pm) or in the Spar **supermarket** (Mon-Sat 6.30am-10pm), opposite, as you won't have such a good selection again until Crianlarich. Inside, is the local **post office** (Mon-Fri 9am-3pm, Sat & Sun 9am-noon); outside, an **ATM**. The **butcher** (Tue-Sat 8.30am-5pm), on the south side of the Green, makes excellent steak pies, perfect for lunch. There's a **health centre** (☎

01360-660203; Mon-Fri 8.30am-noon & 1-6pm, closed Wed afternoon), **pharmacy** (Mon-Fri 9am-6pm, Sat 9am-1pm) and **dentist** (☎ 01360-661097).

### Transport

[See also pp45-9] Drymen is served by McColl's No 309 **bus**. Also see p45 for details of the Demand Responsive Transport service.

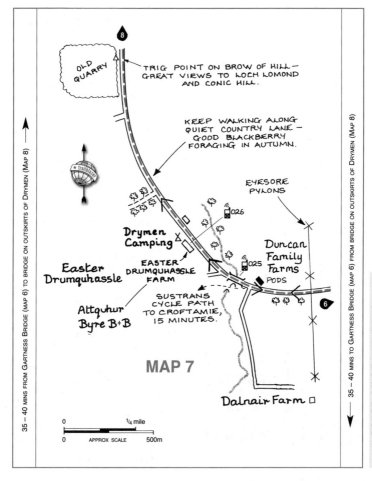

## Where to stay
Most backpackers **camp** at Drymen Camping (see p110, Easter Drumquhassle).

For **B&B**, at the top of the village near the health centre is *Bolzicco's B&B* (☎ 0783 771 8011, 🖳 www.bolziccos.com; 1D/1T, Tr or Qd; WI-FI; ⒧). Rates are £42.50pp for two people sharing, falling to £35pp for four sharing the Studio Room.

*Kip in the Kirk* (☎ 07734-394315, 🖳 kipinthekirk.co.uk; WI-FI) is an excellent place to stay with a range of accommodation. Converted from the old church hall, there are three rooms: Church Window (D or T, from £40pp), Pinwheels (D £40pp, sgl occ £60) and Friendship Star, which is an 8-bed dorm (£30pp) with two shared bathrooms. Rates include continental breakfast.

The *Drymen Inn* (☎ 01360-660321, 🖳 thedrymeninn.com; 5D or T/1F; WI-FI; £55-60pp, sgl occ full room rate) is popular with walkers.

*Buchanan Arms Hotel & Spa* (☎ 01360-660588, 🖳 buchananarms.scot-hotel.com, **fb**; 5T/34D/16Qd; ☛; WI-FI; 🐾; ⒧; £65pp, sgl occ £130) is a smart hotel which offers very good value indeed particularly if booked well in advance. The added attraction is that guests can use the heated swimming-pool and spa bath (open Mon-Thur 7am-10pm, Fri-Sun to 9pm).

The *Winnock Hotel* (☎ 01360-660245, 🖳 winnockhotel.com; 73 rooms; ☛; WI-FI patchy but best in public spaces; ⒧; 🐾 £10/night) is on The Square. Rates (from £92.50pp, sgl £124, sgl occ £152.50) include breakfast. It's worth phoning to see if they have any special deals.

The Clachan Inn

Next door is the old *Clachan Inn* (☎ 01360-660824, 🖳 clachaninndrymen.co.uk; 1T en suite, 2T shared bathroom; WI-FI; ⒧; £37.50pp room only, sgl occ £75), which has always been a trekkers' favourite.

*Ashbank B&B* (☎ 01360-660049, 🖳 ashbank-drymen.co.uk; 1D or T/1D/1Tr; WI-FI; ⒧; from £43.50pp, sgl occ £87) is at 1 Balmaha Rd. One room has a wet room which a previous resident, Eric Liddell (the athlete whose story is told in *Chariots of Fire*), certainly would not recognise.

*Braeside Guest House* (☎ 01360-660989, 🖳 www.braeside-drymen.co.uk; 2D/2T/1D or F; ☛; WI-FI; ⒧; 🐾; £37.50pp, sgl occ full room rate) is a very comfortable place with a pleasant garden (double) room. Note that breakfast is not provided here, but they can book it at the nearby *Drymen Inn* for you.

Long-running and welcoming, *Lander B&B* (☎ 01360-660273, 🖳 bandb.labbs.com; 1T/1Tr, shared facilities; WI-FI; 🐾; ⒧; £32-36pp, sgl occ £46) is at 17 Stirling Rd. *Elmbank* (☎ 01360-661016, 🖳 elmbank-drymen.com; 2D/1T/1D, T or F, en suite, 1D/1T shared bathroom), is at 10 Stirling Rd. Rates are from £30pp for room only; breakfast is not provided here.

A mile south-west of Drymen in the grounds of Buchanan Castle is *Green Shadows* (☎ 01360-660289, 🖳 www.greenshadowsbandb.com; 1D/1Tr; WI-FI), which charges from £47.50pp (sgl occ £95). They offer a pick-up service from Drymen, saving you a long walk, and will drop you back on the trail again the next morning.

## Where to eat and drink
In the village there's *Clachan Inn* (see Where to stay) which claims to be Scotland's oldest licensed pub, established in 1734. It's a popular place to drink and eat (food daily noon-9pm) with something on the menu to suit most tastes from vegetable tagine to a variety of steaks with a range of sauces. They also have a good vegetarian selection. Main courses cost from around £11.

The *Drymen Inn* (see Where to stay;

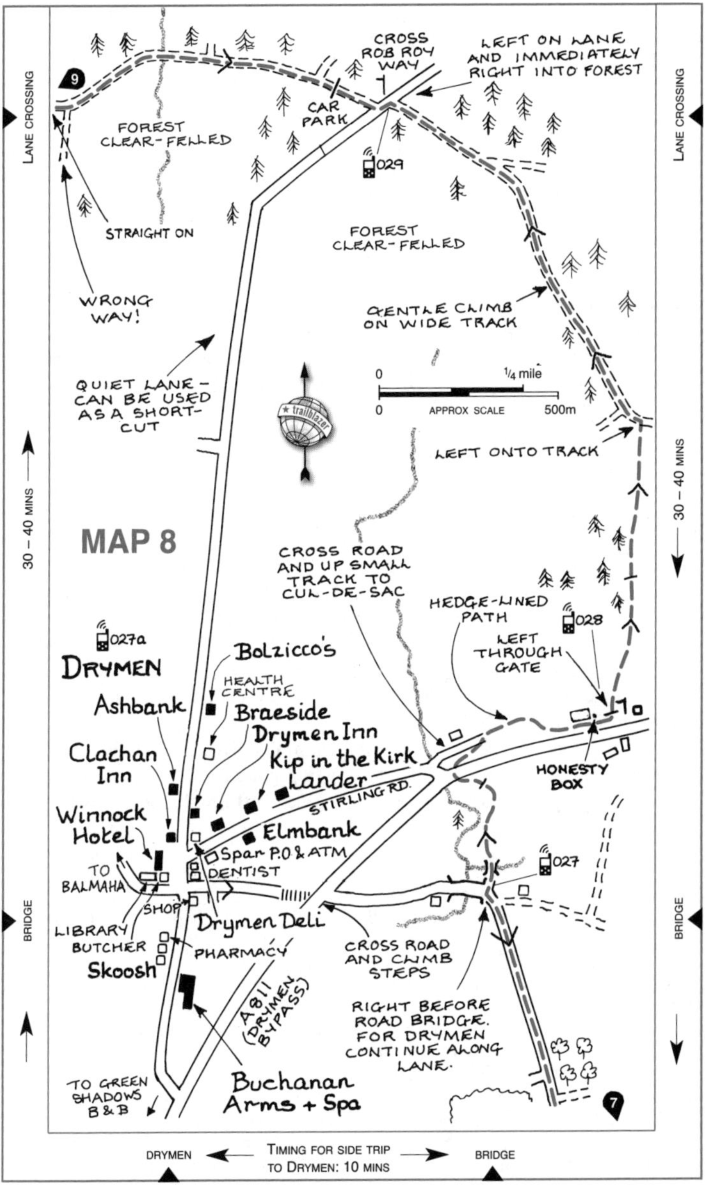

**9**

LANE CROSSING

FOREST CLEAR-FELLED

STRAIGHT ON

WRONG WAY!

QUIET LANE — CAN BE USED AS A SHORT-CUT

**MAP 8**

30 – 40 MINS

BRIDGE

CROSS ROB ROY WAY

CAR PARK

📱029

LEFT ON LANE AND IMMEDIATELY RIGHT INTO FOREST

LANE CROSSING

FOREST CLEAR-FELLED

GENTLE CLIMB ON WIDE TRACK

0    ¼ mile
0    APPROX SCALE    500m

★ trailblazer

LEFT ONTO TRACK

30 – 40 MINS

CROSS ROAD AND UP SMALL TRACK TO CUL-DE-SAC

HEDGE-LINED PATH

📱028

LEFT THROUGH GATE

📱027a

**Drymen**

Bolzicco's

Ashbank

HEALTH CENTRE

Braeside

**Drymen Inn**

Clachan Inn

**Kip in the Kirk**

Lander

STIRLING RD.

Winnock Hotel

**Elmbank**

TO BALMAHA

Spar P.O. & ATM

DENTIST

SHOP

LIBRARY

BUTCHER

**Drymen Deli**

**Skoosh**

PHARMACY

A811 (DRYMEN BYPASS)

TO GREEN SHADOWS B & B

**Buchanan Arms + Spa**

HONESTY BOX

📱027

CROSS ROAD AND CLIMB STEPS

RIGHT BEFORE ROAD BRIDGE. FOR DRYMEN CONTINUE ALONG LANE.

**7**

BRIDGE

DRYMEN ← TIMING FOR SIDE TRIP → BRIDGE
TO DRYMEN: 10 MINS

food daily 9am-8pm; 🐾) has a good restaurant and a bright covered area at the front that's perfect for a coffee. Try their haggis fritters for starter (£5.50), an interesting twist on an old theme.

**Skoosh Tea Room** (☎ 01360-661212, **fb**; 50 Main St; WI-FI, daily 8.30am-4pm) is a popular little café that's excellent value. There are baguettes, hot filled rolls, and home-made cakes to eat in or take away.

*The Ptarmigan Restaurant* at the Winnock Hotel (see Where to stay) has meals (daily noon-8.30pm) including traditional favourites such as haggis, neeps and champ tatties for £8.95.

The *Buchanan Arms* (see Where to stay; daily noon-9pm) has a good restaurant (daily noon-4pm & 5-8.30pm) with main courses starting at just a tenner though steaks are more expensive.

---

❑ **ONE FOOT IN THE HIGHLANDS AND ONE IN THE LOWLANDS**
**Conic Hill** (Map 10, p118) lies on the Highland Boundary Fault, a massive geological fracture separating the Lowlands from the Highlands. Standing on top of the hill you can see the line of islands across Loch Lomond clearly marking the direction of the fault zone which runs right across the width of Scotland from Kintyre to Stonehaven, just south of Aberdeen.

---

## DRYMEN TO BALMAHA                         MAPS 8-11

This is a wonderful **7-mile (11.5km)** section to the edge of the Highlands. Wide tracks climb gently through what remains of **Garadhban Forest** (Map 9) after recent clearance of this conifer plantation, to a clearing where the trail divides (1-1¼hrs). The **easier route** descends to **Milton of Buchanan** and follows the pavement by the B837 road for almost 2 miles (3km) to Balmaha (45-60 mins). The tiring yet spectacular **high route** (1½-2hrs) winds through more forest and then out onto open moorland before ascending to just below the top of **Conic Hill** (Map 10; 361m/1184ft); see box above.

A short climb to one of the multiple summits gives an incredible vantage point over Loch Lomond and the surrounding countryside. The steep descent takes you swiftly down to the honey-pot hamlet of **Balmaha** on the loch shore; a hive of boating activity in summer.

### BALMAHA                         Map 11, p119

This small village at the foot of Conic Hill is situated round an idyllic bay providing a sheltered anchorage for pleasure boats. However, it gets very crowded in summer, particularly at weekends.

It's a convenient departure point for **cruises** round the string of islands stretching across Loch Lomond to the western shore. For details of cruises check 🖳 cruise lochlomond.co.uk or 🖳 sweeneyscruiseco .com.

At the **boatyard** MacFarlane & Son

(☎ 01360-870214, 🖳 balmahaboatyard.co .uk) operate a service to North Pier on Inchcailloch for £7.50 return.

By the water is a statue of **Tom Weir**, the STV broadcaster, environmentalist and climber who lived locally. He wrote a column in *The Scots Magazine* for 50 years.

### Services

The **National Park Visitor Centre** (☎ 01389-722600, 🖳 lochlomond-trossachs .org, Apr-Oct daily 9.30am-4pm, Jul & Aug

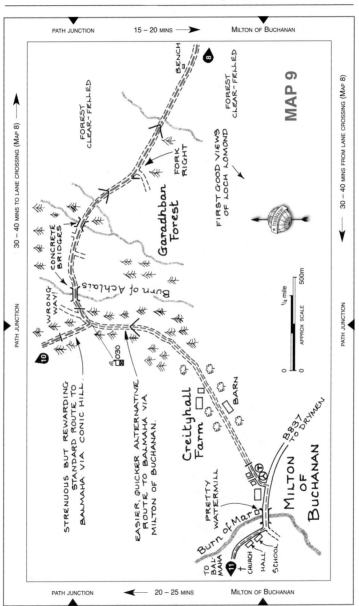

PATH JUNCTION     15 – 20 MINS ⟶     MILTON OF BUCHANAN

30 – 40 MINS TO LANE CROSSING (MAP 8) ⟶

30 – 40 MINS FROM LANE CROSSING (MAP 8)

MAP 9

FOREST CLEAR–FELLED

FOREST CLEAR–FELLED

FOREST CLEAR–FELLED

BENCH

8

FORK RIGHT

FIRST GOOD VIEWS OF LOCH LOMOND

Garadhban Forest

Trailblazer

1/4 mile    500m

APPROX SCALE

0    0

PATH JUNCTION

CONCRETE BRIDGES

WRONG WAY!

Burn of Achlais

10

STRENUOUS BUT REWARDING STANDARD ROUTE TO BALMAHA VIA CONIC HILL.

EASIER, QUICKER ALTERNATIVE ROUTE TO BALMAHA VIA MILTON OF BUCHANAN.

Creityhall Farm

BARN

B837 TO DRYMEN

PRETTY WATERMILL

Burn of Mar

MILTON OF BUCHANAN

TO BALMAHA

11

CHURCH

HALL

SCHOOL

PATH JUNCTION     ⟵ 20 – 25 MINS     MILTON OF BUCHANAN

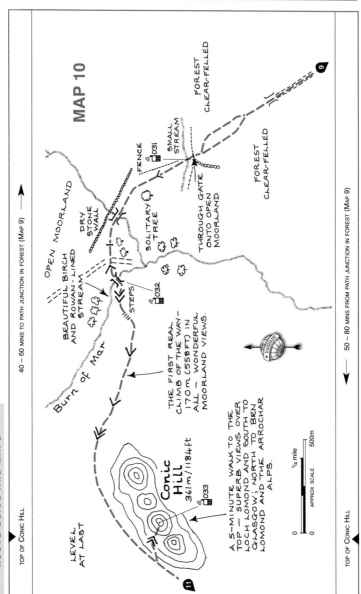

MAP 10

TOP OF CONIC HILL

← 40 – 60 MINS TO PATH JUNCTION IN FOREST (MAP 9)

OPEN MOORLAND

FENCE

□031

SMALL STREAM

FOREST CLEAR-FELLED

FOREST CLEAR-FELLED

9

DRY STONE WALL

SOLITARY TREE

THROUGH GATE ONTO OPEN MOORLAND

BEAUTIFUL BIRCH AND ROWAN-LINED STREAM

STEPS

□032

Burn of Mar

THE FIRST REAL CLIMB OF THE WAY – 170m (558FT) IN ALL – WONDERFUL MOORLAND VIEWS.

50 – 80 MINS FROM PATH JUNCTION IN FOREST (MAP 9) →

TOP OF CONIC HILL

¼ mile
0                500m
0
APPROX SCALE

Conic Hill 361m/1184ft

□033

A 5-MINUTE WALK TO THE TOP – SUPERB VIEWS OVER LOCH LOMOND AND SOUTH TO GLASGOW; NORTH TO BEN LOMOND AND THE ARROCHAR ALPS.

LEVEL AT LAST

11

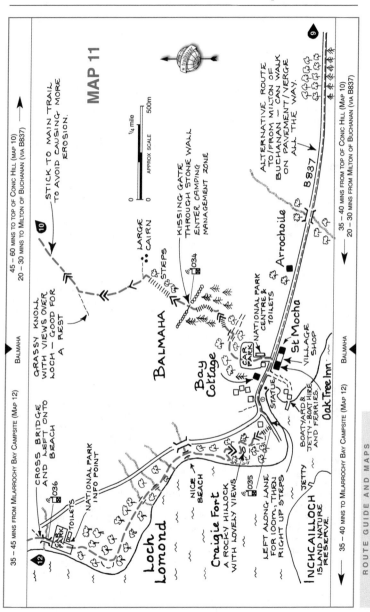

MAP 11

**9**

45 – 60 MINS TO TOP OF CONIC HILL (MAP 10)
20 – 30 MINS TO MILTON OF BUCHANAN (VIA B837) →

BALMAHA

**10** STICK TO MAIN TRAIL TO AVOID CAUSING MORE EROSION.

GRASSY KNOLL WITH VIEWS OVER LOCH – GOOD FOR A REST

LARGE CAIRN

STEPS

KISSING GATE THROUGH STONE WALL ENTER CAMPING MANAGEMENT ZONE

◎034

BALMAHA

Bay Cottage

NATIONAL PARK CENTRE & TOILETS

CAR PARK

STATUE

ALTERNATIVE ROUTE TO/FROM MILTON OF BUCHANAN – CAN WALK ON PAVEMENT/VERGE ALL THE WAY.

B 837

Arrochoile

St Mocha

VILLAGE SHOP

BOATYARD & JETTY/BOAT HIRE AND FERRIES

Oak Tree Inn

APPROX SCALE

0        500m
0    ¼ mile

35 – 40 MINS FROM TOP OF CONIC HILL (MAP 10)
20 – 30 MINS FROM MILTON OF BUCHANAN (VIA B837) →

← BALMAHA

35 – 45 MINS FROM MILARROCHY BAY CAMPSITE (MAP 12)

CROSS BRIDGE AND LEFT ONTO BEACH

◎036

NATIONAL PARK INFO POINT

CAR PARK

TOILETS

**12**

Loch Lomond

NICE BEACH

Craigie Fort
A ROCKY HILLOCK WITH LOVELY VIEWS

◎035

LEFT ALONG LANE FOR 100m, THEN RIGHT UP STEPS

JETTY

INCHCAILLOCH ISLAND NATURE RESERVE.

← 35 – 40 MINS TO MILARROCHY BAY CAMPSITE (MAP 12)

to 6pm; Nov-Mar weekends only 9.30am-4pm; WI-FI) in the car park provides information on the area including an interesting exhibition on the geology of the area. There are free toilets here too.

The **Village Shop** (daily 8am-9pm) is well stocked and has a selection of emergency items for walkers – snacks, socks, plasters, maps. The ATM has gone but they do offer cash back with any purchase.

Garelochhead's No 309 **bus** calls here; see p46 for details.

### Where to stay and eat

Between May and September it is possible to **camp** at Port Bawn on the island of **Inchcailloch**. This simple site (🖳 lochlomond-trossachs.org then search *Inchcailloch campsite*; see also box opposite) has a composting toilet for human waste only; there is no running water and barbecues aren't permitted. Up to 12 people can stay for £9pp per night (max 2 nights) and it is bookable up to 4 weeks in advance. The island can be reached by catching the small ferry operated by MacFarlane & Son (see p116).

As you walk out of the car park into Balmaha, directly opposite is the walker-friendly *Oak Tree Inn* (☎ 01360-870357, 🖳 theoaktreeinn.co.uk; 2S/8T/21D/3Qd; ▼; WI-FI intermittent; £47.50-102.50pp, sgl/sgl occ £85), constructed from local timber and slate but also swathed in ugly astroturf. There are two pods available (£60pp; sgl occ £120) at the rear of the inn. The Inn offers a wide range of **food** (daily noon-9pm) including toasted pretzel baguettes (£7.95), burgers from £11.95 and an excellent creamy cullen skink for £9.95. Nearby is *St Mocha coffee shop and ice-cream parlour* (daily 9am-5pm, may be later in summer), where you can pamper yourself with speciality coffee and cake.

The tariff at *Bay Cottage* (☎ 01360-870346, 🖳 lochlomond-baycottage.co.uk; 3Tr or F; WI-FI; 🐾; ⓛ; £50pp, sgl occ £75; Mar-Oct) includes use of the hot tub on the deck outside and afternoon tea with scones. One room is in the main house, one in an annex and another, the studio, is right next to the hot tub.

On the road from Milton of Buchanan (Map 11) is *Arrochhoile* (☎ 01360-870231, 🖳 whw-bb-lochlomond.com; 1D/1Tr; WI-FI, ⓛ; from £45pp), the owner of which will drop off/pick up at Rowardennan (£10).

---

### ☐ LOCH LOMOND

Loch Lomond is the **largest area of fresh water** in Britain; 23 miles (37km) long, up to 5 miles (8km) wide and 190m (623ft) deep at it deepest point near Rowchoish bothy. It was gouged out by a glacier about 10,000 years ago and at its northern end displays a typical fjord-like landscape with steep mountain walls on each side of the narrow ribbon of water. Its southern end is dotted with most of the 38 islands which have been lived on at one time or another. The loch provides up to 450 million litres of water a day to people in Central Scotland which, incredibly, lowers the water level by only 6mm.

The **wildlife** of the area is exceptionally rich. Naturalists have found a quarter of Britain's flowers, 200 species of birds and 19 species of fish, more than in any other loch. It is renowned for giant pike which grow to huge weights in the depths and you will often see anglers trolling for them behind small motor boats. Two of the more unusual species present are powan (*Coregonus lavaretus*), a type of freshwater herring, and lamprey (*Petromyson marinus*), an eel-like parasite which can grow to almost a metre in length. It latches on to other fish with its sharp teeth and sucker mouth producing a saliva which liquifies the victim's muscles, often killing it in the process.

❏ LOCH LOMOND NATIONAL NATURE RESERVE
Just offshore from Balmaha is the beautiful wooded island of **Inchcailloch** (Map 11, p119) which, along with four small neighbouring islands and the mouth of the Endrick Water just south of Balmaha, forms Loch Lomond National Nature Reserve. Inchcailloch can be visited by boat (see p116) any time of the year and there is a nature trail explaining the natural and human history of the island. The woods are arguably at their most beautiful in spring when the bluebells and primroses are in flower. Inchcailloch, which translates as Island of Nuns, has long been associated with Christianity and specifically St Kentigema, a missionary from Ireland who settled here in the 8th century. A church was built on the island in the 12th century; the remains of it can be seen on the nature trail walk. The associated burial ground was used up until 1947.

## BALMAHA TO ROWARDENNAN                                    MAPS 11-15

This is the first **7 miles (11.5km, 2½-3¼hrs)** of interesting walking along the 'bonnie banks' of **Loch Lomond** (see box opposite). There are no major climbs though the well-maintained path does rise and fall many times as it meanders through beautiful re-established native woodland punctuated by rocky coves and tiny beaches. For short sections it is forced to join the road which runs parallel to the Way as far as Rowardennan. In summer this can be busy with holidaymakers driving between the various caravan sites, car parks and beauty spots.

**Rowardennan** is the starting point for the long but rewarding climb to the top of **Ben Lomond** (see pp126-8) which stands above this tiny scattered settlement.

### CASHEL
#### Map 12 p122 & Map 13 p123
*Milarrochy Bay Campsite* (☎ 01360-870236, 🖳 campingandcaravanningclub.co .uk; WI-FI; 🐾; late Mar to late Oct/early Nov; £6.75-9.70pp) is a large family-orientated **campsite**. A hut is set aside for backpackers; it has showers, toilets and a common room – with a microwave, sink and lockers – which provides extra shelter. The site also has a small **shop**.

*Cashel Caravan and Campsite* (☎ 01360-870234, 🖳 campingintheforest.co .uk/scotland/loch-lomond/cashel-campsite; 🐾; Apr to late Oct) is just under a mile further on and is beautifully located by the loch. Facilities include a **laundry** and a well-stocked **shop** (daily 9am-6pm) which has a good selection of food and also midge

repellent, maps and all fuels for camping stoves. Be warned: stocks may run out towards the end of the season. It's worth noting that the camping area here is rather stony – a fellow camper suggested that this was a cunning way of selling him a mallet!

*Sallochy Campsite* (☎ 01360-870142, 🖳 forestryandland.gov.scot/forest-parks/ queen-elizabeth-forest-park/sallochy; 🐾; £8-9pp; Apr to end Oct) is run by Forestry and Land Scotland (formerly Forestry Commission Scotland). There are pitches both on the main site and 10 more on the lochside. Booking is essential, at least 24 hours in advance. There are composting toilets and a water tap. A warden is on site daily (9am-3.30pm).

ROUTE GUIDE AND MAPS

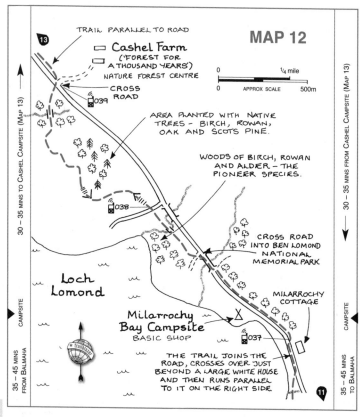

**MAP 12**

TRAIL PARALLEL TO ROAD

🔵13

☐ Cashel Farm
☐ ('FOREST FOR A THOUSAND YEARS')
NATURE FOREST CENTRE

CROSS ROAD

0 ————— ¼ mile
0 ————— APPROX SCALE ————— 500m

039

AREA PLANTED WITH NATIVE TREES - BIRCH, ROWAN, OAK AND SCOTS PINE.

WOODS OF BIRCH, ROWAN AND ALDER - THE PIONEER SPECIES.

038

CROSS ROAD INTO BEN LOMOND NATIONAL MEMORIAL PARK

Loch Lomond

MILARROCHY COTTAGE

Milarrochy Bay Campsite
BASIC SHOP

037

THE TRAIL JOINS THE ROAD, CROSSES OVER JUST BEYOND A LARGE WHITE HOUSE AND THEN RUNS PARALLEL TO IT ON THE RIGHT SIDE

🔵11

★ Trailblazer

30 – 35 MINS TO CASHEL CAMPSITE (MAP 13)

35 – 45 MINS FROM BALMAHA

CAMPSITE

30 – 35 MINS FROM CASHEL CAMPSITE (MAP 13)

CAMPSITE

35 – 45 MINS TO BALMAHA

ROUTE GUIDE AND MAPS

### ☐ CASHEL – THE FOREST FOR A THOUSAND YEARS

The restoration of native woodland is very much in vogue on the shores of Loch Lomond. The project taking place at Cashel Farm (☎ 01316-340043, 🖳 cashel.org.uk; Map 12) is one of the most ambitious, aiming to re-create a native woodland (oak, birch, aspen, alder, hazel, juniper, holly and Scots pine) over 3000 acres of land. Local community involvement and public access is an important objective and will hopefully show the way ahead for sound woodland management which benefits everyone. They have a small, unmanned, visitor centre (Easter-Oct, Tue-Sun 10am-4pm) with an interpretation board and toilets. You can also enjoy one of their three **woodland trails**, each of which showcases the variety of native woodland that exists in the Highlands. A walk around these regenerating woodlands highlights the importance of reforestation projects such as this in righting some of the damage done to our environment. See also box p71.

☐ **IMPORTANT NOTE – WALKING TIMES**
Unless otherwise specified, **all times in this book refer only to the time spent walking**. You will need to add 20-30% to allow for rests, photography, checking the map, drinking water etc, not to mention time simply to stop and stare. When planning the day's hike count on 5-7 hours' actual walking.

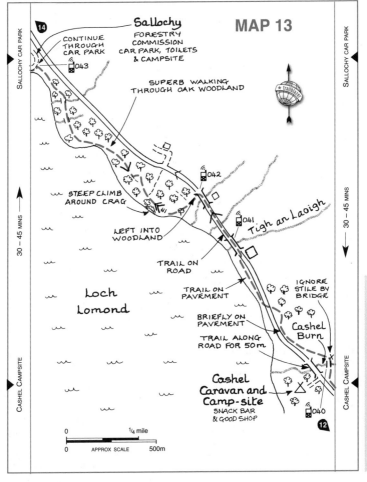

MAP 13

**Sallochy** FORESTRY COMMISSION CAR PARK, TOILETS & CAMPSITE

14 CONTINUE THROUGH CAR PARK

043

SUPERB WALKING THROUGH OAK WOODLAND

042

STEEP CLIMB AROUND CRAG

LEFT INTO WOODLAND

041 *Tigh an Laoigh*

TRAIL ON ROAD

TRAIL ON PAVEMENT

*Loch Lomond*

BRIEFLY ON PAVEMENT

IGNORE STILE BY BRIDGE

*Cashel Burn*

TRAIL ALONG ROAD FOR 50m

*Cashel Caravan and Camp-site* SNACK BAR & GOOD SHOP

040

12

SALLOCHY CAR PARK

SALLOCHY CAR PARK

30 – 45 MINS

30 – 45 MINS

CASHEL CAMPSITE

CASHEL CAMPSITE

0     ¼ mile
0     APPROX SCALE     500m

ROUTE GUIDE AND MAPS

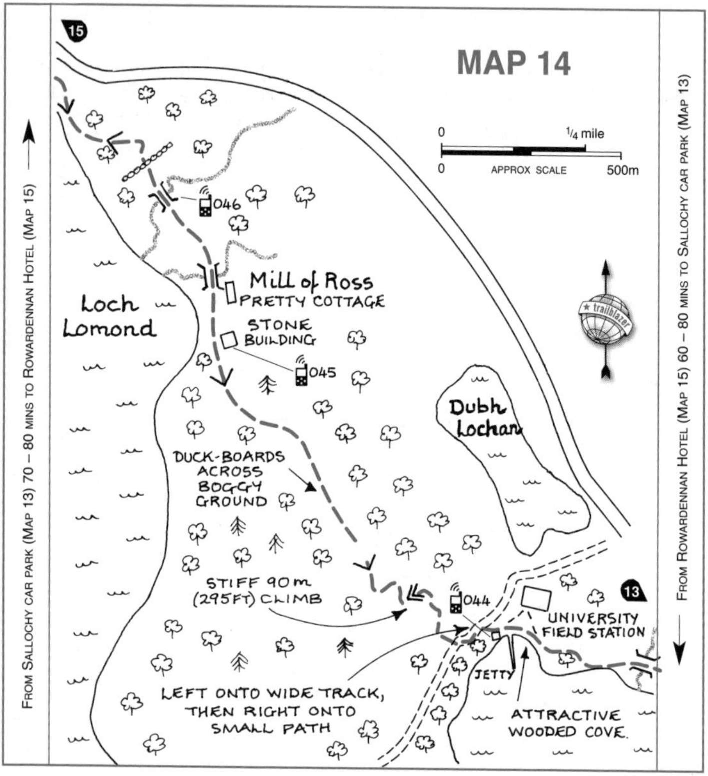
MAP 14
FROM SALLOCHY CAR PARK (MAP 13) 70 – 80 MINS TO ROWARDENNAN HOTEL (MAP 15)
FROM ROWARDENNAN HOTEL (MAP 15) 60 – 80 MINS TO SALLOCHY CAR PARK (MAP 13)
0 1/4 mile
0 APPROX SCALE 500m
15
13
046
045
044
Mill of Ross
PRETTY COTTAGE
STONE BUILDING
Loch Lomond
Dubh Lochan
DUCK-BOARDS ACROSS BOGGY GROUND
STIFF 90m (295FT) CLIMB
LEFT ONTO WIDE TRACK, THEN RIGHT ONTO SMALL PATH
UNIVERSITY FIELD STATION
JETTY
ATTRACTIVE WOODED COVE
trailblazer

## ROWARDENNAN **Map 15**

This tiny settlement provides accommodation for campers and hostellers as well as those with a healthy budget, but nothing in between.

***Rowardennan Hotel*** (☎ 01360-870273, 💻 rowardennanhotel.co.uk; 4D/17D or T/3Tr; £53.50-67.50pp, sgl occ £90-98; ☕; 🐕; Ⓛ; WI-FI in bar only) offers **B&B**. Most walkers only pop into the hotel for a restorative pint and perhaps some 'haggis from the Highlands' in the ***Clansman*** bar. **Food** is served daily noon-8.45pm, Sat to 9.30pm; non-residents are also welcome to join them for breakfast (daily 7-9am). The garden by the loch is perfect for a stop.

Five minutes further on is a beautiful Victorian hunting lodge, now ***Rowardennan Lodge Youth Hostel*** (☎ 01360-870259, 💻 hostellingscotland.org .uk; 63 beds; 3 x 2-, 3 x 3-, 2 x 4-, 5 x 6-, 1 x 10-bed room; WI-FI public spaces only; Ⓛ; from £15.50pp, private room rates on request; one room is en suite; mid Mar to mid Oct); the reception is closed between 10am and 4pm.

It is licensed, meals are provided and there is also a very basic food **shop** (7-10am & 4-10pm). There's a washing machine and drying room.

Just beyond the hostel the old ranger centre has been converted into ***Ben***

*Lomond Bunkhouse, Ardess Lodge* (☎ 07837-784120, 🖥 hostelling scotland.org.uk/hostels/ben-lomond; sleeps 10 in bunk beds – 1 x 4- and 1 x 6-bed room; £25pp; 🐾). Run by the National Trust for Scotland, it has a great living room and wood-burning stove and a communal kitchen. A breakfast of tea, coffee, bread, butter and jam is included in the price. A small honesty shop sells basics.

For details of Cruise Loch Lomond's **ferry services** see p116. The journey between Tarbet and Rowardennan (YH jetty) takes 45 minutes and costs £12/18 single/return; dogs are free. Call in advance to be sure of a place or to check whether the seasonal Rowardennen to Luss service is available.

See pp46-9 for onward **bus** connections from Tarbet (Scottish Citylink Nos 914, 915, 916, 926 & 976) and for the **rail** service (Arrochar & Tarbet station).

If you're planning to climb Ben Lomond visit the Ben Lomond Shelter in the car park en route. Made of straw bales and rendered in lime, it's a low-impact building that has displays on local history and wildlife. There is a drinking-water tap and toilets.

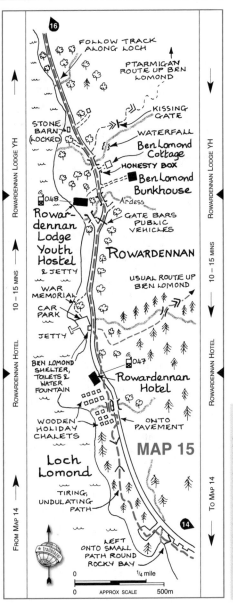

❑ '...THE BONNIE BONNIE BANKS OF LOCH LOMOND'
But for how much longer? This world-famous line was written by a condemned
Jacobite prisoner who lamented that he would never see his true love again on the
shore of the loch. Popularised by William Wordsworth, Gerard Manley Hopkins and
Walter Scott, Loch Lomond is still regarded as one of the most beautiful places in
Scotland and by walking the West Highland Way you get to journey along its entire
length.

In recent years camping by the eastern shore of the loch became hugely popular,
probably thanks to the Scottish Outdoor Access Code which allows greater freedom
for wild camping. Whilst wild camping is a worthwhile way of enjoying the outdoors
it is only acceptable if done so responsibly. Sadly, Loch Lomond seems particularly
vulnerable to hugely irresponsible campers, some of whom arrive with the sole purpose of partying on the beaches, leaving beer cans and other rubbish scattered in the
sand after they have gone. As a result **camping restrictions now apply – see p53**.

The leisure industry is also having a big impact on the area: oil pollution, sewage
and noise from boats is interfering with wildlife and other recreational users such as
bathers and fishermen. The thousands of walkers and picnickers who flock to the
shores in summer leave behind an incredible amount of litter and their cars choke the
roads for miles around. Nearby forestry and farming have also had an effect by pol-
luting the water with fertiliser nutrients and an increasing amount of silt which is
washed into the loch when the drainage of the hillsides is modified.

With such high intensity usage and so many conflicting interests it was the obvious choice for the first National Park in Scotland (see box p61). It is hoped that
increased funding and an integrated management strategy will help conserve the
beauty of this popular area but it also requires campers and the leisure industry to play
their part.

### Ascent of Ben Lomond

Ben Lomond, Scotland's most southerly Munro (see box p35), is the first real
mountain you pass on the Way and is a great excuse for taking a day out from
your progress north. At 974m (3195ft) the summit is an excellent vantage point
from which to view Loch Lomond and a large portion of the West Highland
Way.

**Route options** There are two principal ways to the top. The **most straightforward** but least exciting is to follow the popular well-maintained path beginning opposite the Ben Lomond Shelter at the Rowardennan car park which
ascends through forest onto the broad southerly ridge of the mountain and follows this to the summit. To return do the route in reverse.

The **interesting alternative** ascends via the subsidiary summit of
**Ptarmigan** before climbing the steep north-west ridge to the top and then
descends along the normal route. This route is described below. The whole trip
takes 4½-5½ hours allowing for short stops along the way.

**Safety** Steep corries on the north and north-east flanks of Ben Lomond mean
that you should take particular care when nearing the summit, especially if visibility is poor or when there is snow and ice on the ground. No matter how
good the weather is, you must know how to navigate well with map and com-

pass and be properly equipped, conditions can change quickly and with little warning. You'll need one of the following maps: OS Landranger sheet 56 (1:50,000) or OS Explorer OL39 (1:25,000).

## The Ptarmigan Route

(See also Map 15) The Ptarmigan Route leaves the West Highland Way just after **Ben Lomond Cottage**. Watch for the small trail on the right immediately after crossing the concrete bridge. Take this small trail through the woods passing a **waterfall** on the right and then under the wide branches of an old oak tree. Climb the bracken-covered hillside, go through a **kissing gate** and on up steepening ground keeping a deer-fence on your right; ignore any ladder-stiles over it.

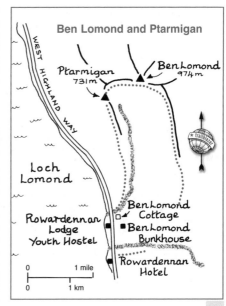

After 15-20 minutes the deer-fence and regenerated woodland veer off to your right; continue along the well-worn trail underneath some small crags with a conifer plantation far below to the left. As you round a small bend the knobbly summit of Ptarmigan appears and the path can be seen zigzagging up to it. In 10-15 minutes go through another kissing gate and continue on the trail along the west side of Ptarmigan's south-reaching ridge.

In five minutes you cross a small burn (fill up with water), then gradually climb onto the south ridge to the zigzags which lead steeply up to **Ptarmigan** (731m/2398ft); 20 minutes. It's then gentle walking round and over rocky hummocks past some small lochans up to the highest hummock marked with a cairn (751m/2463ft); 15 minutes. Descend to the peat-covered **Bealach Buidhe**, crossed on some large stepping stones, and begin the ascent of Ben Lomond's north-west ridge on a good path. Though steep, the path is easy to follow and you'll reach the **summit** in 20-25 minutes. Allowing for short stops you should get to the summit in 2½ to 3 hours from the start.

The wide, easily angled **tourist route** makes a pleasant and quick descent and you can appreciate that it would be a sluggish, uninspiring way up. Fifty minutes to one hour after leaving the summit you pass through a **kissing gate**, descend steeply momentarily, before levelling across the cattle-grazed hillside.

Fifteen minutes later cross the small bridge over the **Ardess Burn** into the coniferous forest. Five minutes further on you descend a rocky step (slippery in the wet) and then continue down some well-made stone steps, over a small

ROUTE GUIDE AND MAPS

bridge, weaving through heather, bracken and birch. You emerge from the forest opposite the Ben Lomond Shelter 15 minutes later.

---

❑ **BEN LOMOND NATIONAL MEMORIAL PARK**
This park runs along 8 miles (13km) of the loch's eastern shore, from Milarrochy to Rowardennan, right up to the summit of Ben Lomond. It was officially opened in 1997 as a reminder of those who have fought for their country and it is held in trust for the public in perpetuity.

The park is jointly managed and owned by the National Trust for Scotland and Foresty and Land Scotland (formerly Forestry Commission Scotland) and is an excellent example of how the priorities of these organisations are changing for the better. Until a few years ago this land was covered in uniform conifer plantation, the purpose of which was purely economic. Now the conifers are being grubbed up and the woodland is slowly being brought back to the native birch and oak which have traditionally covered the banks of Loch Lomond. In the process the number of plants, animals and insects that these woods can support will increase; just compare ground beneath a conifer plantation with the floor of a native woodland. The project will span over 40 years. Pioneer species such as rowan, birch and alder must first get established to naturally prepare the ground for the oak which will then follow. Deer can quickly destroy the young saplings so a high fence has had to be erected until the trees can fend for themselves.

---

## ROWARDENNAN TO INVERSNAID                              MAPS 15-19

Once upon a time, not so long ago, walkers were confronted by a choice of routes on this **7-mile (11.5km, 2¾-3¾hrs) stage**. The easier, high route, stayed on the undulating forestry track as it passes several waterfalls, yielding occasional surprise views through the trees. The alternative trail, on the other hand, was a different kettle of Loch Lomond salmon altogether – a tortuous route (as it was described in the previous edition of this book) that clung as close to the shore as it could, where hikers were forced to clamber over fallen trees, scramble over shifting rockfalls and struggle up some steep climbs if they wanted to continue on the trail.

Surprisingly, the authorities have clearly decided that everyone should now tackle this 'tortuous route', and have made it the official path, having removed the signs that pointed to the higher route; though to be fair, the alternative trail has been smartened up and the addition of wooden steps and bridges have done much to reduce the difficulty of this stretch. So while it may still be more arduous than the old official route, the reward of being immersed in glorious oak woods, away from both traffic and tourists, and with wonderful lochside views permanently on your left, is a more than ample pay-off.

The new route rejoins the old just beyond ***Rowchoish Bothy*** (see Map 17), a simple shelter with sleeping platform and fire. The Way continues on a well-made path along the shore through further stretches of old oak woodland.

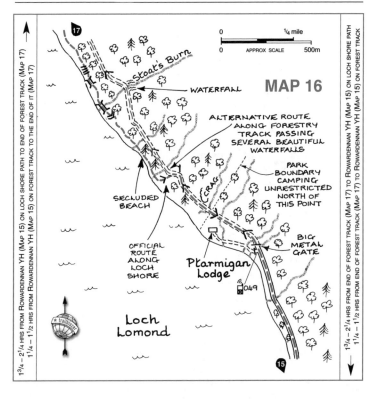

## MAP 16

SKoat's Burn

WATERFALL

ALTERNATIVE ROUTE
ALONG FORESTRY
TRACK PASSING
SEVERAL BEAUTIFUL
WATERFALLS

PARK
BOUNDARY
CAMPING
UNRESTRICTED
NORTH OF
THIS POINT

CRAG

SECLUDED
BEACH

OFFICIAL
ROUTE
ALONG
LOCH
SHORE

Ptarmigan
Lodge

BIG
METAL
GATE

049

Loch
Lomond

0    ¼ mile

0    APPROX SCALE    500m

*left margin:* 1¾ – 2¼ HRS FROM ROWARDENNAN YH (MAP 15) ON LOCH SHORE PATH TO END OF FOREST TRACK (MAP 17)
1¼ – 1½ HRS FROM ROWARDENNAN YH (MAP 15) ON FOREST TRACK TO THE END OF IT (MAP 17)

*right margin:* 1¾ – 2¼ HRS FROM END OF FOREST TRACK (MAP 17) TO ROWARDENNAN YH (MAP 15) ON LOCH SHORE PATH
1¼ – 1½ HRS FROM END OF FOREST TRACK (MAP 17) TO ROWARDENNAN YH (MAP 15) ON FOREST TRACK

## INVERSNAID          Map 19, p133

*Inversnaid Bunkhouse* (☎ 01877-386249, 🖳 inversnaid.com; Mar-Oct open, Nov-Feb group bookings only), housed in what was once a church (some of the stained-glass windows are still in situ), is a remote and cosy place which offers a range of accommodation. A free pick-up service from the Way is available, which is useful, considering its location 800m uphill from the Way (just follow the road up from the hotel). A bed/bunk bed in the **bunkhouse** (27 beds; 2T/4Tr/1x 5-bed dorm; 🐾; WI-FI; ⓛ) costs £25pp. They have a **log cabin** (2D; shared facilities; £60 per cabin). The rate for **campers** starts at £10pp (WI-FI; 🐾; ⓛ) including use of the self-catering kitchen (8-9am & 6-8pm). However, food is served

at the *Top Bunk Bistro*, a licensed restaurant (Mar-Oct daily 7.45-9.15am & 6-9pm; booking recommended for non-residents). A buffet continental breakfast costs £5.95 and an evening meal around £12. They have a hot tub (£2.50 per 15 mins) and a laundry service (wash & dry £5 per load).

Continuing along the road for half a mile past the bunkhouse brings you to Garrison Farm and *Garrison of Inversnaid* (☎ 01877-386341, 🖳 garrisonofinversnaid.co.uk; WI-FI, ⓛ). There are two self-contained apartments available to Way walkers (D, Tr or Qd; from £60pp) which have their own kitchenettes. Transfers (£2 each way) to and from the trail are available if pre-booked. Dogs are sometimes allowed

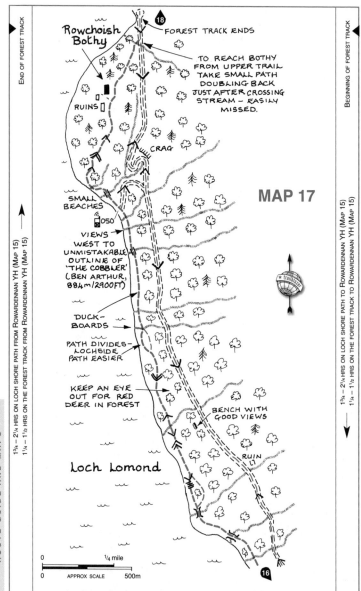

Rowchoish Bothy

18 FOREST TRACK ENDS

TO REACH BOTHY
FROM UPPER TRAIL
TAKE SMALL PATH
DOUBLING BACK
JUST AFTER CROSSING
STREAM — EASILY
MISSED.

RUINS

CRAG

SMALL
BEACHES

050

MAP 17

VIEWS
WEST TO
UNMISTAKABLE
OUTLINE OF
'THE COBBLER'
(BEN ARTHUR,
884m/2900FT)

DUCK-
BOARDS

PATH DIVIDES—
LOCHSIDE
PATH EASIER

KEEP AN EYE
OUT FOR RED
DEER IN FOREST

BENCH WITH
GOOD VIEWS

RUIN

Loch Lomond

0           1/4 mile
0    APPROX SCALE    500m

16

END OF FOREST TRACK

1¾ – 2¼ HRS ON LOCH SHORE PATH FROM ROWARDENNAN YH (MAP 15)
1¼ – 1½ HRS ON THE FOREST TRACK FROM ROWARDENNAN YH (MAP 15)

BEGINNING OF FOREST TRACK

1¾ – 2¼ HRS ON LOCH SHORE PATH TO ROWARDENNAN YH (MAP 15)
1¼ – 1½ HRS ON THE FOREST TRACK TO ROWARDENNAN YH (MAP 15)

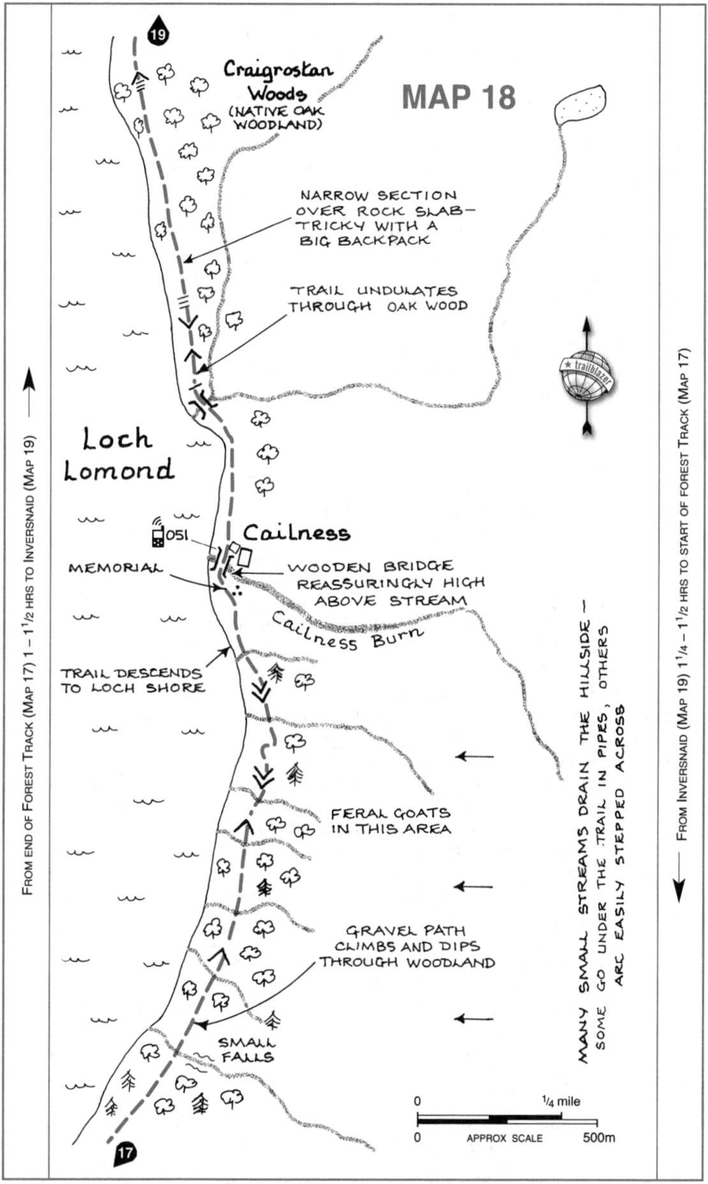

**19**

Craigrostan
Woods
(NATIVE OAK
WOODLAND)

**MAP 18**

NARROW SECTION
OVER ROCK SLAB -
TRICKY WITH A
BIG BACKPACK

TRAIL UNDULATES
THROUGH OAK WOOD

Loch
Lomond

051 Cailness

MEMORIAL

WOODEN BRIDGE
REASSURINGLY HIGH
ABOVE STREAM

Cailness Burn

TRAIL DESCENDS
TO LOCH SHORE

FERAL GOATS
IN THIS AREA

GRAVEL PATH
CLIMBS AND DIPS
THROUGH WOODLAND

SMALL
FALLS

**17**

FROM END OF FOREST TRACK (MAP 17) 1 – 1½ HRS TO INVERSNAID (MAP 19) →

FROM INVERSNAID (MAP 19) 1¼ – 1½ HRS TO START OF FOREST TRACK (MAP 17) ↓

MANY SMALL STREAMS DRAIN THE HILLSIDE —
SOME GO UNDER THE TRAIL IN PIPES, OTHERS
ARE EASILY STEPPED ACROSS

0        ¼ mile
0                    500m
APPROX SCALE

ROUTE GUIDE AND MAPS

but must be kept on a lead due to the resident livestock. Evening meals are available and there's even a hot tub (£5pp per hour).

Owned by coach tour company Lochs & Glens, *Inversnaid Hotel* (☎ 01877-386223, ☐ inversnaidhotel.com; 19S/25D/27T/1Tr/14F; ●; WI-FI in downstairs public areas; ⊕; from £123; Mar-Oct) is a welcome relief for many walkers as it's the only place right on the Way between Rowardennan and Inverarnan that provides food and drink. The walkers' entrance is next to a lounge area where there are coat hooks for wet coats and it's appreciated if you remove muddy boots. The **bar** serves good-value **food** (Easter-Oct daily 11am-4.30pm & from 6.30pm). Take-away meals, such as burgers & chips (£8.25), are served 11am-4.30pm; sandwiches are available all day. There's also a smart **restaurant**.

If you wish to cross Loch Lomond, from the jetty here, to go to Tarbet, contact **Cruise Loch Lomond** (☐ cruiselochlomond.co.uk) whose scheduled West Highland Way Rambler cruises call there. From Tarbet **Scottish Citylink coaches** (Nos 914, 915, 916 & 975) and Garelochhead's No 302 goes to the **railway station** (Arrochar & Tarbet; see p47).

Five minutes north of the hotel is a lovely clearing on the loch shore beyond the boathouse where backpackers can **camp** for free. All that is asked is that you stay only one night and don't light a fire. Campers can use the facilities in the bar (till 11pm).

---

## ❑ ROB ROY'S CAVE

The concealed entrance to Rob Roy's cave (see Map 19), supposedly a hideaway of the Highland hero, lies close to the path. It's quite a scramble to get there and there's not a lot to see. If you want to explore take a torch with you so that you can investigate the nooks and crannies. Judging by the amount of droppings on the floor it's used more by errant sheep and goats than clandestine men.

Rob Roy MacGregor, the Robin Hood of the Highlands, was born in 1671, the third son of a clan chieftain. Like many Highlanders of the time he made a living by dealing cattle, both legally and illegally, and would occasionally set off for the Lowlands on cattle raids. Part of this 'business' was the taking of protection money. By the time he was 40 he had acquired a sizeable amount of land and was prospering as a dealer. He was well known throughout Scotland for being a fair businessman, fine swordsman and for his good looks and wild red hair earning him the Gaelic nickname 'Ruadh', meaning red, which became Anglicised to 'Roy'.

His infamous career as a bandit began when he made one deal too many. He had borrowed the large sum of £1000 from the Duke of Montrose to complete a transaction, but his trusted drover ran off with the money leaving Rob a wanted man. The duke seized his land and declared Rob an outlaw. Given refuge and encouragement by a distant relation, the Duke of Argyll, Rob set off on many rustling raids against their common enemy, Montrose. He was on the run for over 10 years and was captured several times but always managed to escape in daring ways, boosting his image. In the end he turned himself in, was threatened with deportation but was eventually pardoned by the king. He lived out his final years in relative peace at home, with his wife, where he died aged 63.

Sir Walter Scott, the prolific 19th-century Scottish writer, did more for the reputation of Rob MacGregor than a lifetime of brigandry could ever achieve. In 1818 he published the highly romanticised novel, *Rob Roy*, which not only took the tale to a wider audience but also ensured that Loch Lomond became a key sight on any tour of the Highlands. By the time William Wordsworth's sister, Dorothy, came to see the cave in 1822 there was the full tourist set-up of lake steamer, Highland piper and boys selling trinkets. If anything, the cave is a quieter place today.

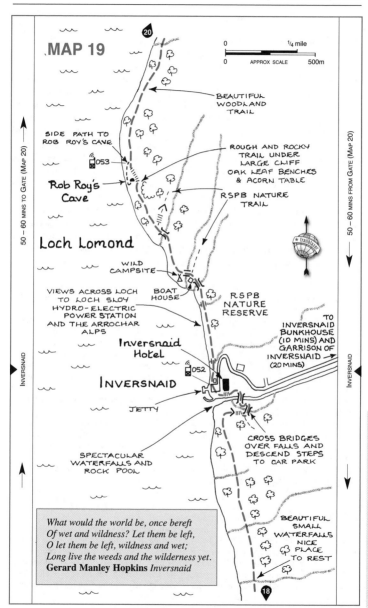

**MAP 19**

0       ¼ mile
0       APPROX SCALE     500m

🔊 053

BEAUTIFUL WOODLAND TRAIL

SIDE PATH TO ROB ROY'S CAVE

ROUGH AND ROCKY TRAIL UNDER LARGE CLIFF OAK LEAF BENCHES & ACORN TABLE

Rob Roy's Cave

RSPB NATURE TRAIL

Loch Lomond

WILD CAMPSITE

BOAT HOUSE

RSPB NATURE RESERVE

VIEWS ACROSS LOCH TO LOCH SLOY HYDRO-ELECTRIC POWER STATION AND THE ARROCHAR ALPS

TO INVERSNAID BUNKHOUSE (10 MINS) AND GARRISON OF INVERSNAID (20 MINS)

Inversnaid Hotel

🔊 052

INVERSNAID

JETTY

CROSS BRIDGES OVER FALLS AND DESCEND STEPS TO CAR PARK

SPECTACULAR WATERFALLS AND ROCK POOL

BEAUTIFUL SMALL WATERFALLS NICE PLACE TO REST

50 – 60 MINS TO GATE (MAP 20)

50 – 60 MINS FROM GATE (MAP 20)

INVERSNAID

INVERSNAID

> *What would the world be, once bereft*
> *Of wet and wildness? Let them be left,*
> *O let them be left, wildness and wet;*
> *Long live the weeds and the wilderness yet.*
> **Gerard Manley Hopkins** *Inversnaid*

ROUTE GUIDE AND MAPS

## INVERSNAID TO INVERARNAN                    MAPS 19-22

These 6½ miles (10.5km, 2½-3hrs) continue in much the same vein as the previous stage (assuming, of course, that you took the 'new', harder official route on the previous section and not the relatively simple forest track). Which means that, for the first 3 miles (5km) at least, you'll be confronted by plenty more tiring climbs and falls as you tackle the rocky path that winds through woodland across steep craggy slopes leading down to Loch Lomond. It is wild scenery marred only by the noise from the busy road on the western shore, now much closer as the loch narrows. Just north of Inversnaid is the **RSPB Inversnaid Nature Reserve** (🖳 www.rspb.org.uk then search 'Inversnaid'), a beautiful ancient oakwood, home to redstarts, pied flycatchers and wood warblers. There is a short nature trail that starts and finishes by the Way. Another mile north from here is **Rob Roy's Cave** (see box p132) which lies a hop and a skip from the main trail amongst a craggy mess of rocks.

Near *Doune Byre Bothy* (see Map 21), which provides very basic free shelter and a fireplace), the woodland opens out giving far-reaching southerly views. The trail then climbs away from Loch Lomond to a wide pass before descending into **Glen Falloch** (Map 22). Soft scenery dominated by water and woodland give way to the rocky fells and mountain views of the Highlands.

### ARDLUI                    Map 21, p136

Ardlui is on the opposite side of Loch Lomond to the trail and provides a useful start or finish for a walk along part of the Way. There are regular **buses** (Scottish Citylink Nos 914, 915 & 916) and **trains** to/from Glasgow and Fort William (for details see p47). The 975 & 977 services also call here en route between Glasgow and Oban. If you are simply looking for somewhere for the night you would be better off continuing to Inverarnan.

The **ferry** (Apr-Sep 9am-7pm, Oct to 6pm, 1/hr to **Ardleish**, run by Ardlui Hotel) costs £5 per person (minimum charge £6) and is summoned by raising the ball on the signal mast during hours of operation and it will come at the scheduled time. In winter you must arrange a ferry by phone via the hotel.

The attractive *Ardlui Hotel* (☎ 01301-704243, 🖳 ardlui.com; 1S/1T/6D/1Tr/2Qd; ▰; WI-FI; 🐾; ℚ; £64.50-74.50pp, sgl £64, sgl occ full room rate), at the head of the loch, has gardens running down to a small anchorage and marina. There is a restaurant and bar with **food** (Easter to Oct Mon-Fri 8am-3pm & 6-9.15pm, Sat & Sun 8am-9.15pm, Nov to Easter Mon-Fri 8am-2pm & 6-8pm, Sat & Sun 8am-9pm). Be aware that some of the rooms are above the bar. There are three **camping pods** (walkers' bothy; 🐾; £37-40 sleeps 3, £63-70 sleeps 5); you'll need your own sleeping bag, or hire one (£7.50).

### INVERARNAN                    Map 22, p137

The Way goes right past the excellent *Beinglas Farm* (☎ 01301-704281, 🖳 beinglascampsite.co.uk; Easter-Oct) where you can pitch your **tent** (£10pp; well-behaved 🐾). The immaculate showers are free, there's a washing machine and dryer and a sheltered area for cooking. They have six

**camping cabins**, each sleeping up to four (£20pp regardless of how many people share the cabin); sleeping bags/bedding can be hired for £5. **B&B** (4T/4Tr, all en suite; ℚ; £43-47.50pp, sgl occ £75) is also available in self-contained rooms in a purpose-built unit.

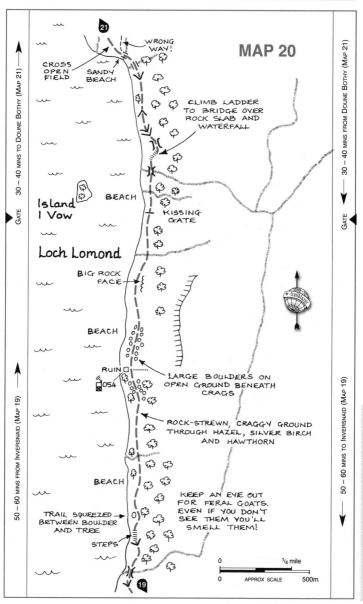

**MAP 20**

21

WRONG WAY!

CROSS OPEN FIELD

SANDY BEACH

CLIMB LADDER TO BRIDGE OVER ROCK SLAB AND WATERFALL

Island I Vow

BEACH

KISSING GATE

Loch Lomond

BIG ROCK FACE

BEACH

RUIN

054

LARGE BOULDERS ON OPEN GROUND BENEATH CRAGS

ROCK-STREWN, CRAGGY GROUND THROUGH HAZEL, SILVER BIRCH AND HAWTHORN

BEACH

KEEP AN EYE OUT FOR FERAL GOATS. EVEN IF YOU DON'T SEE THEM YOU'LL SMELL THEM!

TRAIL SQUEEZED BETWEEN BOULDER AND TREE

STEPS

19

GATE — 30 – 40 MINS TO DOUNE BOTHY (MAP 21) ▲

50 – 60 MINS FROM INVERSNAID (MAP 19) ▲

▲ 30 – 40 MINS FROM DOUNE BOTHY (MAP 21)

GATE ▼

50 – 60 MINS TO INVERSNAID (MAP 19) ▼

0        ¼ mile
0                    500m
APPROX SCALE

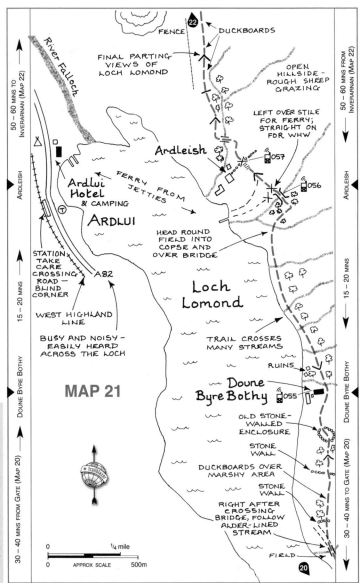

River Falloch

FENCE **22** DUCKBOARDS

FINAL PARTING VIEWS OF LOCH LOMOND

OPEN HILLSIDE – ROUGH SHEEP GRAZING

LEFT OVER STILE FOR FERRY; STRAIGHT ON FOR WHW

057

Ardleish

FERRY FROM JETTIES

056

Ardlui Hotel & CAMPING

ARDLUI

HEAD ROUND FIELD INTO COPSE AND OVER BRIDGE

STATION TAKE CARE CROSSING ROAD — BLIND CORNER

A82

WEST HIGHLAND LINE

Loch Lomond

BUSY AND NOISY – EASILY HEARD ACROSS THE LOCH

TRAIL CROSSES MANY STREAMS

RUINS

**MAP 21**

Doune Byre Bothy  055

OLD STONE-WALLED ENCLOSURE

STONE WALL

DUCKBOARDS OVER MARSHY AREA

STONE WALL

0    ¼ mile
0    APPROX SCALE    500m

RIGHT AFTER CROSSING BRIDGE, FOLLOW ALDER-LINED STREAM

FIELD

**20**

50 – 60 MINS TO INVERARNAN (MAP 22)

ARDLEISH

15 – 20 MINS

DOUNE BYRE BOTHY

30 – 40 MINS FROM GATE (MAP 20)

50 – 60 MINS FROM INVERARNAN (MAP 22)

ARDLEISH

15 – 20 MINS

DOUNE BYRE BOTHY

30 – 40 MINS TO GATE (MAP 20)

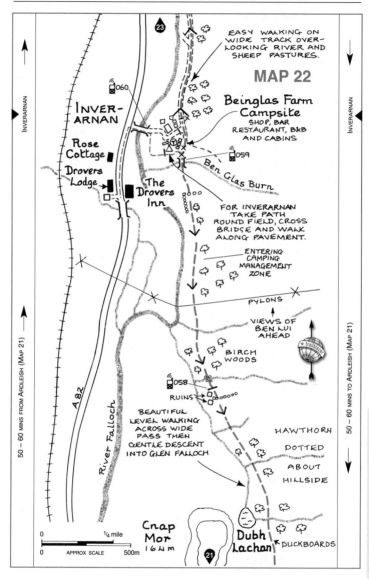

EASY WALKING ON WIDE TRACK OVER-LOOKING RIVER AND SHEEP PASTURES.

**MAP 22**

Beinglas Farm Campsite
SHOP, BAR
RESTAURANT, B&B
AND CABINS

📱060

INVER-ARNAN

Rose Cottage

Drovers Lodge

The Drovers Inn

📱059

Ben Glas Burn

FOR INVERARNAN TAKE PATH ROUND FIELD, CROSS BRIDGE AND WALK ALONG PAVEMENT.

ENTERING CAMPING MANAGEMENT ZONE

PYLONS

VIEWS OF BEN LUI AHEAD

★ trailblazer

BIRCH WOODS

📱058

RUINS

BEAUTIFUL LEVEL WALKING ACROSS WIDE PASS THEN GENTLE DESCENT INTO GLEN FALLOCH

HAWTHORN

DOTTED

ABOUT

HILLSIDE

A 82

River Falloch

Cnap Mor
164m

Dubh Lachan

DUCKBOARDS

21

23

INVERARNAN

INVERARNAN

50 – 60 MINS FROM ARDLEISH (MAP 21)

50 – 60 MINS TO ARDLEISH (MAP 21)

0 ¼ mile
0 500m
APPROX SCALE

ROUTE GUIDE AND MAPS

The small **shop** (daily 7.30am-10pm) stocks all the food campers and walkers could need including essentials such as stove fuel, insect repellent and midge nets. Also on the Beinglas Farm site is a **bar and restaurant** (WI-FI in bar area) – they serve breakfast daily 7.30-9.30am (a full Scottish breakfast is around £8.95); snacks and more filling meals, such as steak pie, are served noon to 9.30pm. Readers have praised both the quality of the food ('proper food no catering packs here') and the friendliness of the staff.

It's a 10-minute walk to the main hamlet where comfortable B&B can be found at the pretty **Rose Cottage** (☎ 01301-704255;

1T /1F/1D some en suite; ☞; Ⓛ; £47.50-50pp, sgl occ full room rate), a popular stop with Way walkers.

A stone's throw away is the self-styled 'world famous' **Drovers Inn** (☎ 01301-704234, 🖥 thedroversinn.co.uk; 5T/8D/1Tr/1Qd, some en suite; ☞; 🐾; WI-FI in public areas; Ⓛ; £52-70pp; sgl occ £55-70) and, opposite, the relatively more modern **Drovers Lodge** (13D/7T; 🐾; Ⓛ; £60pp, sgl occ £70). The reputedly-haunted Drovers is an eccentric mix of smoke-blackened walls, sagging velvet-covered chairs and moulting stuffed animals. The Drovers is certainly worth seeing and the atmosphere in the main part of the pub is great; it's a good

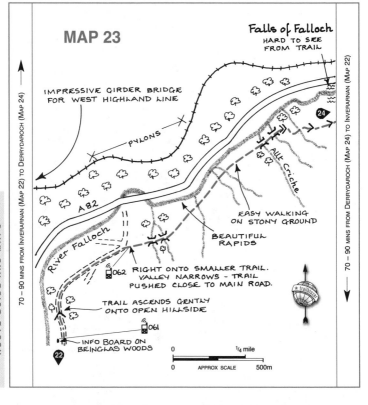

MAP 23

Falls of Falloch
HARD TO SEE FROM TRAIL

IMPRESSIVE GIRDER BRIDGE FOR WEST HIGHLAND LINE

PYLONS

Allt Criche

24

A82

River Falloch

EASY WALKING ON STONY GROUND

BEAUTIFUL RAPIDS

📱062  RIGHT ONTO SMALLER TRAIL. VALLEY NARROWS - TRAIL PUSHED CLOSE TO MAIN ROAD.

TRAIL ASCENDS GENTLY ONTO OPEN HILLSIDE

📱061

INFO BOARD ON BEINGLAS WOODS

22

0                    ¼ mile

0       APPROX SCALE       500m

70 – 90 MINS FROM INVERARNAN (MAP 24) TO DERRYDAROCH (MAP 22)

70 – 90 MINS FROM DERRYDAROCH (MAP 24) TO INVERARNAN (MAP 22)

ROUTE GUIDE AND MAPS

place for a pint. The **food** (summer Mon-Sat 11.30am-10pm, Sun to 9.30pm, winter daily 11.30am-9.30pm) is basic pub grub. Reviews of the accommodation – and hospitality – here are, however, mixed.

Scottish Citylink **coaches** (Nos 914, 915, 916, 975 & 977) stop in the village; see p47 for details.

## INVERARNAN TO CRIANLARICH

MAPS 22-26

The Way shares the next **6½ miles (10.5km, 2-2½hrs)** through **Glen Falloch** with a traffic-laden road, the Highland Line railway, and scores of electricity pylons. If you are able to ignore them the walking is pleasant and undemanding. Good tracks and a section of old military road follow the beautiful River Falloch and then climb easily over rough sheep pasture to the edge of a conifer plantation.

The busy village of **Crianlarich**, the halfway point of the Way, is 15 minutes off the main trail.

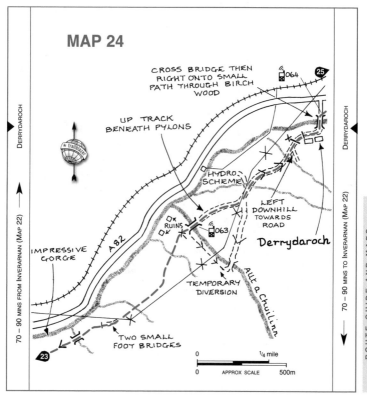

MAP 24

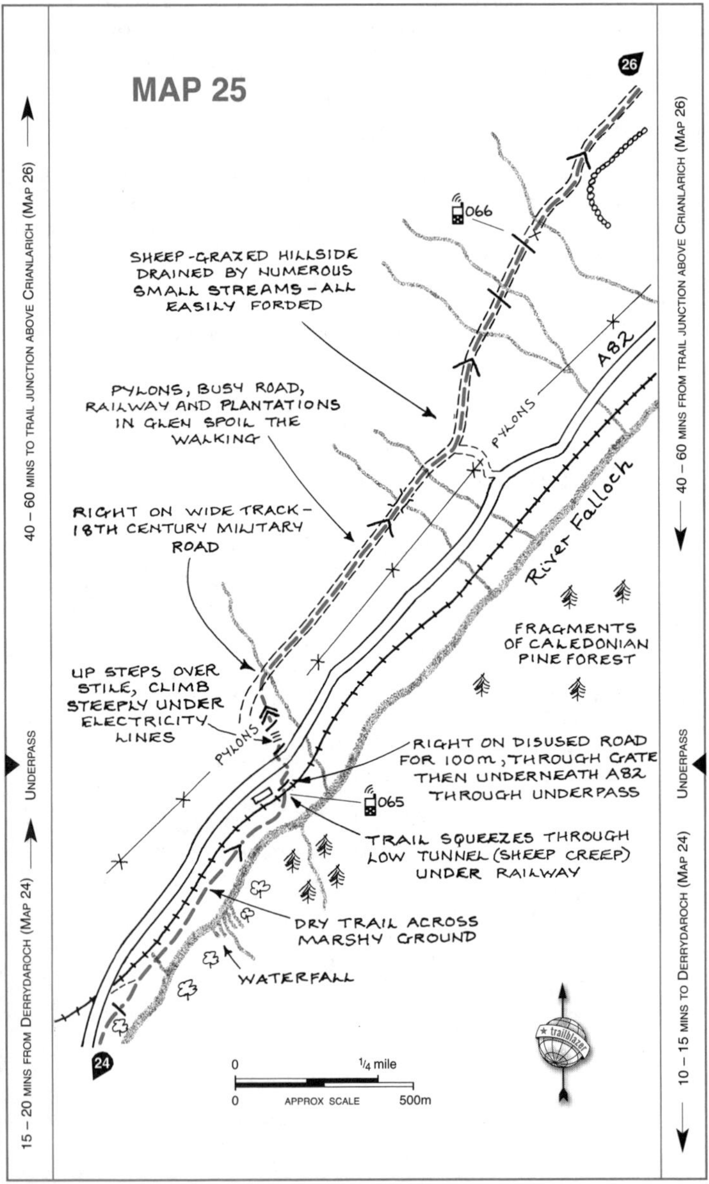

# MAP 25

40 – 60 MINS TO TRAIL JUNCTION ABOVE CRIANLARICH (MAP 26)

40 – 60 MINS FROM TRAIL JUNCTION ABOVE CRIANLARICH (MAP 26)

26

📱066

SHEEP-GRAZED HILLSIDE DRAINED BY NUMEROUS SMALL STREAMS – ALL EASILY FORDED

PYLONS, BUSY ROAD, RAILWAY AND PLANTATIONS IN GLEN SPOIL THE WALKING

RIGHT ON WIDE TRACK – 18TH CENTURY MILITARY ROAD

PYLONS

A82

River Falloch

FRAGMENTS OF CALEDONIAN PINE FOREST

UP STEPS OVER STILE, CLIMB STEEPLY UNDER ELECTRICITY LINES

PYLONS

RIGHT ON DISUSED ROAD FOR 100m, THROUGH CRATE THEN UNDERNEATH A82 THROUGH UNDERPASS

📱065

TRAIL SQUEEZES THROUGH LOW TUNNEL (SHEEP CREEP) UNDER RAILWAY

DRY TRAIL ACROSS MARSHY GROUND

WATERFALL

24

UNDERPASS

UNDERPASS

15 – 20 MINS FROM DERRYDAROCH (MAP 24)

10 – 15 MINS TO DERRYDAROCH (MAP 24)

ROUTE GUIDE AND MAPS

0     1/4 mile

0    APPROX SCALE    500m

★ trailblazer

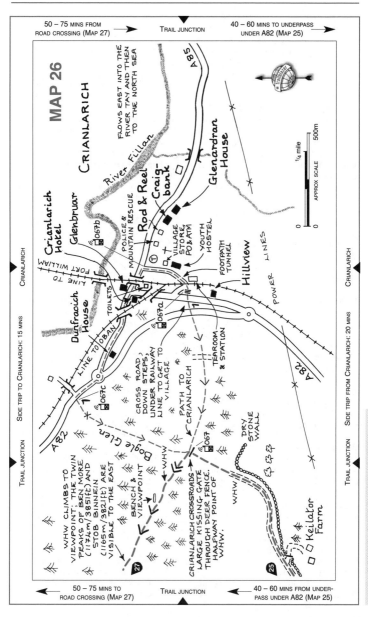

50 – 75 MINS FROM ROAD CROSSING (MAP 27) →

TRAIL JUNCTION

40 – 60 MINS TO UNDERPASS UNDER A82 (MAP 25) →

MAP 26

CRIANLARICH

FLOWS EAST INTO THE RIVER TAY AND THEN TO THE NORTH SEA

River Fillan

A85

Glenardran House

Crianlarich Hotel

Glenbruar

067b

Police & Mountain Rescue

Rod & Reel

Craigbank

VILLAGE STORE PO & ATM

YOUTH HOSTEL

¼ mile

500m

APPROX SCALE

LINE TO FORT WILLIAM

Dunfraoich House

TOILETS

067a

FOOTPATH TUNNEL

Hillview

POWER LINES

LINE TO OBAN

067c

A82

Bogle Glen

CROSS ROAD, DOWN STEPS, UNDER RAILWAY LINE TO GET TO VILLAGE

TEAROOM & STATION

PATH TO CRIANLARICH

067

DRY STONE WALL

WHW CLIMBS TO VIEWPOINT: THE TWIN PEAKS OF BEN MORE (1174m/3851ft) AND STOB BINNEIN (1165m/3821ft) ARE VISIBLE TO THE EAST

BENCH & VIEWPOINT

WHW

WHW

CRIANLARICH CROSSROADS LARGE KISSING-GATE THROUGH DEER FENCE. HALFWAY POINT OF WHW.

WHW

Keilator Farm

27

25

50 – 75 MINS TO ROAD CROSSING (MAP 27)

TRAIL JUNCTION

40 – 60 MINS FROM UNDERPASS UNDER A82 (MAP 25)

CRIANLARICH

SIDE TRIP TO CRIANLARICH: 15 MINS

CRIANLARICH

TRAIL JUNCTION

SIDE TRIP FROM CRIANLARICH: 20 MINS

TRAIL JUNCTION

ROUTE GUIDE AND MAPS

## CRIANLARICH  Map 26, p141

Crianlarich is no beauty spot. Cars and lorries thunder through the heart of the pebble-dashed village along the A85, but don't let this put you off. The village has some pleasant surprises, and essential services.

### Services

Londis **village store** (☎ 01838-300245, 🖥 www.crianlarichstore.co.uk; summer daily 7.30am-6pm; winter Mon-Sat 7.30am-6pm, Sun 8.30am-1pm) is well stocked with a wide range of food, including fruit and veg, basic medicines, maps and guides, footcare, midge repellent, socks and stove fuels. It's also an off-licence, newsagent and **post office** (Mon, Tue, Thur & Fri 9am-12.30pm & 1.30-5.30pm, Wed 9am-1pm, Sat 9am-12.30pm) and it has a Link **cash machine** inside.

The nearest **medical centre** is at Killin (☎ 01567-820213; Mon-Fri 8am-6pm) about 12 miles (19km) east of Crianlarich. Appointments are essential.

### Transport

[See pp45-9]. There are **buses** (Scottish Citylink Nos 914, 915, 916, 975 & 977) to and from Glasgow, Callander, Stirling, Edinburgh, Oban, Dundee and Fort William. In addition, the railway station is served by **trains** (Scotrail) from Glasgow, Fort William and Oban making it another ideal place to start or finish a walk.

The local **taxi** firm is Crianlarich Cars (☎ 0778 7788 360, 🖥 247taxis.co.uk); it is part of the DRT 'bus' service; see p45.

### Where to stay

At *Crianlarich Youth Hostel* (☎ 01838-300260, 🖥 hostellingscotland.org.uk/hostels/crianlarich; 64 beds, 6 x 3-, 4 x 4-, 5 x 6-bed room; 2 en suite rms; 🐾; WI-FI; 🔾; £20-25pp, private rooms from £59), meals are available and the hostel is licensed, has laundry facilities, a drying room and also a small shop (7.30-10am & 3.30-11pm). It's open daily from mid March to late October but Fridays to Sundays only from November to February.

Near the station is deservedly-popular *Hillview B&B* (☎ 01838-300323, 🖥 crian-larichbandb.co.uk; 2D/1T, some en suite; 🐾; WI-FI; 🔾; £40pp, sgl occ £65). It's a very well-run B&B with friendly and helpful owners.

Further along, on the main road is the excellent *Craigbank Guest House* (☎ 01838-300279, 🖥 craigbankguesthouse.com; 2D/2T/1Tr; 🐾; WI-FI 🔾; £42.50-47.50pp, sgl occ £70; mid Mar to mid Oct). Top breakfasts and a most hospitable owner.

Nearby is the comfortable and welcoming *Glenardran House* (☎ 01838-300236; 🖥 glenardran.co.uk; 1T/1D/2F/1 bunkbeds, all en suite; 🐾; WI-FI; 🔾; from £45pp, sgl from £85). The family rooms each have a double and a single bed.

Best Western's *Crianlarich Hotel* (☎ 01838-300272; 🖥 crianlarich-hotel.co.uk; 3S/19D/10T/3Tr/1Qd; 🐾; WI-FI 🐾; 🔾; £40-85pp, sgl/sgl occ £65-170) is a large attractive Victorian hotel in the heart of the village, with a friendly welcome (for humans and dogs). The hotel has an annex across the road: *Glenbruar House* (☎ 01838-300268, 🖥 glenbruar-crianlarich-bandb.co.uk; 5D orT; WI-FI; 🐾; from £52.50pp).

### Where to eat and drink

Don't miss the chance to visit the *Station Tearoom* (☎ 01838-300204, 🖥 crianlarich-station-tearoom.co.uk; Mar-Nov Mon-Sat 9.30am-2.30pm), a rare treat of a café in the old waiting rooms on the platform. As well as great cakes there's hot food, including West Highland breakfasts (£7) and hot filled rolls (£2.20).

The *Rod and Reel* (☎ 01838-300271; Easter to end Oct Mon-Sat 11am-11pm, Sun 12.30pm-11pm, food served till 8pm, Nov to Easter Fri & Sat 11am-11pm, Sun 12.30-11pm) is a popular meeting place with good cheap pub food – everything from toasties (£5.75) to neeps and tatties (£9.85).

Food is available all day at the *Crianlarich Hotel* (see Where to stay; daily 7.30-9.30am & noon-9pm) where non-residents are welcome. They can also provide takeaway picnic bags if preordered.

## CRIANLARICH TO TYNDRUM                    MAPS 26-29

The first 2½ miles (4km) of this **6-mile (10km)** section are through a large conifer plantation high on the valley side with views over the *strath*. The trail descends to the flat valley bottom, crosses the main road and River Fillan and makes a circuitous route through farmland.

It then goes past the ruined priory of St Fillan (see box below) before crossing the road again. The Way follows the river briefly and then heads across a compact moorland into the small but busy village of **Tyndrum (2-2½hrs)**.

### STRATHFILLAN          Map 28, p145

Two miles west of Crianlarich where the main trail crosses the A82 is *Ewich House* (Map 27; ☎ 01838-300536, 🖳 ewich.co.uk; 2S/1T/3D, all en suite; ☛; WI-FI; ①; ✖; £40-45pp, sgl/sgl occ £50/60), a large, comfortable, rambling farmhouse which dates from 1811. It's a great place to stay.

*Strathfillan Wigwams* (Map 28; ☎ 01838-400251, 🖳 www.wigwamholidays.com/strathfillan; ✖; WI-FI £3/24hrs for two devices), at Auchtertyre Farm, just over half a mile after crossing the A82, has accommodation to suit all budgets. **Camping** costs £8pp (booking essential). They have 22 **wigwam cabin** (two sizes, sleep 2-5, £40-50 per cabin). The rate includes electric heating and lighting; the wigwams have power sockets and mattresses (bedding can be hired for £15) and the large ones also have a fridge. There is a toilet, shower (£1) and kitchen block; the kitchen is fully equipped and has a washing machine and dryer (metered). **En suite wigwams** (sleep 4, £75) have a kitchenette with cooking facilities and a fire pit/BBQ. In addition there are five **lodges** (sleep up to 8, £60-80 per lodge) and **yurts** (sleep 5,

£70) with a log-burning stove. Note that all prices are based on two sharing, it's £10 for each additional adult, and bedding hire is extra.

Their **farm shop**, The Trading Post (daily Apr-Oct 9am-6.30pm; Nov-Mar to 6pm), sells the essentials for campers as well as a large variety of meats (lamb, beef and pork as well as buffalo, crocodile, kangaroo, zebra etc) which can be cooked on a camp fire. Their **café** sells hot drinks, hot pies and bacon rolls.

As it's near the trail, don't resist stopping at *Artisan Café* (Map 28; ☎ 01838-400391, 🖳 artisancafetyndrum.co.uk; WI-FI; Mar-Oct daily 10am-4pm, winter Thur-Mon), an excellent family-run coffee shop and craft studio in the old church. Top class homemade cakes!

On the outskirts of Tyndrum is the excellent *Glengarry Guest House* (Map 28; ☎ 01838-400224, 🖳 glengarryhouse.com; 1T/1D or T/1D, T or Tr, some en suite; WI-FI; ①; £42.50pp, sgl occ full room rate). The owners are most welcoming, there's a drying room and they'll do a load of laundry for £5.

---

### ❏ ST FILLAN

St Fillan was an Irish evangelist who, like many other missionaries, had come to Scotland to convert the Picts and the Scots to Christianity in the 7th century. He was active throughout the region of Breadalbane and it is possible that he had a chapel on the site of the priory remains on Kirkton Farm (Map 28). A 12th-century monastery on this site was made into a priory in 1318 by Robert the Bruce who was a strong believer in the cult of St Fillan, even taking a holy relic of the saint into battle at Bannockburn in 1314. Many miracles are associated with him and there is a nearby pool in the River Fillan, known as the Holy Pool, said to cure insanity.

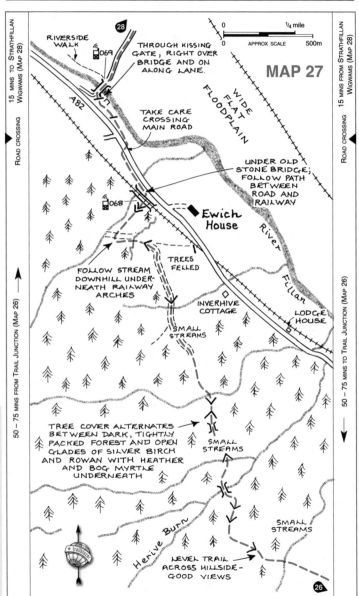

MAP 27

RIVERSIDE WALK

28

📱069

THROUGH KISSING GATE, RIGHT OVER BRIDGE AND ON ALONG LANE.

A82

TAKE CARE CROSSING MAIN ROAD

WIDE FLAT FLOODPLAIN

UNDER OLD STONE BRIDGE; FOLLOW PATH BETWEEN ROAD AND RAILWAY

📱068

Ewich House

River Fillan

FOLLOW STREAM DOWNHILL UNDERNEATH RAILWAY ARCHES

TREES FELLED

INVERHIVE COTTAGE

LODGE HOUSE

SMALL STREAMS

TREE COVER ALTERNATES BETWEEN DARK, TIGHTLY PACKED FOREST AND OPEN GLADES OF SILVER BIRCH AND ROWAN WITH HEATHER AND BOG MYRTLE UNDERNEATH

SMALL STREAMS

SMALL STREAMS

Henive Burn

LEVEL TRAIL ACROSS HILLSIDE - GOOD VIEWS

26

0 ... 1/4 mile
0 ... APPROX SCALE ... 500m

trailblazer

ROAD CROSSING ► 15 MINS TO STRATHFILLAN WIGWAMS (MAP 28)

15 MINS FROM STRATHFILLAN WIGWAMS (MAP 28) ◄ ROAD CROSSING

50 – 75 MINS FROM TRAIL JUNCTION (MAP 26) ▲

50 – 75 MINS TO TRAIL JUNCTION (MAP 26) ▼

ROUTE GUIDE AND MAPS

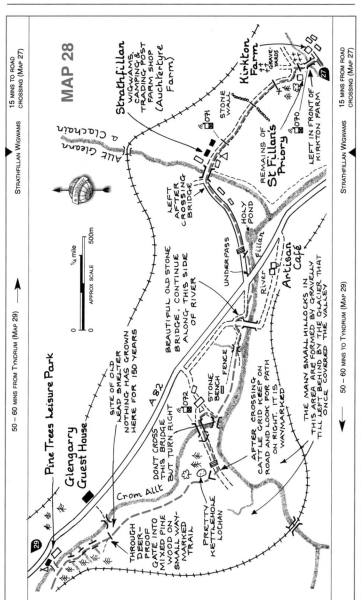

MAP 28

Strathfillan

WIGWAMS, CAMPING & TRADING POST FARM SHOP (Auchtertyre Farm)

Allt Gleann a Clachain

Kirkton Farm

GRAVE-YARDS

STONE WALL

REMAINS OF St Fillan's Priory

LEFT IN FRONT OF KIRKTON FARM

LEFT AFTER CROSSING BRIDGE

HOLY POND

River Fillan

UNDERPASS

Artisan Café

BEAUTIFUL OLD STONE BRIDGE. CONTINUE ALONG THIS SIDE OF RIVER

THE MANY SMALL HILLOCKS IN THIS AREA ARE FORMED BY GRAVEL TILL LEFT BEHIND BY THE GLACIER THAT ONCE COVERED THE VALLEY

STONE BENCH

FENCE

AFTER CROSSING CATTLE GRID KEEP ON ROAD AND LOOK FOR PATH ON RIGHT. IT IS WAYMARKED

Pine Trees Leisure Park

Glengarry Guest House

SITE OF OLD LEAD SMELTER NOTHING HAS GROWN HERE FOR 150 YEARS

A 82

¼ mile

0          500m
APPROX SCALE

DON'T CROSS THIS BRIDGE BUT TURN RIGHT

Crom Allt

PRETTY KETTLEHOLE LOCHAN

THROUGH DEER-PROOF GATE INTO MIXED PINE WOOD ON SMALL WAY-MARKED TRAIL

50 – 60 MINS FROM TYNDRUM (MAP 29)

STRATHFILLAN WIGWAMS

15 MINS TO ROAD CROSSING (MAP 27)

15 MINS FROM ROAD CROSSING (MAP 27)

STRATHFILLAN WIGWAMS

50 – 60 MINS TO TYNDRUM (MAP 29)

## TYNDRUM                          Map 29

The tiny village of Tyndrum has grown so rapidly that it has come to resemble one vast car park. It has traditionally been a stopping-off point for travellers heading to or from Oban and Fort William and as such it has been subject to an array of developments attempting to lure sedentary holiday-makers to part with their money: two vast coach-tour hotels, a roadside restaurant, and The Green Welly Stop shopping emporium have all brought acres of tarmac for parking.

Thankfully people walking can by-pass most of this and still find somewhere to stay.

### Services

Don't forget to stock up on supplies here. Apart from in Glencoe Village, there are no more shops until Kinlochleven. **Brodie's** (**fb**; 9am-5pm) is a family-run village **store** and **post office** (Mon-Fri 9.30am-1.30pm) open a staggering 363 days a year, with plenty of food for backpackers.

There's another **mini grocery store** (daily 7am-9pm) in the Green Welly petrol station where you'll also find a **cash machine** (£1.50). The **outdoor equipment store** in the Green Welly Stop (☎ 01301-702089; daily 8.30am-5.30pm) sells all the kit you could need including fuels.

### Transport

[See also pp45-9] Tyndrum is blessed with two railway stations, Tyndrum Lower for the Glasgow–Oban line and Upper Tyndrum for Glasgow–Fort William/Mallaig **trains**.

There are also **buses** (Scottish Citylink Nos 914, 915 & 916) to and from Glasgow, Callander, Stirling, Edinburgh, Oban, Dundee and Fort William.

### Where to stay

On entering the village, next to the lower station, is the *By The Way Hostel and Campsite* (☎ 01838-400333, 🖳 tyndrumbytheway.com; WI-FI; Mar/Apr-Oct, though group bookings welcome in winter) which offers a variety of accommodation and a small **shop** (summer daily, winter hours vary), selling walkers' essentials, on site. **Camping** costs £12pp, though they don't take anything bigger than a two-person tent. They also have: **trekker huts** (sleep 2-5, £15-25pp; 🐾); **camping cabins** (sleep 2, £20pp; sgl occ £30; 🐾) and **hobbit houses** (sleep 2-4, £15-20pp), the latter being the most luxurious. There's a shower/toilet block and other facilities, also provided for campers. Everyone, however, must provide their own bedding (sleeping-bag hire £4 per night) and cooking utensils.

The modern, functional **hostel** has rooms (3T/1D shared facilities; £25pp, sgl occ £40) and dormitories (18 beds; £25pp); there are also catering facilities and bedding is provided. By The Way is owned by walkers so they have all the facilities walkers need. Their website is also worth a look as it contains lots of practical info for West Highland Way walkers.

*Pine Trees Leisure Park* (Map 28; ☎ 01838-400349, 🖳 pinetreescaravanpark.co .uk; 🐾) was originally more of a caravan park but they've now built some wooden **huts** and **lodges** (£40-65 per hut for 2-4 people; en suite huts from £70, min 2 nights) for hikers and they also cater for **campers** (£10/18 for 1/2-person tent; book by phone only), including free showers and wi-fi.

On Lower Station Rd there are a couple of quiet B&Bs. *Tigh-na-Fraoch* (☎ 01838-400354, 🖳 tigh-na-fraoch.com;

> 🖵 **LEAD MINING**
> Just before crossing the A82 in Tyndrum (Map 29) heading north, you pass a row of old miners' cottages known as Clifton village. It is named after Sir Robert Clifton who discovered a vein of lead nearby in the 1740s, the mining of which provided employment for the village for over a century.

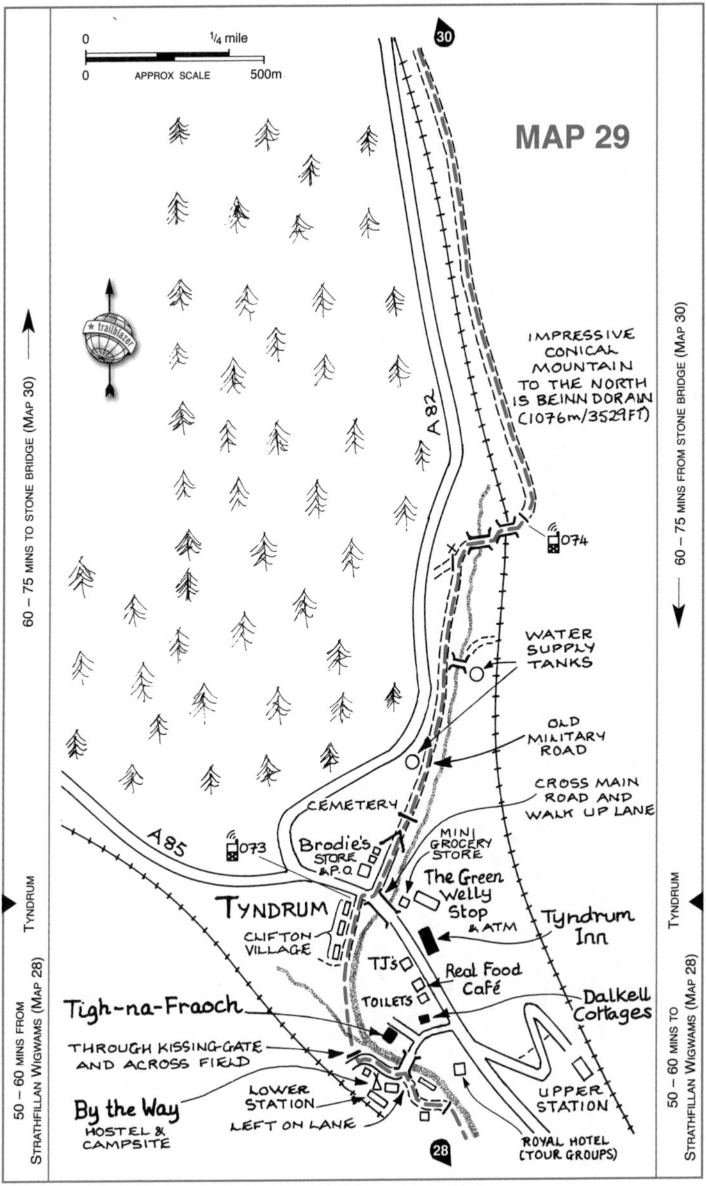
MAP 29
0
1/4 mile
0
APPROX SCALE
500m
trailblazer
30
28
60 – 75 MINS TO STONE BRIDGE (MAP 30)
60 – 75 MINS FROM STONE BRIDGE (MAP 30)
50 – 60 MINS FROM STRATHFILLAN WIGWAMS (MAP 28)
50 – 60 MINS TO STRATHFILLAN WIGWAMS (MAP 28)
TYNDRUM
TYNDRUM
A82
A85
IMPRESSIVE CONICAL MOUNTAIN TO THE NORTH IS BEINN DORAIN (1076m/3529FT)
074
073
WATER SUPPLY TANKS
OLD MILITARY ROAD
CROSS MAIN ROAD AND WALK UP LANE
CEMETERY
Brodie's STORE &P.O.
MINI GROCERY STORE
The Green Welly Stop &ATM
TYNDRUM
CLIFTON VILLAGE
Tyndrum Inn
TJ's
Real Food Café
TOILETS
Dalkell Cottages
Tigh-na-Fraoch
THROUGH KISSING-GATE AND ACROSS FIELD
By the Way HOSTEL & CAMPSITE
LOWER STATION
LEFT ON LANE
UPPER STATION
ROYAL HOTEL (TOUR GROUPS)

1S/3D/1T/1Tr; ☛; WI-FI; ⓛ; from £40pp)
is the first you reach. Nearby is *Dalkell
Cottages* (☎ 01838-400285, 🖳 dalkell
.com; 1S/1T/2D/3D or T; most en suite; WI-
FI; from £36.50pp, sgl £47, sgl occ £65).
They also have a **cottage** (1D/1D or T,
extra bed possible; ☛) which can be
rented nightly on a B&B basis (from £37-
52.50pp).

On the busy A82 is *The Tyndrum Inn*
(☎ 01838-400219, 🖳 thetyndruminn.co.uk;
5S/6T/6D/3Tr/1Qd; ☛; WI-FI; 🐾 bar area
only; ⓛ; £55pp, sgl £45-60). Three of the
single rooms share facilities but all the
other rooms are en suite. They have a drying room for walkers.

### Where to eat and drink

The oldest of Tyndrum's eateries, *The
Tyndrum Inn* serves food year-round in the
bar (daily 11am-9pm, to 10pm in summer)
and in the restaurant in the peak season
only. Huge mains (from £11.50) and delicious burgers from the burger menu (from

£9.45) are their speciality.

There are Scottish breakfasts for £9.95
and a haggis supper from £7.05 at *The Real
Food Café* (☎ 01838-400235, 🖳 thereal-
foodcafe.com, **fb**; Mar-Oct daily 7.30am-
9pm, Nov-Mar daily 7.30am-9.15pm). The
name makes it sound like a health food café
but they do at least use fresh ingredients.
Next door is *TJ's* (☎ 01838-400557, 🖳 tjs-
diner.co.uk; Tue-Sun 10am-9pm), an
American-style burger joint serving all-day
breakfasts (£6.50 for the full Scottish), pancakes (from £4.95), hot dogs and, of course,
burgers (from £10.55).

*The Green Welly Stop* self-service
restaurant (see also Services; 🖳 thegreen-
wellystop.co.uk; daily 8.30am-4pm) is fine
for a quick, cheap meal. You can also buy
sandwiches, fruit and cakes to take away.
Next door is the *Snack Stop* (Apr-Oct daily
7am-9pm, Nov-Mar daily 4-9pm), also part
of the Green Welly complex, serving fast
food.

---

### ❏ A SCOTTISH GOLD RUSH

In addition to being a major transport crossroads, Tyndrum has become the centre of
a Scottish goldrush and you may see people panning in local streams. The town, of
course, has long had an association with lead mining: you walk past some remnants
of the industry just before entering the village, while the nearby hamlet of Clifton is
made up of former mining cottages. In early 2018, however, a commercial gold- and
silver-mine opened at Cononish, a couple of miles south-west of Tyndrum. The min-

ing company Scotgold (which, despite the
name, is largely Australian-owned) plans
to extract around four and a half tonnes of
gold after initial drilling in 2012 produced
positive results.

The seam itself was actually discovered
about 30 years ago, but had never been
mined commercially due to the difficulty
in extracting the gold from the quartz rock
in which it is embedded. However, given
the high price that the precious metal now
fetches on the commodity market, opening the mine finally became a viable –
indeed profitable – proposition.

Panning for gold in Tyndrum

## TYNDRUM TO BRIDGE OF ORCHY     MAPS 29-32

This stage consists of nearly **7 miles (11.5km, 1¾-2¼hrs)** of good, mostly level walking along the worn cobbled surface of the old military road, with wonderful mountain scenery on all sides. There is no shelter along this open stretch so be prepared in poor weather. Once again the valley is shared with the main road and railway.

Fortunately the road soon parts company with the Way to run on the western side of the valley, while the trail follows the Glasgow to Fort William line along the east side. It is a little-used railway and those trains that do pass are more of a curiosity than an annoyance.

### BRIDGE OF ORCHY     Map 32, p153

Little more than a hotel, a bunkhouse, camping pods and a railway station, Bridge of Orchy is a tranquil hamlet under the spectacular slopes of Beinn an Dothaidh and Beinn Dorain (see p154).

There aren't any shops in the village and the **post office** opens only one morning a week (Tue 9.30-11.30am), in the old church.

**Trains** (Scotrail's Glasgow to Mallaig service) and **buses** (Scottish Citylink Nos 914, 915 & 916) call here; see pp45-9 for details.

#### Where to stay and eat

Across the elegant 18th-century bridge over the River Orchy is a popular free **campsite**.

*[continued on p152]*

According to the surveys, a tonne of rock would yield up to ten grams of gold. This means that the mine could yield hundreds of millions of pounds. Given that they also think that there is an estimated 25 tonnes of silver in the mine, the time seems right to extract the minerals.

The village will also benefit, with the mine employing around 60 people for eight years. In addition the mine could also be a boon to tourism, with plans being mooted for a gold-mining visitor centre in the village, as well as opportunities for tourists to go on 'gold-panning experiences'. Jewellery shops selling items made from Tyndrum gold are also expected to open.

It is hoped that the mine will produce around 200kg of gold a year – enough to produce 30,000 wedding rings per annum – with another 500kg being extracted each year by sending rocks for processing elsewhere. Early indications are good: in December 2021 the company announced that its production in the fourth quarter of that year totalled 1508 ounces (almost 43kg) of gold – a record for the mine.

Nor is this the end of the story, for Scotgold has licences to explore a 2200 sq km area of the southern Highlands for gold. Indeed, forecasters are predicting that there could be as much as five times more gold in the region than there is in Tyndrum.

If you fancy trying to offset the costs of your hike rent a gold pan and try a bit of prospecting while you're here.

ROUTE GUIDE AND MAPS

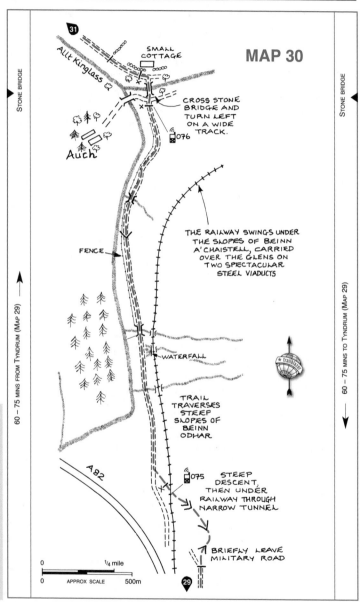

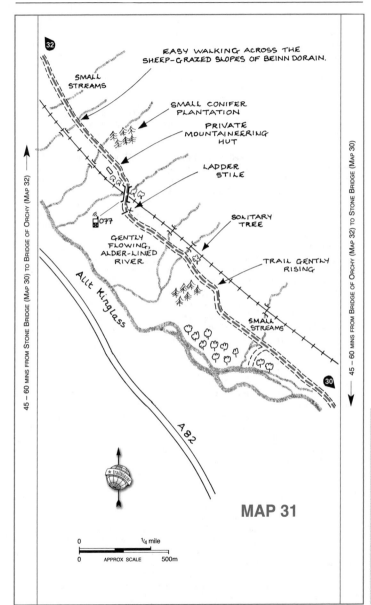

EASY WALKING ACROSS THE
SHEEP-GRAZED SLOPES OF BEINN DORAIN.

SMALL STREAMS

SMALL CONIFER PLANTATION

PRIVATE MOUNTAINEERING HUT

LADDER STILE

077

GENTLY FLOWING, ALDER-LINED RIVER

SOLITARY TREE

TRAIL GENTLY RISING

SMALL STREAMS

Allt Kinglass

A 82

**MAP 31**

0        ¼ mile

0    APPROX SCALE    500m

45 – 60 MINS FROM STONE BRIDGE (MAP 30) TO BRIDGE OF ORCHY (MAP 32)

45 – 60 MINS FROM BRIDGE OF ORCHY (MAP 32) TO STONE BRIDGE (MAP 30)

ROUTE GUIDE AND MAPS

## ❏ DROVE ROADS, MILITARY ROADS AND THE RAILWAY

For much of its route the West Highland Way makes use of historical lines of communication, in particular drove roads and military roads. The growth of cattle rearing in the Highlands in the 17th and 18th century created a network of drove roads through the mountains. These stretched from as far north as Skye to the main markets at Falkirk and Crieff where the cattle would be sold on to Lowland and English cattle dealers.

Many of the old inns along the Way sprang up at this time to provide accommodation for the drovers and grazing for the animals. Inverarnan, Tyndrum, Inveroran, Bridge of Orchy and Kingshouse all saw almost 100,000 sheep and 10,000 cattle moved past each year.

The metalled military roads that the West Highland Way follows for substantial distances from Inverarnan northwards were built in the 18th century after the uprisings in 1715 and 1745 by the Jacobites, as the supporters of the Stuart kings were known. Better roads were needed to move the English troops quickly through the mountains if they were to have any success in suppressing this rebellion. General Wade started the frenetic building in 1725 and gave his name to them but it was his successor, Major Caulfeild, who completed the most difficult roads through the Highlands which walkers now tread.

The West Highland Line from Glasgow to Fort William, which the Way also follows for much of its distance, was completed in stages from 1880 to 1901. The railway linked many of the isolated communities in the Highlands to the rest of Scotland and encouraged the farmers to specialise in sheep as they could be moved quickly to market. It also heralded the start of mountain tourism opening up the Highlands to walkers and climbers from the industrial towns and cities.

There are fantastic mountain walks right from the train beginning at stations such as Crianlarich and Bridge of Orchy and the remote moorland stations such as Rannoch and Corrour give access to wild walking country far from civilisation.

However, there are no facilities and it can be midgy at times.

Some years ago the station building was converted into the *West Highland Way Sleeper* (☎ 07778-746600, 🖳 westhighlandwaysleeper.com; Ⓛ; Easter-Oct), a tiny 10-bed **bunkhouse** (£33pp inc bedding) with a separate en-suite twin room (£42.50pp, sing occ £60 inc breakfast). Meals can be arranged. Booking ahead of time is also advised especially in the main season. It may lack the facilities of some of the more modern, sophisticated hostels, but it's still a quirky, charming place to stay.

Immediately below it is the *Bridge of Orchy Outdoors* (☎ 01838-400208, book via AirBnB; 2T), two simple wooden pods that can be booked on a nightly basis (£35pp). The shower and toilet are just a few seconds away and there's a small kitchen area too with microwave and some provisions (with an honesty box).

The imposing *Bridge of Orchy Hotel* (☎ 01838-400208, 🖳 bridgeoforchy.co.uk; 2T/8D/2Tr main building, 21T or D in annex, cottage sleeps 4; WI-FI; 🐾 charge applies; Ⓛ) is a very comfortable place to stay with a good restaurant. B&B rates vary dramatically (low season from approx £40pp, high season from approx £90pp) so it's best to contact the hotel for an accurate price. There is some wonderful **food** on offer (daily 7-9.30am, noon-8.45pm, winter breakfast from 8am), including traditional haggis, neeps and tatties for £14, or butter-roasted hake with carrot puree, spinach, mussels and bacon crumb for £18.

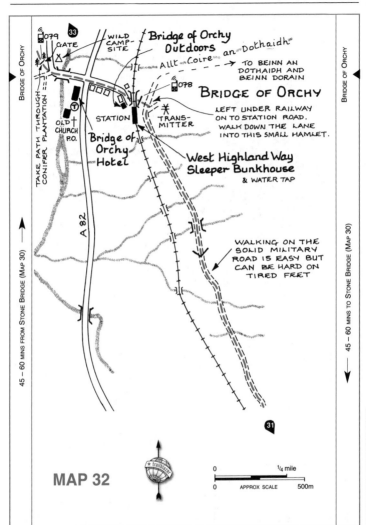

079

33

WILD CAMP-SITE

GATE

Bridge of Orchy Outdoors

Allt Coire an Dothaidh

→ TO BEINN AN DOTHAIDH AND BEINN DORAIN

078

BRIDGE OF ORCHY

LEFT UNDER RAILWAY ON TO STATION ROAD. WALK DOWN THE LANE INTO THIS SMALL HAMLET.

TAKE PATH THROUGH CONIFER PLANTATION

STATION

OLD CHURCH

P.O.

Bridge of Orchy Hotel

TRANS-MITTER

West Highland Way Sleeper Bunkhouse

& WATER TAP

A 82

WALKING ON THE SOLID MILITARY ROAD IS EASY BUT CAN BE HARD ON TIRED FEET

31

MAP 32

trailblazer

0          1/4 mile

0     APPROX SCALE     500m

BRIDGE OF ORCHY (left margin)

BRIDGE OF ORCHY (right margin)

45 – 60 MINS FROM STONE BRIDGE (MAP 30)

45 – 60 MINS TO STONE BRIDGE (MAP 30)

ROUTE GUIDE AND MAPS

❑ **IMPORTANT NOTE – WALKING TIMES**
Unless otherwise specified, **all times in this book refer only to the time spent walk-ing.** You will need to add 20-30% to allow for rests, photography, checking the map, drinking water etc. When planning the day's hike count on 5-7 hours' actual walking.

### Ascent of Beinn Dorain and Beinn an Dothaidh

This is a moderately strenuous climb of two Munros above Bridge of Orchy with wonderful views over Rannoch Moor from Beinn an Dothaidh; 7½ miles (12km), 6-7 hours with short breaks.

**Beinn Dorain**
(1076m/3529ft)

You need to be an experienced hillwalker as navigation can be difficult in poor visibility (see p182). Take care not to wander onto the steep ground on the western side of the mountains. You will need one of the following maps: OS Explorer 377 (1:25,000) or OS Landranger sheet 50 (1:50,000).

From Bridge of Orchy station go through the underpass and head east into Coire an Dothaidh towards the obvious *bealach* (744m/2440ft). Turn right (south) along a path to climb the broad north ridge of Beinn Dorain to the summit (1076m/3529ft).

Note that the true summit is 200m beyond a false summit. Return to the bealach and climb north-north-east up the steep south ridge of Beinn an Dothaidh to its summit (1004m/3293ft). Retrace your steps to Bridge of Orchy.

For more information see Trailblazer's *Scottish Highlands Hillwalking Guide* by Jim Manthorpe.

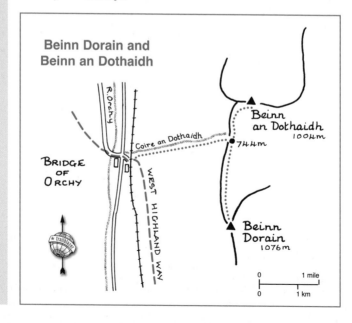

**Beinn Dorain and Beinn an Dothaidh**

## BRIDGE OF ORCHY TO KINGSHOUSE          MAPS 32-38

This superb, challenging **13-mile (21km, 4-5hrs)** section starts easily with three miles (5km) of pleasant walking over a small ridge to the **Inveroran Hotel** and then round the head of **Loch Tulla** (Map 34).

Just beyond Victoria Bridge an old cobbled drove road slowly ascends on to **Black Mount**, a rising of high moorland between the large mountains surrounding Coire Bà (see box p156) west of the trail and the vast expanse of **Rannoch Moor** to the east. This track carries you direct and dry-shod across this desolate landscape. This is the remotest and wildest section of the whole Way; there are no escape routes, nor is there much shelter, for the next 10 miles (16km), so come prepared as the weather here is notoriously cruel. From the highest point of 445m (1460ft) the Way descends to the main road and the isolated **Kings House Hotel** with views to the stunning mountains of **Glen Coe**.

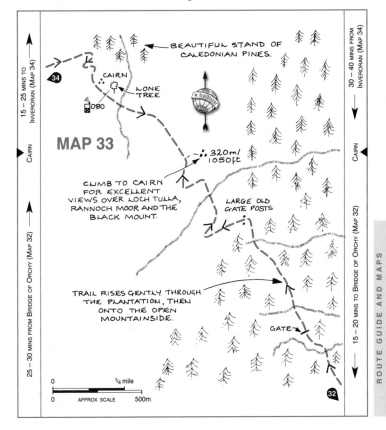

MAP 33

BEAUTIFUL STAND OF CALEDONIAN PINES.

CAIRN

LONE TREE

080

320m/ 1050ft

CLIMB TO CAIRN FOR EXCELLENT VIEWS OVER LOCH TULLA, RANNOCH MOOR AND THE BLACK MOUNT.

LARGE OLD GATE POSTS

TRAIL RISES GENTLY THROUGH THE PLANTATION, THEN ONTO THE OPEN MOUNTAINSIDE.

GATE

34

32

CAIRN

CAIRN

15 – 25 MINS TO INVERORAN (MAP 34)

25 – 30 MINS FROM BRIDGE OF ORCHY (MAP 32)

30 – 40 MINS FROM INVERORAN (MAP 34)

15 – 20 MINS TO BRIDGE OF ORCHY (MAP 32)

0        ¼ mile
0     APPROX SCALE     500m

ROUTE GUIDE AND MAPS

## ❏ TRAVERSING THE BLACK MOUNT HILLS – THE CLACHLET RIDGE

For strong, experienced hillwalkers with good map-reading skills there is a magnificent high-ridge walk between Inveroran and Kingshouse which can be used as an alternative to the Way. It goes over the tops of Stob Ghabhar, Aonach Mor, Clach Leathad and Meall a' Bhuiridh to the west of the route taken by the Way. This is a long day's outing of between 11 and 15 miles (18-24km) depending on which route you take – make sure you are well prepared. You will need either OS Explorer Maps 377 and 384 (1:25,000) or OS Landranger sheets 41 and 50 (1:50,000).

### INVERORAN                Map 34

If location is everything, *Inveroran Hotel* (☎ 01838-400220, 🖳 inveroran.com; 1S/3T/2D/2Tr/1Qd, most en suite 🛏; ⑤; from £57pp; mid Mar to end Oct) has it all. Built in 1708 and at the beautiful western end of Loch Tulla, this is as secluded and 'off-grid' as you could wish as there's no wi-fi and you are 'unlikely' to even get a mobile phone signal. Dorothy Wordsworth visited in 1803 and was not impressed by the food ('the butter not eatable, the barley cakes fusty, the oat-bread so hard I could not chew it') but things have improved greatly since then. The staff are friendly, the food and service excellent. Coffee, tea and snacks are available 10am-5pm; the

*Walkers' Bar* (entrance around the back) is open 11am-11pm and evening meals are served daily 6-7pm. Feast on Scottish salmon or braised venison, enjoy the solitude, the conversation with other intrepid trekkers, and look forward to tomorrow ... and Glen Coe.

The spectacular **camping** area 400 metres west of the hotel by the bridge is free; however, it is sometimes subject to flooding so camping may be less appealing in wet weather. Campers are welcome for breakfast in the hotel (from 7.30am). There's a **water tap** on the outside wall at the back if you need to fill up your bottles.

## ❏ COIRE BÀ

As you cross a part of the moor, aptly named **The Moss** (Map 36, p159), look west into Coire Bà, the largest mountain amphitheatre in Scotland, cradled by the stunning hills of the Black Mount Deer Forest, rising to a height of 1108m (3634ft) at the summit of Meall a' Bhuiridh on the northern rim. To the east the more modest cone of Meall Beag (476m/1561ft) rises beyond the shore of the lochan.

### GLENCOE MOUNTAIN RESORT
###                     Map 38, p161

The West Highland Way does not descend into Glen Coe but skirts to the east of its mountain entrance passing close to *Glencoe Mountain Resort* (01855-851226, 🖳 glencoemountain.co.uk, **fb**), a particularly insensitive development in such immensely beautiful surroundings. The chairlift (daily 9am-4.30pm; £13.20 return) takes walkers, skiers and snowboarders up the slopes of Meall a'Bhuiridh; there is a

viewpoint at 720m/2400ft. There is a brand new **café** (daily 8am-8pm) here to replace the original one which burnt down on Christmas Day 2019. They also have a **campsite** with 20 pitches (£8pp) and 14 **microlodges** (sleep up to 6; £65-80; sleeping bag required; 🐾). Showers (£1 for 5 mins) are available for all.

Scottish Citylink's 914, 915 & 916 **bus** services call here en route between Glasgow and Fort William; see p47 for details.

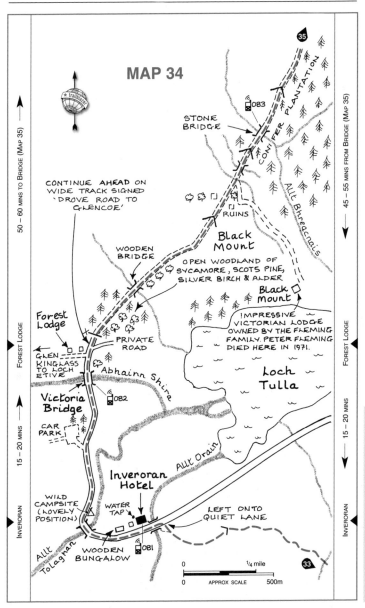

MAP 34

50 – 60 MINS TO BRIDGE (MAP 35)

45 – 55 MINS FROM BRIDGE (MAP 35)

35

083

STONE BRIDGE

CONIFER PLANTATION

Allt Bhreacnais

CONTINUE AHEAD ON WIDE TRACK SIGNED 'DROVE ROAD TO GLENCOE'

RUINS

Black Mount

WOODEN BRIDGE

OPEN WOODLAND OF SYCAMORE, SCOTS PINE, SILVER BIRCH & ALDER

Black Mount

IMPRESSIVE VICTORIAN LODGE OWNED BY THE FLEMING FAMILY. PETER FLEMING DIED HERE IN 1971.

Forest Lodge

PRIVATE ROAD

GLEN KINGLASS TO LOCH ETIVE

Abhainn Shira

Loch Tulla

Victoria Bridge

082

CAR PARK

Allt Orain

FOREST LODGE

FOREST LODGE

15 – 20 MINS

15 – 20 MINS

Inveroran Hotel

WILD CAMPSITE (LOVELY POSITION)

WATER TAP

LEFT ONTO QUIET LANE

Allt Tolaghan

081

WOODEN BUNGALOW

INVERORAN

INVERORAN

33

0        ¼ mile
0        APPROX SCALE    500m

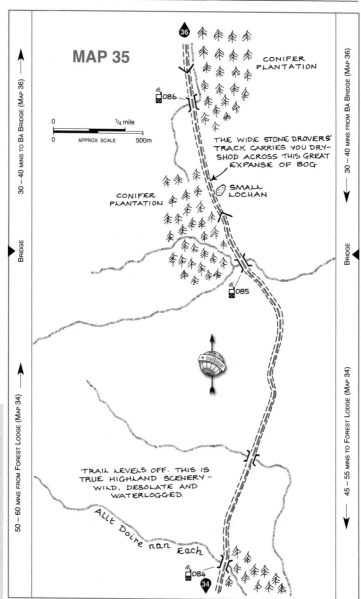

MAP 35

CONIFER PLANTATION

086

THE WIDE STONE DROVERS' TRACK CARRIES YOU DRY-SHOD ACROSS THIS GREAT EXPANSE OF BOG

SMALL LOCHAN

CONIFER PLANTATION

085

TRAIL LEVELS OFF. THIS IS TRUE HIGHLAND SCENERY – WILD, DESOLATE AND WATERLOGGED.

Allt Doire nan Each

084

0 ¼ mile
0    APPROX SCALE    500m

30 – 40 MINS TO BA BRIDGE (MAP 36)

BRIDGE

50 – 60 MINS FROM FOREST LODGE (MAP 34)

30 – 40 MINS FROM BA BRIDGE (MAP 36)

BRIDGE

45 – 55 MINS TO FOREST LODGE (MAP 34)

ROUTE GUIDE AND MAPS

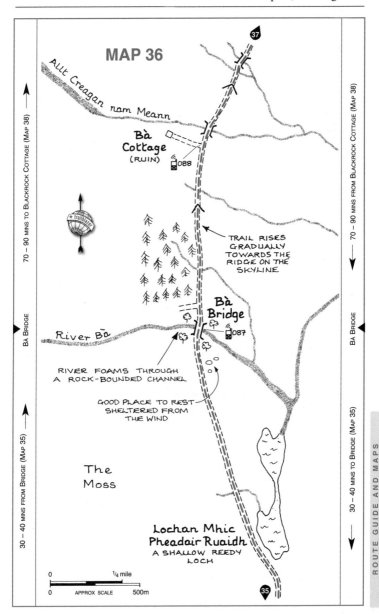

MAP 36

Allt Creagan nam Meann

Bà Cottage (RUIN) 088

TRAIL RISES GRADUALLY TOWARDS THE RIDGE ON THE SKYLINE

Bà Bridge 087

River Bà

RIVER FOAMS THROUGH A ROCK-BOUNDED CHANNEL

GOOD PLACE TO REST SHELTERED FROM THE WIND

The Moss

Lochan Mhic Pheadair Ruaidh A SHALLOW REEDY LOCH

37

35

70 – 90 MINS TO BLACKROCK COTTAGE (MAP 38)

BÀ BRIDGE

30 – 40 MINS FROM BRIDGE (MAP 35)

70 – 90 MINS FROM BLACKROCK COTTAGE (MAP 38)

BÀ BRIDGE

30 – 40 MINS TO BRIDGE (MAP 35)

ROUTE GUIDE AND MAPS

0        1/4 mile
0    APPROX SCALE    500m

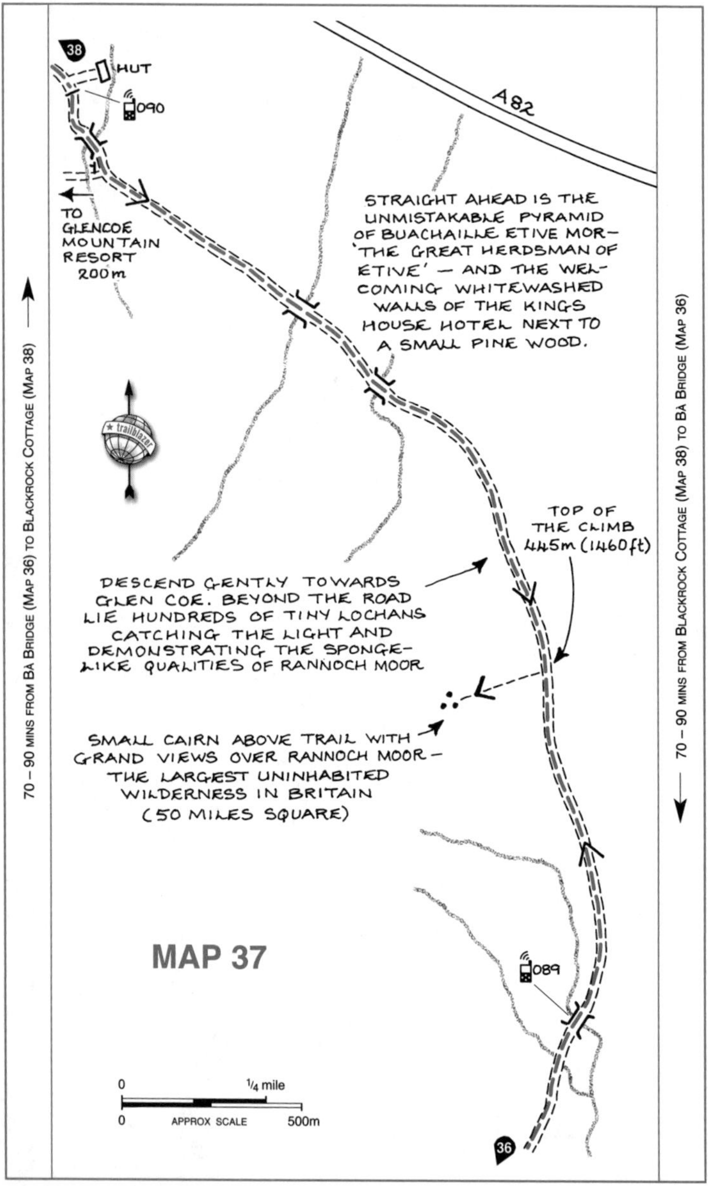

38

HUT

📱090

TO
GLENCOE
MOUNTAIN
RESORT
200m

A82

STRAIGHT AHEAD IS THE
UNMISTAKABLE PYRAMID
OF BUACHAILLE ETIVE MOR —
'THE GREAT HERDSMAN OF
ETIVE' — AND THE WEL-
COMING WHITEWASHED
WALLS OF THE KINGS
HOUSE HOTEL NEXT TO
A SMALL PINE WOOD.

★ trailblazer

TOP OF
THE CLIMB
445m (1460ft)

DESCEND GENTLY TOWARDS
GLEN COE. BEYOND THE ROAD
LIE HUNDREDS OF TINY LOCHANS
CATCHING THE LIGHT AND
DEMONSTRATING THE SPONGE-
LIKE QUALITIES OF RANNOCH MOOR.

SMALL CAIRN ABOVE TRAIL WITH
GRAND VIEWS OVER RANNOCH MOOR —
THE LARGEST UNINHABITED
WILDERNESS IN BRITAIN
(50 MILES SQUARE)

**MAP 37**

📱089

| 0 | | ¼ mile |
|---|---|---|
| 0 | APPROX SCALE | 500m |

36

70 – 90 MINS FROM BA BRIDGE (MAP 36) TO BLACKROCK COTTAGE (MAP 38)

70 – 90 MINS FROM BLACKROCK COTTAGE (MAP 38) TO BA BRIDGE (MAP 36)

ROUTE GUIDE AND MAPS

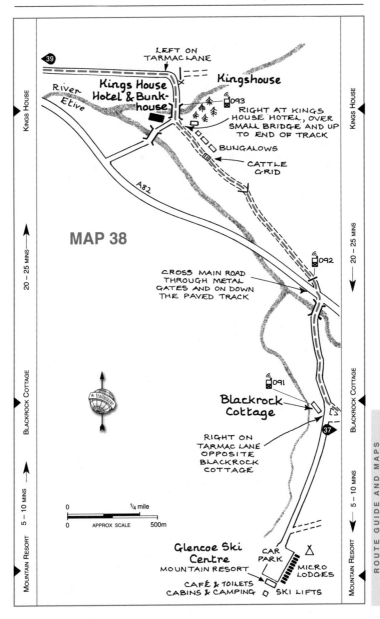

39

LEFT ON
TARMAC LANE

Kingshouse

Kings House
Hotel & Bunk-
house

River
Etive

093

RIGHT AT KINGS
HOUSE HOTEL, OVER
SMALL BRIDGE AND UP
TO END OF TRACK

BUNGALOWS

CATTLE
GRID

A82

MAP 38

092

CROSS MAIN ROAD
THROUGH METAL
GATES AND ON DOWN
THE PAVED TRACK

trailblazer

091

Blackrock
Cottage

37

RIGHT ON
TARMAC LANE
OPPOSITE
BLACKROCK
COTTAGE

0        ¼ mile
0        APPROX SCALE    500m

Glencoe Ski
Centre

MOUNTAIN RESORT

CAFÉ & TOILETS
CABINS & CAMPING

CAR
PARK

MICRO
LODGES

SKI LIFTS

KINGS HOUSE
20 – 25 MINS
BLACKROCK COTTAGE
5 – 10 MINS
MOUNTAIN RESORT

KINGS HOUSE
20 – 25 MINS
BLACKROCK COTTAGE
5 – 10 MINS
MOUNTAIN RESORT

ROUTE GUIDE AND MAPS

## KINGSHOUSE          Map 38, p161

After Glencoe Mountain Resort, the only other **accommodation** on the Way before Kinlochleven, 8 miles (13km) away, is the *Kings House Hotel & Bunkhouse* (☎ 01855-851259, 🖳 kingshousehotel.co.uk; patchy WI-FI; 🐾). This 18th-century drovers' stop is a long-time favourite with walkers. The hotel now boasts 57 **rooms** (D/T/Tr/Qd, £60-144pp; ➥), two restaurants, a pub and a **bunkhouse** with 33 beds (£35pp, breakfast extra) in 10 small dormitories, which has shared showering facilities, a drying room, and a communal kitchen. You can also eat in the hotel pub, **The Way Inn**, or, for more substantial meals in the **Kingshouse Bar** (more commonly known as the **Climbers Bar**).

As the hotel website (🖳 kingshouse hotel.co.uk/wild-camping) explicitly states, walkers can **wild-camp** on the other side of the bridge, using the £1 showers round the back of the bunkhouse. The nearest official campsite is now at Glencoe Mountain Resort Centre (see p156).

At busy times of the year Kingshouse is a notorious bottle-neck on the West Highland Way. You could, however, hitch-hike or catch a **bus** from the stop on the A82 (jct with Glencoe Mountain Resort road, near WPT 092), to Glencoe village where there is more choice.

## GLEN COE

Although the West Highland Way doesn't run through either the valley of Glen Coe or Glencoe village it's well-worth making a side trip for a day if your schedule allows. There's no finer introduction to the Scottish mountaineering scene than to tick off a Glen Coe Munro and finish the day in the Boots Bar of Clachaig Inn. If you're feeling the need for a day without walking there's plenty to do in the valley, or simply laze around in beautiful surroundings.

### Getting to Glencoe Village

Walking from Kingshouse to Glencoe is only for masochists. It is 9 miles (14km) of walking on or very close to the busy A82. It's better to hitch or catch a Citylink **bus** (see public transport map and table pp46-9). To hitch from Kingshouse first walk half a mile towards Glencoe to the layby otherwise cars can't stop for you on this busy road.

Places to stay and eat are spread along 3 miles (5km) of the bottom of the glen so decide where you want to be. For the centre of the village, where there are shops and B&Bs, ask to be dropped at Glencoe Inn & Gathering. For Clachaig Inn, the campsite, hostel and bunkhouse get off the bus earlier, either at the western end of Loch Achtriochtan from where you can walk along the minor road to Clachaig Inn or, if you miss that, at the next car park on the right from where you can cross the river on a footbridge and walk through the small forest to the lane. There is also a stop between the two near the Visitor Centre.

Local **taxi companies** include Alistair's (☎ 01855-811136, 🖳 alistairstaxis.co.uk).

### Glencoe Village

Supplies can be bought at **Nisa General Store** (Mon-Thur 10am-5pm, Fri-Sat to 7pm, Sun to 4pm) and there's also a **cash machine** inside. The **medical centre** (☎ 01855-811226; Mon, Tue, Thur & Fri 8am-6pm, Wed to 1pm) is a mile west in Ballachulish.

The little **Glencoe and North Lorn Folk Museum** (☎ 01855-811664, 🖳 glencoemuseum.com; May-Oct Thur-Sun 11am-3pm; £3), in a heather-

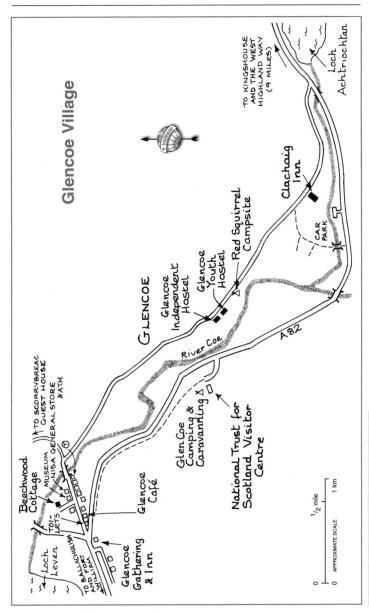

Glencoe Village

thatched cottage next to Nisa, has a quirky mixture of artefacts. The **National Trust for Scotland Visitor Centre** (☎ 01855-811307, 🖳 www.nts.org.uk/ visit/places/glencoe; Apr-Nov daily 10am-5pm, Dec-Mar to 4pm) has an exhibition (admission £4; NT members free) with an interesting short video on the massacre (see box opposite) as well as displays on mountaineering and natural history. There is also a *café*, free WI-FI and an outlook station where it is possible to get weather reports and advice on walks in the area. However, it's difficult to get to on foot being 1½ miles south along the A82. There is a footpath partly through the woods but it's not a great walk being quite close to the busy road.

### Where to stay and eat

*Clachaig Inn* (☎ 01855-811252, 🖳 clachaig.com; 1S/7T/10D/3Tr/2Qd; ➘; unreliable WI-FI in public areas only; ⽊; Ⓛ; £30-75pp, sgl £59.50; summer weekends min 2 nights) has been a meeting place for outdoor addicts for years and is deservedly popular. There's always a good range of independent ales and up to 400 malt whiskies which you can either sip in the Bidean Lounge or down one after the other in the Boots Bar, where there's live music every Saturday night, or The Snug, a converted beer cellar. Great **food** is available (bar menu noon-9pm) from haggis, neeps and tatties (£11.95) to Highland game pie (£14.95).

Walking west along the lane towards the main village, in 10 minutes you pass *Red Squirrel Campsite* (☎ 01855-811256, 🖳 redsquirrelcampsite.co.uk; ⽊; £12.50pp; open all year). It is by a swimming hole in the river and is a pleasant farm site popular with walkers and climbers. There are shower and toilet facilities and gullies to ignite fires in. *Glencoe Camping & Caravanning Club* (☎ 01855-811397, 🖳 campingandcaravanningclub.co.uk; £8.35-14.20pp) by the Visitor Centre also takes campers though a minimum stay of two nights is often required.

Five minutes further on is *Glencoe Youth Hostel* (☎ 01855-811219, 🖳 hostellingscotland.org.uk/hostels/glencoe; open all year; 39 beds, 9 rooms 1T, 2 x 3-beds, 2 x 4-beds, 2 x 5-beds, rest 6-7 beds; ⽊ in private rooms only; WI-FI; Ⓛ) where a dorm bed costs £24pp and it's open all year. 'Cook yourself' meals available. Reception sells some grocery essentials and there is a washing machine (£2), tumble dryer and a drying room.

Accommodation is good value at *Glencoe Independent Hostel* (☎ 01855-811906, 🖳 glencoehostel.co.uk; usually Jan-Oct, check re Nov-Dec as sometimes open at weekends; WI-FI). Their Alpine **bunkhouses** (£16-40pp; 3 rooms sleep up to 14), have access to a kitchen, toilets and drying room. However, they are often booked up with groups, particularly at weekends and in the main season. The former hostel is now set up as two self-catering '**bothies**' (sleep 5/6; £21-35pp; min 2 nights; ⽊). For longer stays there are three **log cabins** (sleep 2-3; approx £120 per night per cabin; ⽊) and four **caravans** (sleep 4, £70-120 per night per caravan). Both are for minimum three-nights; bedding and towels are provided.

Just before crossing the bridge into the village a road on the right goes to *Scorrybreac Guest House* (☎ 01855-811354, 🖳 scorrybreacglencoe.com; 1T or D/4D, all en suite; ➘; WI-FI; Ⓛ; £40-57.50pp, sgl occ £72) which has comfortable accommodation and a drying room. Walkers must be aware that

*Scorrybreac* is at least a 30-minute walk from the nearest bus-stop and 45 minutes from the nearest eatery so this must be taken into consideration if opting to stay. They usually require a minimum two-night stay during the busy season.

On Lower Carnoch Rd and open year round is *Beechwood* (☎ 01855-811062, 🖥 beechwoodcottage.scot; 2D/1D or T, all en suite, WI-FI; £42.50-49.50). One night stops are an option in one room though between April and September they require a commitment of two nights.

*The Glencoe Café* (☎ 01855-811168, 🖥 glencoecafe.co.uk; WI-FI) is open Mon-Fri 11am-4pm, Sat & Sun to 5pm). They serve a range of soups, cakes and light lunches to eat in or take away. Nearby is the large *Glencoe Inn and Gathering* (☎ 01855-811625, 🖥 crerarhotels.com/glencoe-gathering; daily 8am-8pm) with a menu including burgers (venison burger £15) and pizzas from £10.

Information on other accommodation and dining options in the local area can be found at 🖥 discoverglencoe.scot.

## DAY WALKS AROUND GLEN COE                    see map p167
Here are some suggestions with grid references to help those with hillwalking experience plan a walk (see also p57); the times given below are approximate and include essential short stops. You'll need one of the following maps, each of which covers the area: OS Explorer 384 (1:25,000), OS Landranger sheet 41 (1:50,000), Harvey's Superwalker 'Glencoe' (1:25,000), Harvey's Ultrampa 'Glencoe' (1:40,000). Further hill-walking ideas for Glen Coe and the rest of the Highlands can be found in Trailblazer's *Scottish Highlands Hillwalking Guide*.

### Allt Coire Gabhail
(Grid square 1655) A beautiful and easy walk of 3 miles (5km, 2hrs) up to a hidden valley where the MacDonalds hid their stolen cattle. Start at the car park at GR171568 and return the same way.

### ❑ MOUNTAINS AND MASSACRE
Glen Coe is one of the most scenically impressive valleys in Scotland. Standing guard at its entrance is the spectacular arrowhead mountain Buachaille Etive Mor, 'the great herdsman of Etive.' As you descend into the glen towards Loch Achtriochtan the road is squeezed by the precipitous walls of the Bidean nam Bian massif to the south and the incredible line of the Aonach Eagach ridge to the north. It is a perfect playground for climbers and hill-walkers and arguably the home of Scottish mountaineering.

However, the notoriety of the valley has more to do with the events of 1692 than gymnastic exploits on the crags. The massacre of the MacDonalds by Highland troops is a bloody tale of deception. While Highland history is full of such awful events the Glencoe massacre is the one that everyone remembers. One reason for this infamy is the horrific nature of the premeditated plan to exterminate the MacDonald clan in cold blood after they had provided hospitality to their potential murderers for two weeks. This was sanctioned by men in high office, including the crown. The other reason is that the dreadful episode has been exploited by generations of writers and provides ample fuel for the tourist industry of today.

### Circuit of Buachaille Etive Beag
(9 miles/14.5km; 4½-6 hours) A long low walk round the 'little herdsman of Etive' via Lairig Eilde and Lairig Gartain. There are several stream crossings making the circuit difficult after heavy rain. Start/finish at GR187563 by the Scottish Rights of Way Society sign to Loch Etiveside.

### Ascent of Buachaille Etive Beag
(5½ miles/9km; 5-6 hours) A straightforward, moderately strenuous climb taking in two Munros. Start at GR187563 by the Scottish Rights of Way Society sign to Loch Etiveside and follow this path for about 500m. Leave it and head south up the side of the mountain to the pass at GR188545. From here climb steeply north-east to the summit of Stob Coire Raineach (925m/3034ft), then return to the pass and climb south-west to a minor summit (902m/2959ft) and continue along the narrow ridge to Stob Dubh (958m/3142ft). Return the same way.

### Ascent of Buachaille Etive Mor
(9 miles/14.5km; 6½-8½ hours) A full, strenuous walk on one of Scotland's best-loved mountains. Start at Altnafeadh GR221563, cross the footbridge over the River Coupall and follow the path all the way to the back of Coire na Tulaich.

The route ascends up the steep scree-covered headwall of the corrie (take care) and onto a flat pass. Head east to the summit of Stob Dearg (1022m/3352ft), the first Munro. Most walkers then retrace their steps to the top of Coire na Tulaich and, rather than descending, continue west and then south-west along the wide ridge over Stob na Doire (1011m/3316ft) and Stob Coire Altruim (941m/3086ft) to the second Munro, Stob na Broige (956m/3136ft).

The usual descent is from the pass between Stob Coire Altruim and Stob na Doire down into Lairig Gartain and then back along the path to Altnafeadh.

---

### ❑ CARNIVOROUS PLANTS ON THE WEST HIGHLAND WAY
In the large swathes of acid peat bog and damp moorland present on the West Highland Way live two of Britain's more unusual species of flora. Nutrients are limited in these saturated lands so the plants that do survive here have to find them from somewhere other than the ground on which they stand – with sometimes ingenious results.

Two, in particular – the **sundew** (*Drosera rotundifolia*, see photo opposite p64) and **butterwort** (also known as the **bog violet**; *Pinguicula vulgaris*) have resorted to snacking on the local fauna for their nutrition. Using sticky droplets of digestive enzymes on their hairs, they trap and digest any small insects that should happen to land on them, including midges, thereby providing the plants with the essential nitrogen they need for healthy growth. Butterworts are so-called as it was thought that the juice from the leaves, when rubbed onto cows' udders, would charm the milk from the cow. What is true is that the bactericide that stops the insects from decomposing before they are digested would have helped to prevent udder infections. The other use of this bacteria on the leaves was to curdle the milk to turn it into a type of yoghurt. Sundews are also useful. The plant contains plumbagin, a naturally occurring antibiotic, and is used by modern herbalists to treat a number of respiratory conditions.

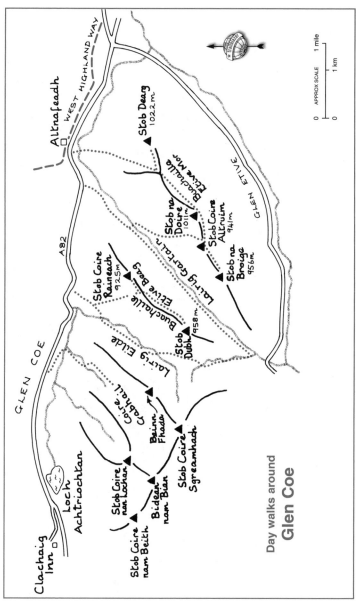

Day walks around
**Glen Coe**

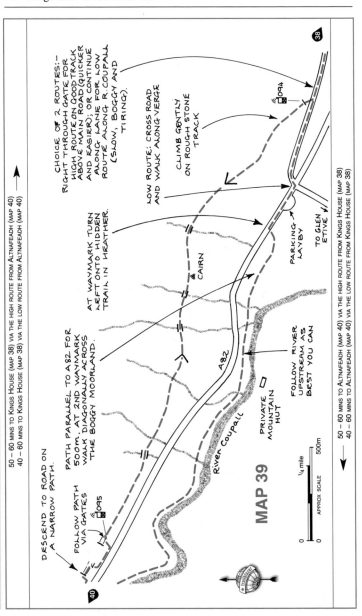

50 – 60 MINS TO KINGS HOUSE (MAP 38) VIA THE HIGH ROUTE FROM ALTNAFEADH (MAP 40)
40 – 60 MINS TO KINGS HOUSE (MAP 38) VIA THE LOW ROUTE FROM ALTNAFEADH (MAP 40)

CHOICE OF 2 ROUTES:- RIGHT THROUGH GATE FOR HIGH ROUTE ON GOOD TRACK ABOVE MAIN ROAD (QUICKER AND EASIER); OR CONTINUE ALONG LANE FOR LOW ROUTE ALONG R.COUPALL (SLOW, BOGGY AND TIRING).

LOW ROUTE: CROSS ROAD AND WALK ALONG VERGE

CLIMB GENTLY ON ROUGH STONE TRACK

094

38

AT WAYMARK TURN LEFT ONTO HIDDEN TRAIL IN HEATHER.

CAIRN

PARKING LAYBY

TO GLEN ETIVE

PATH PARALLEL TO A82 FOR 500m. AT 2ND WAYMARK WALK DIAGONALLY ACROSS THE BOGGY MOORLAND.

A82

FOLLOW RIVER UPSTREAM AS BEST YOU CAN

PRIVATE MOUNTAIN HUT

River Coupall

MAP 39

¼ mile

0

0        500m

APPROX SCALE

DESCEND TO ROAD ON A NARROW PATH.

FOLLOW PATH VIA GATES

095

40

50 – 60 MINS TO ALTNAFEADH (MAP 40) VIA THE HIGH ROUTE FROM KINGS HOUSE (MAP 38)
40 – 60 MINS TO ALTNAFEADH (MAP 40) VIA THE LOW ROUTE FROM KINGS HOUSE (MAP 38)

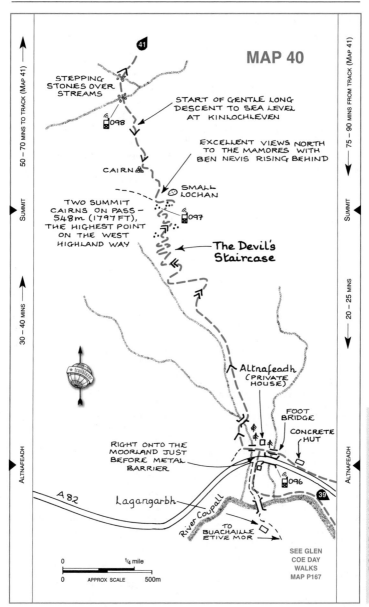

## KINGSHOUSE TO KINLOCHLEVEN                    MAPS 38-42

This **8½ miles (14km, 2½-3¼hrs)** gives spectacular walking across inspiring mountainous terrain. The route is easy to follow but can be extremely exposed in wet, windy or snowy conditions as there is nowhere to shelter.

The unpleasant walk parallel to the A82 from Kingshouse to Altnafeadh is over quickly and the climb to the highest point on the West Highland Way begins: the **Devil's Staircase** (Map 40). This ascent of 259 metres (850ft) up the south side of the ridge between Kingshouse and Kinlochleven is feared by Way walkers but although it's a sustained climb, it's not nearly as hard as the name would suggest. In all likelihood it was christened by the soldiers who had to carve this sinuous military road up the bleak hillside in the 1750s. You follow the old road as it climbs to the pass (548m/1797ft) where there are views over the Glen Coe peaks and, in good weather, north over the Mamores to Ben Nevis.

From the top it's a long descent across rugged mountainside and then on a steep four-wheel-drive track down to **Kinlochleven**, an ugly, modern village set amidst dramatic Highland scenery.

### KINLOCHLEVEN          Map 42, p173

The planned factory village of Kinlochleven was called 'the ugliest on two thousand miles of Highland coast' by WH Murray in his 1968 guide to the West Highlands. Things have improved considerably now the aluminium smelter (see box opposite) which necessitated its construction has closed. It still has a utilitarian feel but it's a pleasant place to stay largely because of the magnificent surroundings and the friendliness of the people.

Kinlochleven has reinvented itself as a major outdoor activity centre, which fits in well with the Lochaber region's unofficial status as the 'Outdoor Capital of the UK'. The location is certainly ideal for such an ambition and the transformation of the old smelter building into **The Ice Factor** (☎ 01855-831100, 🖳 ice-factor.co.uk; daily 9am-6pm), the biggest indoor articulated rock climbing wall and ice wall in Britain, draws the outdoor fraternity to the village when the weather outside is too foul.

The **Aluminium Story Visitor Centre** (☎ 01855-831021; summer Mon, Tue, Thur & Fri 10am-12.30pm & 1.30-4pm, Wed & Sat 10am-1pm; winter closed) has displays telling the story of this part of the town's history.

Another worthwhile sight is the impressive **Grey Mares Tail waterfall**, a short walk along the path that starts beside the Scottish Episcopal Church.

If you're walking over the first week in May you'll hear the **Scottish Six Day Motorcycle Trials** (🖳 ssdt.org), based here, even before you see them. B&Bs will be booked out.

### Services

The **cash machine** is outside the Aluminium Story Visitor Centre which houses the **post office** (Mon, Tue & Fri 10am-12.30pm & 1.30-4pm; Wed & Sat 10am-1pm, Thur 10am-12.30pm & 1.30-5.30pm). The library (☎ 01855-832047; term time Mon-Wed 10am-noon & 2-4pm, Thur & Fri 10am-1pm; **internet access** free) is in the High School.

For supplies there's the Co-op **supermarket** (daily 7am-10pm). The Ice Factor is home to a small **outdoor equipment store**.

### Transport

[See pp45-9] Kinlochleven is isolated at the head of Loch Leven and gets little through traffic. Shiel's N44 **bus** goes to

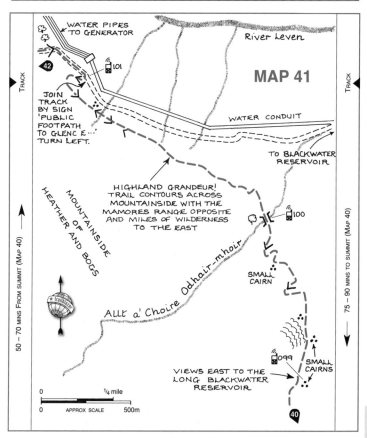

## ALUMINIUM AND BLACKWATER RESERVOIR

The eight-mile (13km) long Blackwater Reservoir (off Map 41) was created by the Blackwater dam, the largest in Europe at the time, which was built between 1905 and 1909. The muscle power came from unemployed migrants and 3000 skilled navvies, the itinerant labourers who constructed so much of industrial Britain. It was designed to supply the water to power the hydro-electric (HEP) plant at the new aluminium smelter in the purpose-built village of Kinlochleven.

At the time, the smelter was one of the largest in the world and the newly formed village thrived and steadily expanded as its prosperity grew. But by the end of the 20th century competition from more modern plants and newer methods of smelting meant that it was no longer viable.

ROUTE GUIDE AND MAPS

Fort William via Glencoe Junction.

For a **taxi** phone Levenside Taxi (☎ 07786-863230).

## Where to stay
**Budget accommodation**  The best **campsite** (£10pp; 11x2-person tent pitches; 🐾; Apr-Oct) is behind *MacDonald Hotel & Cabins* (Map 43; ☎ 01855-831539, 🖳 macdonaldhotel.co.uk), Fort William Rd, with beautiful views down the loch. They also have nine **cabins** (sleep 2-4; from £20pp; bedding hire from £2.50; 🐾). There are showers, toilets, a laundry and a drying room.

There is also **camping** (30 pitches; £15pp; Mar-Oct) at *Blackwater Hostel* (☎ 01855-831253, 🖳 blackwaterhostel.co.uk; WI-FI; 🐾), and **bunkhouse** accommodation (39 beds; 1T/3 x 3-, 5 x 4-, 1 x 8-bed room; all en suite; WI-FI) with prices from £25pp depending how many are sharing a room, inclusive of bedding and with full cooking facilities. They also have three sizes of glamping **pods** (sleep 2-4, £55-100 per pod; 🐾) which have electric sockets, fridge and kettle, though crockery, cutlery and bedding aren't provided. The bunkhouse and pods are open all year. They also have another bunkhouse, *West Highland Lodge Bunkhouse* (32 beds; 8x 4-bed rooms), high up on the hillside, which they open when necessary. Both bunkhouses and the campsite have a drying room. Towels are not provided.

**B&Bs**  There is a choice of B&B accommodation here. As you enter the village the estate of houses on the right has several places. The first you reach is *Forest View* (☎ 01855-831302, 🖳 forestviewbnb.co.uk; 2T/1D/2Tr, most en suite; WI-FI; ⏾; £37.50-45pp, sgl occ £65), at 24 Wades Rd. They have a drying room and laundry service.

Ideally situated both near the pub and on the way is *Lochaber Crescent B&B* (☎ 01855-831294, 🖳 www.lochabercrescent bandb.co.uk; fb; 1D/T shared bathroom ⏾; WI-FI; ⏾; £35pp). Though they are letting just one room at present, plans are afoot to install a glamping pod in the garden – call them for details.

At the time of research **Highland Getaway** (☎ 01855-831258) was closed and up for sale, but previously had 10 B&B rooms and a restaurant so it's worth calling them to check the latest.

Nearby is *Allt-Na-Leven* (☎ 01855-831366, 🖳 bedandbreakfastkinlochleven .co.uk; 23-24 Leven Rd; 5 flexible rms sleep 2-4; WI-FI; ⏾; from £43pp, a popular place run by friendly, helpful people. They will do a load of washing for £10; use of the drying room for wet boots and clothes is free. They will pick up from Kings House Hotel (see p162), if walkers book a two-night stay; phone them for the latest prices for this service.

One of the plushest places is *Tigh-na-Cheo Guest House* (off Map 42; ☎ 01855-831434, 🖳 tigh-na-cheo.co.uk, Garb-hein Rd; 1S/1D/6D or T/1Tr; ⏾; WI-FI; ⏾; £50pp; sgl £69; Mar to Nov) on a rise overlooking the loch and mountains. They have a drying room and laundry service, and all except the triple room has a bath.

Close by, on the same road and with similar views is *Edencoille* (☎ 01855-831358, 🖳 kinlochlevenbedandbreakfast .co.uk; 4D or T/1Tr/1Qd; WI-FI; ⏾; £42pp, sgl occ £84). Each room has a foot spa – a nice touch – and they will do a load of washing for you for a small fee.

**Hotels**  *Tailrace Inn* (☎ 01855-831777, 🖳 thetailraceinn.co.uk; 6 flexible rooms sleeping 2-5; 🐾; WI-FI; ⏾; from £45pp, sgl occ £70) is in the centre of the village. They have a drying room and laundry service (£10).

*MacDonald Hotel & Cabins* (Map 43; see Budget accommodation; 6T/3D/2Tr; ⏾; WI-FI; 🐾; from £55pp, slg occ £85) is beautifully located on the outskirts of town.

## Where to eat and drink
In the main part of the village *Tailrace Inn* (see Hotels) serves food virtually all day: breakfast is served 8am-10am (Apr-Oct); main meals are served 11am to 9pm. They also do packed lunches (order the night before). Among the reasonably extensive menu in the restaurant and bar there are haggis fritters (£6.95) for lunch and mince

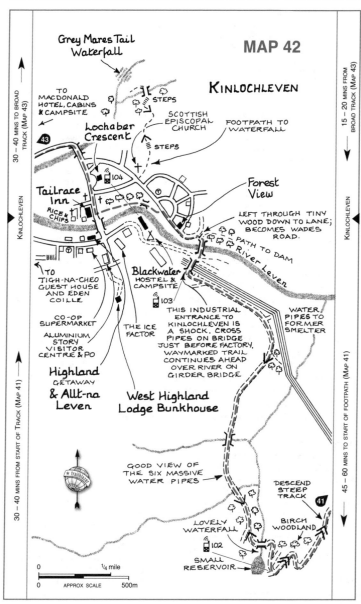

MAP 42

Grey Mares Tail Waterfall

KINLOCHLEVEN

STEPS

TO MACDONALD HOTEL, CABINS & CAMPSITE

Lochaber Crescent

SCOTTISH EPISCOPAL CHURCH

FOOTPATH TO WATERFALL

STEPS

104

Forest View

LEFT THROUGH TINY WOOD DOWN TO LANE; BECOMES WADES ROAD.

Tailrace Inn

RICE & CHIPS

PATH TO DAM

River Leven

TO TIGH-NA-CHEO GUEST HOUSE AND EDEN COILLE

Blackwater HOSTEL & CAMPSITE

103

WATER PIPES TO FORMER SMELTER

CO-OP SUPERMARKET

THE ICE FACTOR

ALUMINIUM STORY VISITOR CENTRE & PO

Highland GETAWAY & Allt-na Leven

THIS INDUSTRIAL ENTRANCE TO KINLOCHLEVEN IS A SHOCK. CROSS PIPES ON BRIDGE JUST BEFORE FACTORY. WAYMARKED TRAIL CONTINUES AHEAD OVER RIVER ON GIRDER BRIDGE

West Highland Lodge Bunkhouse

GOOD VIEW OF THE SIX MASSIVE WATER PIPES

DESCEND STEEP TRACK

41

BIRCH WOODLAND

LOVELY WATERFALL

102

SMALL RESERVOIR

43

trailblazer

0          1/4 mile

0        APPROX SCALE        500m

30 – 40 MINS TO BROAD TRACK (MAP 43)

KINLOCHLEVEN

30 – 40 MINS FROM START OF TRACK (MAP 41)

15 – 20 MINS FROM BROAD TRACK (MAP 43)

KINLOCHLEVEN

45 – 60 MINS TO START OF FOOTPATH (MAP 41)

ROUTE GUIDE AND MAPS

and tatties (£9.95) for dinner.

Nearby, the former chippy has become a Chinese takeaway called *Rice & Chips* (☎ 01855-831349, **fb**; Tue-Sun 4-9pm, also Thur-Sat noon-2pm).

Food is available all day inside The Ice Factor: in the daytime from the *Ice Factor Café* (daily 9am-5pm; eat in or takeaway) including hot breakfast rolls from £3.95; and in the evenings their *Chillers Bar & Grill* (Sun-Thur 5-11pm, Fri & Sat 5pm-1am) has a range of burgers from £7.95 amongst other mains, is licensed and has occasional live music nights.

At the *MacDonald Hotel & Cabins* (see Where to stay) there's a good restaurant and the *Bothy Bar*. It has wonderful views down the length of Loch Leven and very good pub grub (eg The Highlander

home-made burger with haggis and black pudding for £11.50, or cullen skink and a roll for £6-7) is served daily 8am-9pm. Campers' breakfasts (from 7am; booking recommended; £12.50, or £15 for non-residents and those not camping) are served in the restaurant.

Four miles from Kinlochleven, by the loch is one of the best fish restaurants in this part of Scotland: *Lochleven Seafood Café* (off Map 43; ☎ 01855-821048; 🖥 lochlevenseafoodcafe.co.uk; Wed-Mon 10am-8.45pm). The local mussels cooked in cider (£7.25/14 for 500g/kilo) are superb and there are are Scottish lobsters (£19.50/39.50, half/full) and whole brown crabs (£12.95) to consider also. You'd have to get a taxi to get here (about £12) but it's well worth it.

## KINLOCHLEVEN TO FORT WILLIAM                          MAPS 42-49

The final tough but rewarding **15 miles (24km, 4¾-6½hrs)** crosses a beautiful high pass and then undulates through repetitive forests to the end of the West Highland Way, now right in the centre of Fort William.

It's a long sustained 250m (820ft) climb out of Kinlochleven on a steep winding trail through birch trees. At the top you continue on a wide track, the old military road, which traverses the mountain side with glorious views over **Loch Leven** to the mountains of Glencoe. From here the trail rises gently through a wide U-shaped valley to a broad pass, the **Lairigmor** (Map 45) at 330m/1082ft. This can be exposed in bad weather. The Way descends and then climbs again through a series of dense conifer plantations with occasional views of **Ben Nevis**, Britain's highest mountain. A final descent on forest tracks takes you into **Glen Nevis** from where it's only a short walk along the road (or one of the better options listed on pp186-7) to **Fort William**.

### GLEN NEVIS
#### Map 48 p181 & Map 49 p187

Pastoral Glen Nevis is surrounded by some of the finest mountains in Britain and as a result has an excited buzz of activity year round. For those who'd prefer to end their walk in the open countryside rather than on the streets of Fort William there's a B&B, youth hostel, a couple of bunkhouses and a large campsite, the only one in the area – all perfectly situated for a Ben Nevis ascent.

### Services
The Ben Nevis **visitor centre** (Map 49;

☎ 01349-781401, 🖥 www.highlifehighland .com/bennevis/visitor-centre; daily 8.30am to 4pm) is well worth a look in if only to get an accurate **weather forecast**. There is an excellent exhibition on the natural history and environment of the area, a bookshop and they stock outdoor gear; the staff also have a wealth of local knowledge.

Shiel's N41 **bus** service runs up and down the glen and can be flagged down if it is safe to stop. The N42 also calls here in the summer months; see p46 for details.

*(cont'd on p179*

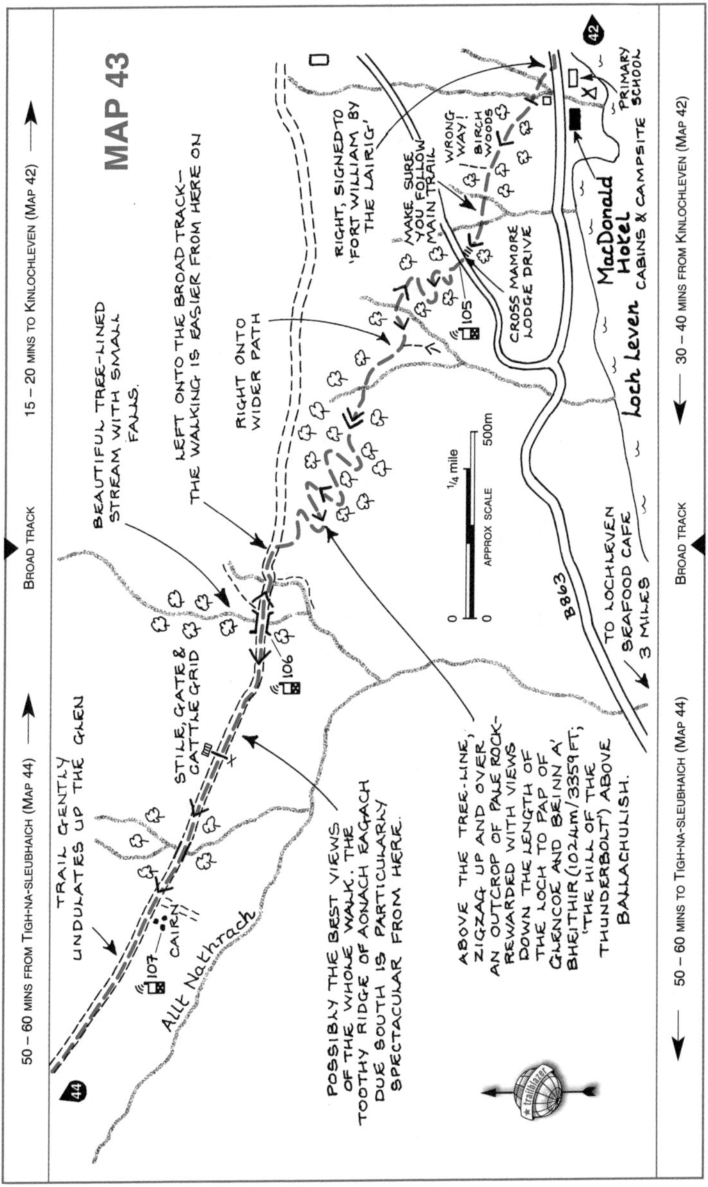
MAP 43
50 – 60 MINS FROM TIGH-NA-SLEUBHAICH (MAP 44) →
BROAD TRACK
15 – 20 MINS TO KINLOCHLEVEN (MAP 42) →
44
TRAIL GENTLY UNDULATES UP THE GLEN
107
CAIRN
Allt Nathrach
STILE, GATE & CATTLE GRID
106
BEAUTIFUL TREE-LINED STREAM WITH SMALL FALLS.
LEFT ONTO THE BROAD TRACK– THE WALKING IS EASIER FROM HERE ON
RIGHT ONTO WIDER PATH
RIGHT, SIGNED TO 'FORT WILLIAM BY THE LAIRIG'
MAKE SURE YOU FOLLOW MAIN TRAIL
WRONG WAY!
BIRCH WOODS
105
CROSS MAMORE LODGE DRIVE
42
PRIMARY SCHOOL
POSSIBLY THE BEST VIEWS OF THE WHOLE WALK. THE TOOTHY RIDGE OF AONACH EAGACH DUE SOUTH IS PARTICULARLY SPECTACULAR FROM HERE.
ABOVE THE TREE-LINE, ZIGZAG UP AND OVER AN OUTCROP OF PALE ROCK– REWARDED WITH VIEWS DOWN THE LENGTH OF THE LOCH TO PAP OF GLENCOE AND BEINN A' BHEITHIR (1024M/3359FT; 'THE HILL OF THE THUNDERBOLT') ABOVE BALLACHULISH.
APPROX SCALE
0 1/4 mile
0 500m
B863
TO LOCHLEVEN SEAFOOD CAFE 3 MILES
Loch Leven
MacDonald Hotel
CABINS & CAMPSITE
trailblazer
← 50 – 60 MINS TO TIGH-NA-SLEUBHAICH (MAP 44)
BROAD TRACK
← 30 – 40 MINS FROM KINLOCHLEVEN (MAP 42)

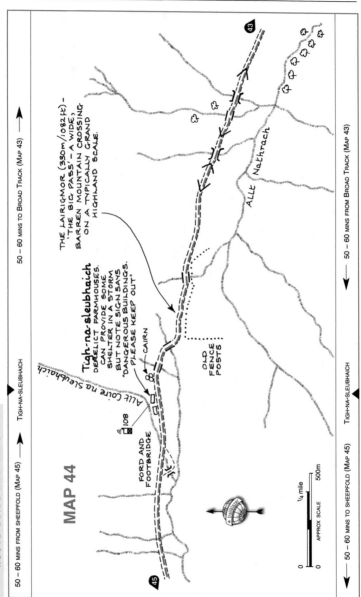

50 – 60 MINS TO BROAD TRACK (MAP 43) →

50 – 60 MINS FROM BROAD TRACK (MAP 43) ←

◄ TIGH-NA-SLEUBHAICH

TIGH-NA-SLEUBHAICH ◄

50 – 60 MINS FROM SHEEPFOLD (MAP 45) →

50 – 60 MINS TO SHEEPFOLD (MAP 45) ←

THE LAIRIGMOR (330m/1082ft) – "THE BIG PASS" – A WIDE, BARREN MOUNTAIN CROSSING ON A TYPICALLY GRAND HIGHLAND SCALE.

Tigh-na-sleubhaich
DERELICT FARMHOUSES.
CAN PROVIDE SOME
SHELTER IN A STORM
BUT NOTE SIGN SAYS
"DANGEROUS BUILDINGS.
PLEASE KEEP OUT"

CAIRN

ALLT Coire na Sleubhaich

108

FORD AND
FOOTBRIDGE

ALLT Nathrach

OLD
FENCE
POSTS

MAP 44

¼ mile
500m
APPROX SCALE
0
0

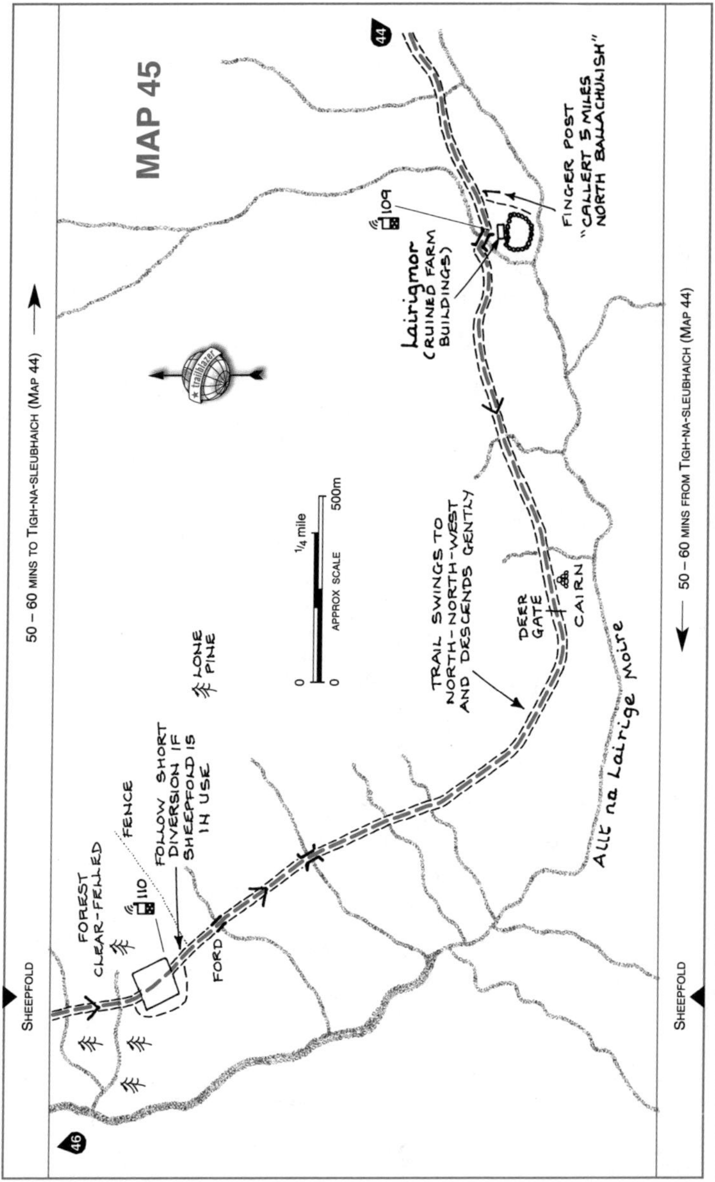

MAP 45

← 50 – 60 MINS TO TIGH-NA-SLEUBHAICH (MAP 44)

50 – 60 MINS FROM TIGH-NA-SLEUBHAICH (MAP 44) →

44

FINGER POST
"CALLERT 5 MILES
NORTH BALLACHULISH"

109

Lairigmor
(RUINED FARM
BUILDINGS)

TRAIL SWINGS TO
NORTH-NORTH-WEST
AND DESCENDS GENTLY

DEER
GATE

CAIRN

Allt na Lairige Moire

¼ mile

500m

APPROX SCALE

0

0

LONE
PINE

FOLLOW SHORT
DIVERSION IF
SHEEPFOLD IS
IN USE

FENCE

110

FOREST
CLEAR-FELLED

FORD

SHEEPFOLD ◀

SHEEPFOLD ◀

46

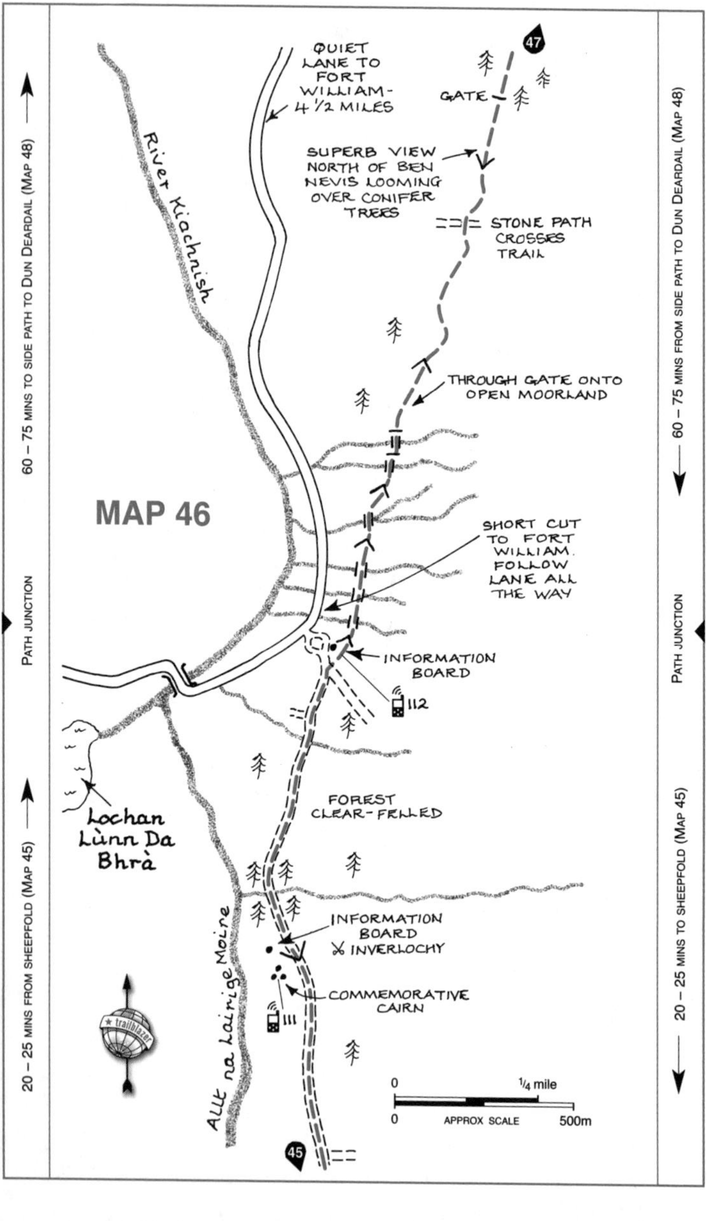

QUIET LANE TO FORT WILLIAM- 4 1/2 MILES

47

GATE

SUPERB VIEW NORTH OF BEN NEVIS LOOMING OVER CONIFER TREES

STONE PATH CROSSES TRAIL

River Kiachnish

THROUGH GATE ONTO OPEN MOORLAND

MAP 46

SHORT CUT TO FORT WILLIAM. FOLLOW LANE ALL THE WAY

INFORMATION BOARD

112

Lochan Lùnn Da Bhrà

FOREST CLEAR-FELLED

INFORMATION BOARD & INVERLOCHY

COMMEMORATIVE CAIRN

Allt na Lairige Moire

111

45

0          1/4 mile
0     APPROX SCALE     500m

60 – 75 MINS TO SIDE PATH TO DUN DEARDAIL (MAP 48)

PATH JUNCTION

20 – 25 MINS FROM SHEEPFOLD (MAP 45)

60 – 75 MINS FROM SIDE PATH TO DUN DEARDAIL (MAP 48)

PATH JUNCTION

20 – 25 MINS TO SHEEPFOLD (MAP 45)

ROUTE GUIDE AND MAPS

## Where to stay and eat

***Glen Nevis Caravan and Camping Park***
(Map 48; ☎ 01397-702191, 🖳 glen-
nevis.co.uk; from £11pp; 🐾; mid Mar to
end Oct/early Nov) is a vast acreage of
neatly cut grass and conifers sprawling over
the bottom of the glen. It has a laundry (£3
for wash) and a well-stocked **shop** (daily
8am-8pm, till 9pm in July/Aug). There are
also 2- and 3-bed camping **pods** available
(£80-120 per pod per night; bring your own
bedding). In the high season there is a
**snack van** here (daily 8-10am & 5-10pm),
peddling breakfast rolls and burgers.

Just up the glen from here is the popular ***Glen Nevis Youth Hostel*** (Map 48; ☎
01397-702336, 🖳 hostellingscotland.org
.uk/hostels/glen-nevis; 73 beds; 7T, 1Tr, 6x

4-bed & 4x 8-bed rooms, some en suite; WI-
FI; Ⓛ; £20-40pp) which is open all year.
**Meals** are available, the hostel is licensed
and it has laundry facilities (£2 per wash) as
well as a drying room.

***Glen Nevis Restaurant and Lounge
Bar*** (☎ 01397-705459, 🖳 glennevisrest
aurant.co.uk); Mar/Apr to end Oct, daily 3-
9pm) is a modern building with the air of a
motorway service station and is located
between the camping park and the youth
hostel. The menu features burgers, pies and
fish & chips plus four different variations
on 'mac & cheese' (from £12).

Another good place to stay in a beautiful position at the start of the Ben Nevis
path is ***Ben Nevis Inn*** (Map 49; ☎ 01397-
701227, 🖳 ben-nevis-inn.co.uk; WI-FI), a

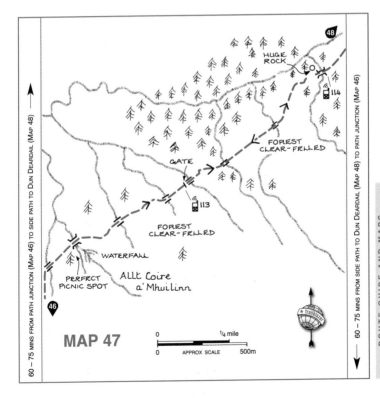

MAP 47

60 – 75 MINS FROM PATH JUNCTION (MAP 46) TO SIDE PATH TO DUN DEARDAIL (MAP 48)

60 – 75 MINS FROM SIDE PATH TO DUN DEARDAIL (MAP 48) TO PATH JUNCTION (MAP 46)

HUGE ROCK

114

FOREST CLEAR-FELLED

GATE

113

FOREST CLEAR-FELLED

WATERFALL

PERFECT PICNIC SPOT

Allt Coire a' Mhuilinn

0        ¼ mile
0    APPROX SCALE    500m

carefully renovated barn. Its **bunkhouse** has been converted into three separate self-contained en-suite bunk-bed rooms, sleeping six (£150), eight (£200) or ten (£250) people. Each room comes with a kitchenette (including microwave, toaster and fridge) and a drying cupboard; bedding and towels are provided too. Booking is recommended, particularly in the summer months. Excellent **food** is available here (summer daily noon-9pm, winter Thur-Sun only); the menu changes regularly but during the day may include chicken tandoori flatbread (£9.25) and in the evening ale-battered haddock & chips (£16.50) and chicken & haggis rumbledethumps (see box p23; £16.50).

Light snacks are served till closing time at 11pm. It's the kind of place where you could spend all day, listening to (the occasional) live acoustic music, warming yourself by the woodburner and luxuriating in the glorious views up the glen. It can get very busy, so best to book ahead for dinner.

Next door, ***Achintee Farm*** (Map 49; ☎ 01397-702240, 🖥 achinteefarm.com) has self-catering units (1D/1T, shared facilities; £50-70pp) and **B&B** (3D en suite; ➽; WI-FI; Ⓛ; from £67.50pp, sgl occ full room rate) accommodation in the farmhouse. Everyone can use their drying rooms. Booking is recommended and two-night bookings are preferred.

## BEN NEVIS                                                            See map p183

*You remember your first mountain in much the same way you remember having your first sexual experience, except that climbing doesn't make as much mess and you don't cry for a week if Ben Nevis forgets to phone next morning.*
**Muriel Gray** *The First Fifty – Munro-bagging without a beard*

It is impossible to say who first climbed the highest mountain in Britain. Locals have been walking these hills since the beginning of time and would have been guides to the visitors who first left a record of their ascents in the 18th century. Although nowhere near the first to ascend the mountain, some credit must go to Clement Wragge who climbed the peak every day without fail for two years to take weather readings. Happy to set out in all conditions, he soon became known as 'inclement Wragge'. He was no doubt glad when a weather observatory was built on the summit in 1883 and a substantial path made to service it; now the 'tourist route'. The observatory was abandoned in 1904.

Today 75,000 walkers a year attempt to reach the summit so don't think you'll get the place to yourself. Mass tourism has been a part of the Ben's life since the railway reached Fort William in 1894. Thankfully the tackiness of a summit hotel and pony rides to the top were abandoned soon after the ideas were conceived.

### Climbing Ben Nevis
Climbing the highest mountain in Britain after walking the entire West Highland Way makes a superb ending to your Highland adventure. However, do not underestimate those 1344 metres (4406ft) to the summit. It may not sound that high in comparison with the highest peaks in other countries but it

---

❑ **IMPORTANT NOTE – WALKING TIMES**
Unless otherwise specified, **all times in this book refer only to the time spent walking**. You will need to add 20-30% to allow for rests, photography, checking the map, drinking water etc. When planning the day's hike count on 5-7 hours' actual walking.

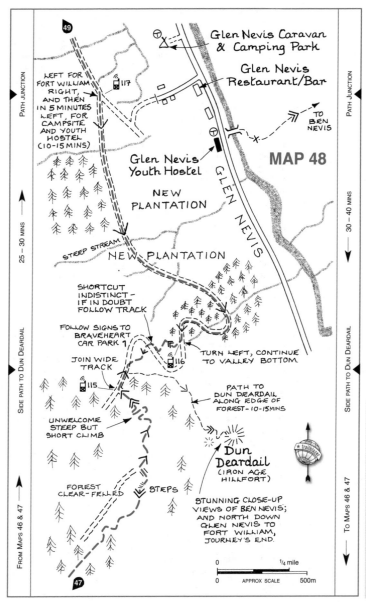

**49**

PATH JUNCTION

LEFT FOR
FORT WILLIAM
RIGHT,
AND THEN
IN 5 MINUTES
LEFT, FOR
CAMPSITE
AND YOUTH
HOSTEL
(10-15 MINS)

117

Glen Nevis Caravan
& Camping Park

Glen Nevis
Restaurant/Bar

TO
BEN
NEVIS

PATH JUNCTION

Glen Nevis
Youth Hostel

GLEN NEVIS

**MAP 48**

NEW
PLANTATION

25 – 30 MINS

STEEP STREAM

NEW PLANTATION

30 – 40 MINS

SHORTCUT
INDISTINCT –
IF IN DOUBT
FOLLOW TRACK

FOLLOW SIGNS TO
BRAVEHEART
CAR PARK 1

TURN LEFT, CONTINUE
TO VALLEY BOTTOM.

JOIN WIDE
TRACK

116

SIDE PATH TO DUN DEARDAIL

115

PATH TO
DUN DEARDAIL
ALONG EDGE OF
FOREST-10-15MINS

SIDE PATH TO DUN DEARDAIL

UNWELCOME
STEEP BUT
SHORT CLIMB

Dun
Deardail
(IRON AGE
HILLFORT)

FOREST
CLEAR-FELLED

STEPS

STUNNING CLOSE-UP
VIEWS OF BEN NEVIS;
AND NORTH DOWN
GLEN NEVIS TO
FORT WILLIAM,
JOURNEY'S END.

FROM MAPS 46 & 47

TO MAPS 46 & 47

**47**

trailblazer

0            ¼ mile

0       APPROX SCALE       500m

ROUTE GUIDE AND MAPS

has a fearsome reputation for accidents and as with all mountains in the Highlands, you should not contemplate climbing it unless you are suitably equipped and knowledgeable (see pp56-8).

There are several routes to the top. By far the most popular is the badly named **Tourist Route** (significantly harder than its belittling name would suggest) ascending from Glen

On the Tourist Route to the summit

Nevis along the well-trodden line of the former pony track all the way to the summit. This route (see p184) takes about 5½ to 6½ hours in total. Some find it a relentless slog, particularly on the upper reaches of the mountain and especially when accompanied by scores of other walkers, as you will be on most days in summer. It is, however, the only option for those who would not class themselves experienced hillwalkers.

For the latter category there is a superb route that provides a tough, long, but grand day out, befitting of Britain's highest mountain. The **Carn Mor Dearg Arête Route** (see p185) follows the normal route initially and then detours under the spectacular north face to climb Carn Mor Dearg (CMD), a significant mountain in its own right. From here it follows the narrow, rocky, crescent line of the Carn Mor Dearg Arête and then up the Ben's boulder-covered south-eastern slopes to the summit plateau. Descent is down the normal route. The whole trip takes about 8½ to 9½ hours.

## Safety

The normal route is along a well-graded trail, easy to follow in good visibility, but a mountain path none the less. Expect loose rock and scree underfoot, patches of snow even late in the year and some steep sections. The alternative CMD route is largely on steep, rough ground with a fair bit of exposure in places. It is a long route, requiring stamina with some sections of easy scrambling. Neither route is suitable in snow or ice unless you are an accomplished winter mountaineer.

The main difficulties on Ben Nevis occur on the summit plateau in poor visibility. The plateau is broad, relatively featureless and fringed to the north by a wall of crags which drop precipitously into Coire Leis below. The gullies that cut into this rock wall have too frequently ensnared lost walkers and climbers wandering round the plateau in white-out conditions. The other real danger is that in an effort to avoid these gullies the walker aims too far south,

### ❏ POOR VISIBILITY NAVIGATION NOTES

To get safely off the summit in severe conditions you must walk from the summit trig point on a **grid** bearing of 231° for 150 metres. Then follow a **grid** bearing of 281° to get off the plateau and onto the Tourist Route. **Remember** to add the number of degrees of magnetic variation to your compass to obtain the magnetic bearing you should follow.

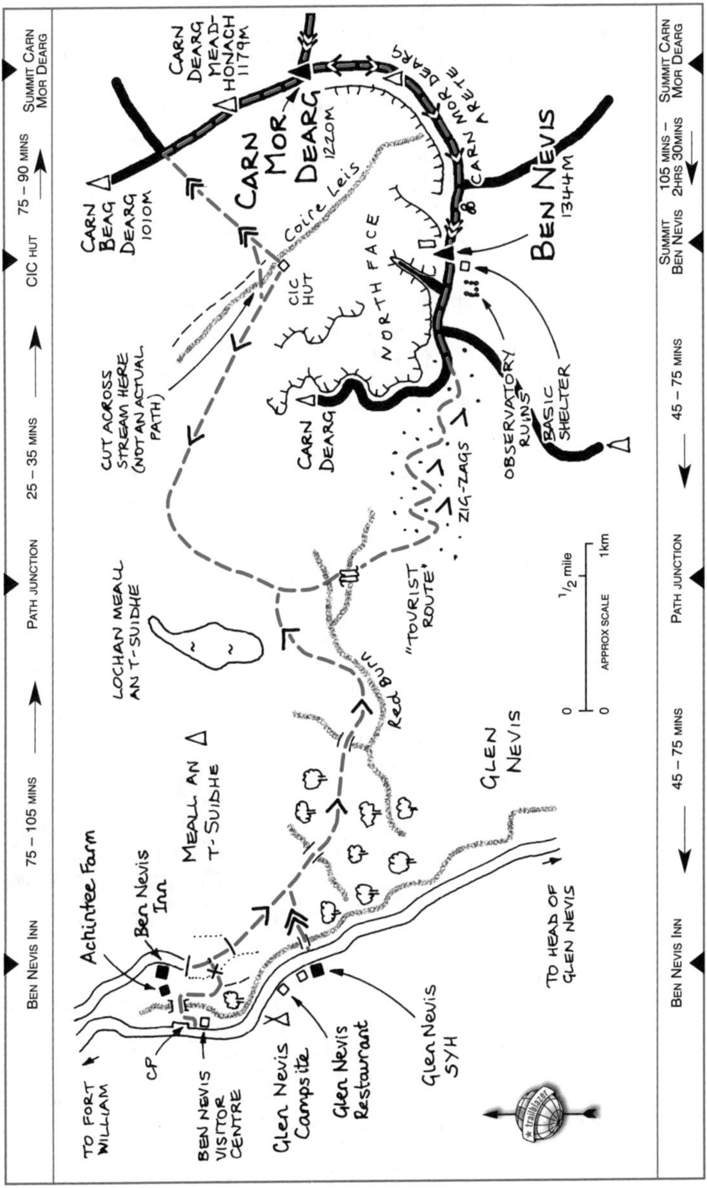

BEN NEVIS INN
75 – 105 MINS
PATH JUNCTION
25 – 35 MINS
CIC HUT
75 – 90 MINS
SUMMIT CARN MOR DEARG
BEN NEVIS INN
45 – 75 MINS
PATH JUNCTION
45 – 75 MINS
SUMMIT BEN NEVIS
105 MINS – 2HRS 30MINS
SUMMIT CARN MOR DEARG
TO FORT WILLIAM
BEN NEVIS VISITOR CENTRE
CP
Glen Nevis Campsite
Glen Nevis Restaurant
Glen Nevis SYH
TO HEAD OF GLEN NEVIS
Achintee Farm
Ben Nevis Inn
MEALL AN T-SUIDHE
GLEN NEVIS
LOCHAN MEALL AN T-SUIDHE
Red Burn
"TOURIST ROUTE"
ZIG-ZAGS
CUT ACROSS STREAM HERE (NOT AN ACTUAL PATH)
CARN DEARG
NORTH FACE
CIC HUT
Coire Leis
CARN BEAG DEARG 1010M
CARN DEARG MEADHONACH 1179M
CARN MOR DEARG 1220M
CARN MOR DEARG ARETE
BEN NEVIS 1344M
OBSERVATORY RUINS
BASIC SHELTER
APPROX SCALE
0
1/2 mile
0
1km

missing the descent path and straying onto the dangerous ground at the top of the notorious Five Finger Gully on the west side of the plateau. In poor visibility, a frequent occurrence as the summit is in cloud an average of 300 days a year, your navigation must be spot on. Snow and cloud together can create a lethal formula. See the box on p182 with instructions for poor visibility navigation.

For either route you must take one of the following maps: OS Landranger Sheet 41 (1:50,000), OS Explorer 392 (1:25,000), or Harvey's Superwalker 'Ben Nevis' (1:25,000). If you have a choice, the last one is the best with its enlarged map of the summit of Ben Nevis; a real help in getting off the mountain in poor visibility.

### Tourist route

From the youth hostel in Glen Nevis, cross the footbridge over River Nevis and turn left over a ladder-stile. Take heed of any pertinent safety or weather information on the notice board here. The path climbs steeply to join the main trail from the visitor centre and Achintee Farm.

The trail climbs gently across the side of Meall an t-Suidhe, up two zigzags and over three small bridges. Follow it into the ravine created by the Allt na h-Urchaire (Red Burn) which falls off the western flanks of the Ben and then up onto a broad grassy pass on which **Lochan Meall an t-Suidhe** (Halfway Lochan) sits. Don't be tempted to cut across the zigzags as this causes further erosion on this intensively used path. South-east of the lochan the trail divides by a short, low stone wall. This junction is about 1½ hours' walking from the start including one or two essential stops. It's at least another 2 to 2½ hours from here to the summit. An indistinct trail continues straight ahead across the col above Lochan Meall an t-Suidhe. This is the start of the route via Carn Mor Dearg (see opposite). The main trail doubles back on itself and climbs easily across the western slopes of Carn Dearg. Cross the **Red Burn** below a waterfall (fill up with water) and begin ascending the interminable zigzags up the severely eroded flank of the mountain. There are lots of short cuts but they do not make the going easier or quicker either on the ascent or coming back down. They are steep, extremely slippery and best avoided.

As you ascend, the huge shoulder of Carn Dearg (1221m/4005ft) spreads out to your left. You may be able to make out the orange emergency shelter just west of its summit. Eventually the route crosses a rock band and at last you climb more gen-

Emergency shelter at the summit

tly onto the vast **summit plateau** (3½ to 4 hours from the start). Among the boulder-strewn landscape are all manner of man-made structures: an emergency shelter, cairns, memorial plaques, the ruins of an observatory and the trig point. The summit is no place for quiet reflection. On most days you will be surrounded by the trappings of the modern world, crackling crisp packets, chirping mobile phones, yet if the cloud is high the views are superb. The descent is back the way you came and takes about 2 to 2½ hours.

## Carn Mor Dearg Arête Route

Follow the Tourist Route to Lochan Meall an t-Suidhe. Where the paths divide, continue straight on across the col. After five minutes there's a large cairn where a faint trail branches left towards the outflow of the lake. Ignore this, keeping straight on along the main trail which climbs gently to another large cairn on the horizon. The trail begins to descend and turns sharply east (right) into Coire Leis under the impressive northern crags of Ben Nevis. Leave the path after a few hundred metres picking your way down over the rough heather- and bilberry-covered slopes to the **Allt a' Mhuilinn**. This is the last reliable place for water until you descend off the Ben.

Choose a safe crossing point and head directly up the grassy, boulder-covered slopes ahead of you, climbing steeply to the ridge between Carn Beag Dearg and Carn Dearg Meadhonach. Continue climbing, more gently now, to the pink granite summit of **Carn Dearg Meadhonach** where there's a cairn and small stone windbreak. The views of the fearsome northern cliffs of Ben Nevis are awe-inspiring from here with snow lingering all year in shaded pockets. To the east the Nevis Range chairlift transports summer tourists and winter skiers up the northern slopes of Aonach Mor.

Descend south to a small col, then up and over the summit of **Carn Mor Dearg** (1220m/4002ft) and onto the spine of the arête. This sweeps round to the south-west dropping to a col and then ascends to some aluminium abseil posts. From here there are wonderful views south over the Mamores. Climb steeply up the grey south-east slopes of Ben Nevis on broken rock and boulders. The paths are indistinct. Take care in poor visibility not to stray too close to the corrie edge. Rejoin the mass of humanity on the summit. The trip time so far including a few short stops is about six to seven hours. The descent is down the Tourist Route (see).

If the ascent of Ben Nevis inspires you to discover more of Scotland's hills take a look at Trailblazer's *Scottish Highlands Hillwalking Guide*.

---

❏ **THE WISHING STONE**                                    Map 49 (see p187)

More accurately called the Counsel Stone (*Clach Chomhairle*) or Samuel's Stone (*Clach MicShomhairle*), this erratic boulder at the side of the Glen Nevis road is said to have been placed here to commemorate the victory of a Highland chieftain. A much more alluring legend, however, says that it has the power to give advice or counsel and at certain times of the year can be found revolving. If you catch it in the act you will discover the answers to three questions asked before it comes to rest.

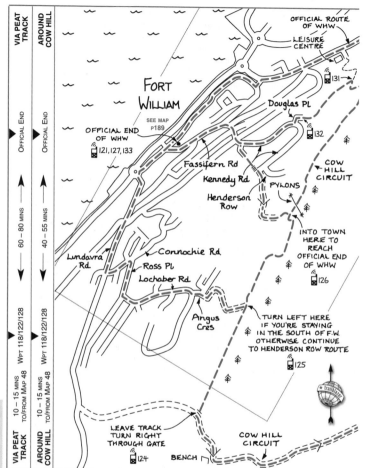

VIA PEAT TRACK

AROUND COW HILL

OFFICIAL END

OFFICIAL END

← 60 – 80 MINS →

← 40 – 55 MINS →

VIA PEAT TRACK    10 – 15 MINS TO/FROM MAP 48    WPT 118/122/128

AROUND COW HILL    10 – 15 MINS TO/FROM MAP 48    WPT 118/122/128

OFFICIAL ROUTE OF WHW

LEISURE CENTRE

131

FORT WILLIAM

SEE MAP P189

OFFICIAL END OF WHW

121,127,133

Douglas Pl

132

Fassifern Rd

Kennedy Rd

Henderson Row

PYLONS

COW HILL CIRCUIT

INTO TOWN HERE TO REACH OFFICIAL END OF WHW

126

Lundavra Rd

Connochie Rd

Ross Pl

Lochaber Rd

Angus Cres

TURN LEFT HERE IF YOU'RE STAYING IN THE SOUTH OF F.W. OTHERWISE CONTINUE TO HENDERSON ROW ROUTE

125

LEAVE TRACK TURN RIGHT THROUGH GATE

124

BENCH

COW HILL CIRCUIT

ROUTE GUIDE AND MAPS

## ☐ A BETTER WAY TO END THE WAY?

Long-distance paths have a tendency to peter out in unspectacular fashion rather than end with a grand flourish and the West Highland Way is no exception, finishing its winding course with a two-mile pavement trudge partly along the traffic-laden A82 into Fort William, an anticlimax to say the least. The official end used to be by the roundabout at the start of the Glen Nevis road but it was moved to the town square.

If you don't feel you have to follow every step of an 'official' route, we'd strongly suggest you take one of the routes away from the road to give your West Highland Way the ending it deserves. (Thanks to reader Nigel Toye for suggesting we research this).

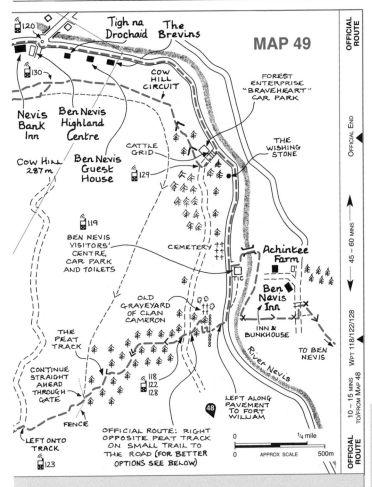

MAP 49

Tigh na Drochaid    The Brevins

120

130

COW HILL CIRCUIT

FOREST ENTERPRISE "BRAVEHEART" CAR PARK

Nevis Bank Inn

Ben Nevis Highland Centre

CATTLE GRID

THE WISHING STONE

Cow Hill 287m

Ben Nevis Guest House

129

119

BEN NEVIS VISITORS' CENTRE, CAR PARK AND TOILETS

CEMETERY

Achintee Farm

TIC

Ben Nevis Inn

OLD GRAVEYARD OF CLAN CAMERON

THE PEAT TRACK

INN & BUNKHOUSE

TO BEN NEVIS

River Nevis

CONTINUE STRAIGHT AHEAD THROUGH GATE

118 122 128

48

LEFT ALONG PAVEMENT TO FORT WILLIAM

FENCE

LEFT ONTO TRACK

123

OFFICIAL ROUTE: RIGHT OPPOSITE PEAT TRACK ON SMALL TRAIL TO THE ROAD (FOR BETTER OPTIONS SEE BELOW)

0          ¼ mile
0    APPROX SCALE    500m

OFFICIAL END

45 – 60 MINS

WPT 118/122/128

10 – 15 MINS TO/FROM MAP 48

OFFICIAL ROUTE

ROUTE GUIDE AND MAPS

● **Peat Track option** (WPTs 122-7) – Leave the West Highland Way at WPT 122 and climb steeply up the Peat Track and over the saddle south of Cow Hill (WPT 123). There are great views over Loch Linnhe as you descend and you can go down into the town from several points (WPTs 125-6) off the path via quiet side streets.

● **Around Cow Hill option** (WPTs 128-133) – Follow signs to Braveheart car park (WPT 129) then around the northern end of Cow Hill and via Douglas Place (WPT 132) into town. It's easier than the Peat Track, and it's far better than the official option as it's away from the road as long as you **don't** go via the Leisure Centre.

● **WHW official route** (WPTs 118-121) – Along Glen Nevis road and the busy A82.

## FORT WILLIAM

Spoilt by thoughtless modern development and a busy ring road, few would make a special journey to visit Fort William were it not for the magnificent natural treasures that surround it. Its stunning location near the foot of the highest mountain in Britain, overlooking Loch Linnhe and at the western end of the Great Glen, manages to overpower the concrete and industrial sprawl. The original c1650 fort was demolished in the 19th century to make way for the railway, heralding the start of mass tourism which still plays an important role in the local economy.

The pedestrian-only High St now panders to the eclectic taste of the Highland tourist, from tartan and tweeds to the latest petroleum-derived high fashion for the mountains and plenty of West Highland Way memorabilia. The official route of the West Highland Way leads you past all this – rather like having to walk through the gift shop as you leave any tourist attraction today. There are, however, pubs and restaurants in which to celebrate the completion of your walk, countless B&Bs for resting your weary legs and convenient transport connections to the rest of Scotland for the journey home.

### Services

The **tourist information**, or iCentre (☎ 01397-701801, 🖥 visitscotland.com; daily 9am-5pm) is at 15 High St.

The excellent **Highland Bookshop** (☎ 01397-705931; 🖥 highlandbookshop.com; Mon-Sat 9.30am-5pm, Sun 11am-4pm) at 60 High St, has a good outdoors section and a second-hand department upstairs.

If you need a **supermarket**, at the north end of the High St there's a Tesco Metro (Mon-Sat 7am-9pm, Sun 10am-5pm) and over by the station is Morrison's (Mon-Sat 7am-10pm, Sun 8am-8pm).

There are several **banks** along the High St, three **chemists**, a **post office** (Mon-Fri 9am-5.30pm, Sat to 2pm) in WH Smith's and a **library** (Mon & Thur 10am-8pm, Tue & Fri 10am-6pm, Wed & Sat 10am-1pm) – a good place to while away the hours or surf the **internet** on a miserable

day. On Belford Rd there's a **hospital** (☎ 01397-702481) with a casualty department. If your dog needs some attention after all its exertions, the only **vet surgery** for many miles around is Crown Vets (☎ 01397-702727, 🖥 www.crownvetsfortwilliam.co.uk; Glen Nevis Pl; Mon-Fri 8.30am-6pm, Sat 9am-noon).

Another popular activity in the rain is gear shopping. Fort William has several large **outdoor equipment shops** all open daily, including Mountain Warehouse, Cotswold, and Regatta on the High St, Nevisport which also has a café and bar (see Where to eat) and Ellis Brigham Mountain Sports near the station. Up-to-date **weather forecasts** are posted at many of them.

Campers, or anyone feeling sweaty after their exertions, can take a shower (£2) at the **Nevis Centre** (☎ 01397-700707; 🖥 neviscentre.co.uk; daily 9am-10pm), behind Morrison's. It also houses a concert hall and a 10-pin bowling alley and plays host to a number of annual events, including Fort William Mountain Festival (see p14) in February. There are also showers at the train station.

### Transport

[See also pp45-9]  The bus station and railway station are at the northern end of town. Scottish Citylink **coaches** (914, 915, 916 & 919) & West Coast Motors (918) operate to and from Glasgow, Edinburgh, Inverness, the Isle of Skye, Oban & Mallaig.

Scotrail **trains** (West Highland Line; Glasgow–Mallaig) also call here. Note that if you're going back to Glasgow, buses are considerably quicker than trains – but don't allow dogs, of course.

Shiel Buses (N41, N42 & N44) go to Glen Nevis, Kinlochleven & Glencoe.

For a **taxi** there's Greyhound (☎ 01397-705050, 🖥 greyhound-taxis.co.uk) or Alistair's (☎ 01397 252525, 🖥 alistairstaxis.co.uk). Alternatively you could **hire a car** for the day from Easydrive (☎ 01397-701616, 🖥 easydrivescotland.co.uk).

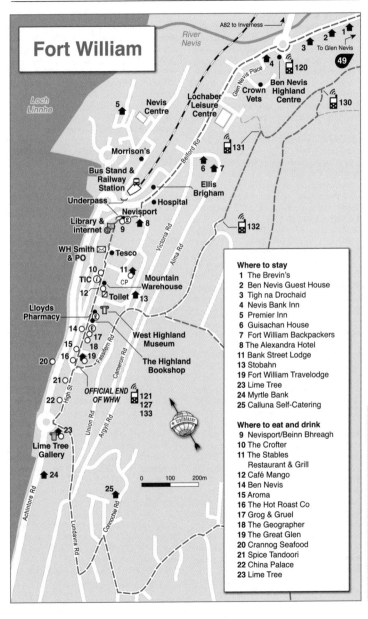

# Fort William

*River Nevis*

*Loch Linnhe*

A82 to Inverness

To Glen Nevis

**49**

Glen Nevis Place

Nevis Centre

Lochaber Leisure Centre

Crown Vets

Ben Nevis Highland Centre

120

130

131

Belford Rd

Morrison's

Bus Stand & Railway Station

Ellis Brigham

Underpass

Hospital

Nevisport

Library & internet @

8

9

132

WH Smith & PO

Tesco

Victoria Rd

Alma Rd

10

11

TIC

CP

12

Toilet

Mountain Warehouse

13

Lloyds Pharmacy

14

17

West Highland Museum

15

18

16

19

The Highland Bookshop

20

21

OFFICIAL END OF WHW

121
127
133

22

Fassifern Rd

Cameron Rd

High St

Union Rd

Argyll Rd

23

Lime Tree Gallery

24

0   100   200m

25

Achintore Rd

Lundavra Rd

Cononchie Rd

trailblazer

**Where to stay**

1 The Brevin's
2 Ben Nevis Guest House
3 Tigh na Drochaid
4 Nevis Bank Inn
5 Premier Inn
6 Guisachan House
7 Fort William Backpackers
8 The Alexandra Hotel
11 Bank Street Lodge
13 Stobahn
19 Fort William Travelodge
23 Lime Tree
24 Myrtle Bank
25 Calluna Self-Catering

**Where to eat and drink**

9 Nevisport/Beinn Bhreagh
10 The Crofter
11 The Stables
   Restaurant & Grill
12 Café Mango
14 Ben Nevis
15 Aroma
16 The Hot Roast Co
17 Grog & Gruel
18 The Geographer
19 The Great Glen
20 Crannog Seafood
21 Spice Tandoori
22 China Palace
23 Lime Tree

## What to see and do

**In town** The **West Highland Museum** (☎ 01397-702169, 🖳 westhighlandmuseum .org.uk; Cameron Sq; Mon-Fri 10am-4pm; free) is a treasure trove of fascinating artefacts on the Highlands, well worth a visit. There's a secret portrait of Bonnie Prince Charlie, displays about the crofting life and lots of information on Ben Nevis, including the story of Henry Alexander who drove his Model T Ford to the summit in 1911.

By the roundabout on Achintore Rd is the **Lime Tree Gallery** (see also Where to stay: Guest houses and hotels). Entrance is free and the gallery is open daily 10am-10pm except November.

There's an indoor swimming pool, sauna, steam room, and gym at **Lochaber Leisure Centre** (☎ 01397-704359; Mon & Wed 7.15am-9.00pm, Tue & Thur from 6.30am, Fri to 7.15am-8.30pm, Sat 7.15am-4pm, Sun 10.15am-4.30pm).

On the opposite side of Cameron Sq from the High St is the swish independent **Highland Cinema** (🖳 highlandcinema .co.uk), with its own café and bar as well as two screens.

**Out of town** Also available are: a 60-minute **cruise** (☎ 01397-700714, 🖳 crannog.net/cruises/our-cruises; Mar-Oct daily 10am, noon, 2pm and 4pm; £12.50) down Loch Linnhe on Crannog's (see Where to eat and drink) boat, *Souter's Lass*; a tour of **Ben Nevis Distillery** (☎ 01397-700200, 🖳 bennevisdistillery.com; Mon-Fri 9am-5pm, also Jun- & Aug Sat 10am-6pm, Sun noon-6pm; from £5) with a chance to sip a whisky at the end; **canoeing** on the Caledonian Canal (☎ 01463-725500; 🖳 scottishcanals.co.uk); **Caledonian Canal Visitor Centre** (☎ 01463-725581, 🖳 visitinvernesslochness.com/listings/Caledonian-Canal-Visitor-Centre; daily 9am-5pm) in Fort Augustus; or riding *The Jacobite* **steam train** to Mallaig (☎ 0333-996 6720, 🖳 westcoastrailways.co.uk; late April to late Oct daily); visit the TIC for more information on these and other possible day trips in the area.



## Where to stay

**Bunkhouses and hostels** On Alma Rd there's the busy ***Fort William Backpackers*** (☎ 01397-700711, 🖳 fortwilliambackpackers.com; 38 beds; WI-FI; £25-30pp), a colourful independent hostel. Continental breakfast costs £3. The rate includes bedding and guests can use the kitchen and sitting room during the day. Note that you need photographic ID to check in.

As long as you are happy to stay for a minimum of three nights, ***Calluna Self-Catering*** (☎ 01397-700451, 🖳 fortwilliamholiday.co.uk; WI-FI; 🐕; mid Dec to Oct) has four apartments sleeping up to 4/6/7/7 people. Bedding is provided and there are full cooking facilities. Apartments are £96-192 per night.

**B&Bs** The difference in price between the hostels/bunkhouses and some of the less expensive bed and breakfasts is negligible when you take the cost of breakfast into account.

Some of the nicest places are located at the top of the Glen Nevis road. The first one you reach, ***The Brevins*** (☎ 01397-701412, 🖳 thebrevins.co.uk; 1T/6D; WI-FI; Ⓛ; around £90pp), is one of the best in Fort William. All the rooms are clean and comfortable.

Just on from here is the smart ***Ben Nevis Guest House*** (☎ 01397-708817, 🖳 bennevisguesthouse.co.uk; 4D/1T/1Tr; ☕; WI-FI; Ⓛ; £35-67.50pp, sgl occ full room rate). There's a nice conservatory to sit in and a drying room. Room-only rates available on request.

Next is tidy, comfortable ***Tigh na Drochaid*** (☎ 01397-704177, 🖳 glennevisbb.co.uk; 1D/1T; WI-FI; Ⓛ; £35-45pp), which is excellent value and run by friendly people.

Fassifern Rd is packed with B&Bs, though most of those we contacted now take bookings solely through AirBnB. One that doesn't is ***Stobahn*** (☎ 01397-702790, 🖳 stobahnguesthouse.co.uk; 1T/2D en suite, 1S/1D/1F with shared facilities; WI-

FI; £32.50-47.50pp, sgl/sgl occ £35-40/50-55) with comfortable rooms.

Alma Rd is also a good area for accommodation as it's quiet, centrally located and has views overlooking the town, including smart *Guisachan House* (☎ 01397-703797, 💻 guisachanguesthouse.co.uk; 2S/5T/6D/2Tr/1Qd; ✎; WI-FI; Ⓛ; £46-49pp, sing occ £82-88).

Below here on Bank St is *Bank Street Lodge* ☎ 01397-700070, 💻 bankstreetlodge.co.uk; WI-FI; 1S/8D/5T/3Tr/3Qd/1 x 5-bed/1 x 6-bed) with different-sized rooms, all en suite save for two twins with private facilities. Twins/doubles are priced at £54.50pp, the single is £60 (room only).

**Guest houses and hotels** Right beside the official end of the West Highland Way is the *Fort William Travelodge* (Fort William ☎ 0871 984 6419, booking line ☎ 0871 984 8484; 💻 travelodge.co.uk; 30D/32Qd; ✎; WI-FI; 30 mins free, £3/24hrs; 🐾 £20 per stay) on the High St. The other large hotel chain, Premier Inn, has a hotel near the railway station: *Premier Inn* (☎ 0333-777 7268; 💻 premierinn.com; 42D/43Tr/18Qd, all en suite; ✎; WI-FI). For both chains, room rates vary hugely depending on demand; if you book early you may get a room for £25 but could pay anything up to £130. The beds are very comfortable in these places.

Further back along the Way, just as it enters the town but by the noisy A82, there's *Nevis Bank Inn* (☎ 01397-705721, 💻 nevisbankinn.co.uk, Belford Rd; 5S/5D/11D or T/4Qd; ✎; WI-FI; 🐾; from £59.50pp, sgl £19).

*The Alexandra Hotel* (☎ 01397-702241, 💻 strathmorehotels-thealexandra .com; 93 rms; contact hotel for rates; ✎; WI-FI) is a large old hotel in the centre. They sometimes have special packages, so it's always worth contacting them.

If you're unlucky and everywhere is booked, try looking on Achintore Rd, the A82 south to Glencoe and Glasgow. Here are wall-to-wall guest houses overlooking Loch Linnhe, but it's an unnecessarily long

way to walk if you don't have to. At the start of Achintore Rd, by the roundabout, is *Lime Tree* (☎ 01397-701806, 💻 limetree fortwilliam.co.uk; 2T/7D; ✎; WI-FI; 🐾; £57.50-72.50pp, sgl occ full room rate) which has luxurious rooms, a restaurant (see Where to eat) and an art gallery (see opposite). They have a map room (with historical maps) and a mountaineering library but perhaps of more practical use to walkers is their drying room.

A cheaper option is *Myrtle Bank* (☎ 01397-702034, 💻 myrtlebankguesthouse .co.uk; 11D/4T; WI-FI; £47.50pp, sgl occ £75; Mar-Nov).

**Where to eat and drink**
All along the High St there is a wide selection of **take-away places** including Indian, fish and chips, and burger bars as well as several **pubs**. There are some **coffee shops**, too, including the big names, or try busy independent *Aroma* (☎ 01397-700182; **fb**) on the High St, open daily 10am-9pm.

There are numerous pubs to choose from. *Grog & Gruel* (☎ 01397-705078, 💻 grogandgruel.co.uk), halfway along the High St, is a cosy traditional pub with a good range of local beers. Food is served in the pub (Mon-Sat noon-9pm) and in the restaurant (evenings 5-9pm). Dishes include their popular Grog (hot) dog from £9.95, quesadillas from £12.25 and venison burgers (£13.75). Almost opposite is the *Ben Nevis* (☎ 01397-702295, 💻 bennevis barfortwilliam.com; food daily noon-9.30pm), with good pub grub such as steak and ale pie for £11.99. Also on the High St, *The Crofter* (💻 crofterbar.co.uk) is a popular, excellent-value pub with Sky Sports and special offers such as curry and a pint for £6.99.

Open long hours and conveniently located below the Travelodge is a branch of the family-friendly pub chain, Wetherspoon – *The Great Glen*. They serve food here daily from 8am until 10pm.

*Beinn Bhreagh* (**fb**; Mon-Sat 9am-4pm, Sun 10am-3pm), the café upstairs at **Nevisport**, is popular, with good value lunches and a carvery at weekends. In the evenings the bar and bistro (**fb**; Wed-Sun 4-11pm/midnight) takes over.

*The Stables Restaurant & Grill* (**fb**; ☎ 01397-700730; summer daily 5-10.30pm, winter hours vary) below Bank Street Lodge (see Where to stay: B&Bs) has a range of steaks, burgers and fish; they also do a good Caesar salad (£14.50).

*Café Mango* (☎ 01397-701367, 💻 cafemango.co.uk; daily noon-10pm) is a BYOB Indian restaurant in the heart of the High St at No 26, and a great place to celebrate the end of your adventure, with vegetarian mains just £8.95.

*The Geographer* (☎ 01397-705011, 💻 geographerrestaurant.co.uk; Mon-Sat noon-2pm & 5-9pm, Sun 5-9pm), 88 High St, is a restaurant 'inspired by travel, food and great people.' Their menu is less eclectic than it used to be; there are several burger options now, plus local dishes including steamed mussels (£16) and Highland venison stew (£18.50).

If you're looking for somewhere to celebrate in style one of the best places for local food is the perfectly-located *Crannog Seafood Restaurant* (☎ 01397-705589, 💻 crannog.net; daily noon-2.30pm & 5.30-9.30pm). Freshly caught seafood such as hake (£19.50) is superbly cooked and reasonably priced. There is always one meat dish (such as lamb, venison or beef) on the menu.

Some of the finest dining in Fort William can be found at *Lime Tree* (see Where to stay; daily 6.30 & 8.30pm); main dishes are around £20. Their Isag Bree (fish stew, £22.50) is superb. Booking advised.

At the southern end of the High St are a couple of takeaways including *China Palace* (daily noon-2.30pm & 5-11pm) and, at 141 High St, glitzy *Spice Tandoori* (☎ 01397-705192, 💻 spice-tandoori.com; daily 4-10.30pm), which has indoor seating and great views over Loch Linnhe as well as a takeaway service.

# APPENDIX A – GAELIC

Gaelic was once spoken all over Scotland but there are now only about 57,000 Gaelic speakers mainly in the north-west of Scotland. Gaelic names of geographical features are found all along the West Highland Way; some of the most common words are listed below.

| | | | |
|---|---|---|---|
| *abhainn* | river | *coille/choille* | wood/forest |
| *acarsaid* | anchorage | *coire/coireachan/choire* | corry/corries |
| *achadh/achaidh* | field | | (cirque) |
| *adhar/adhair* | sky | *craobh* | tree |
| *àite/àiteachan* | place/places | *creag* | rock/cliff/crag |
| *Alba* | Scotland | *crom* | crooked |
| *Albannach/Albannaich* | Scot | *cruach* | stack |
| *allt/uillt* | stream/burn | *cumain* | bucket |
| *aonach* | ridge/moor | | |
| *àrd/àird* | high | *dearg* | red |
| | | *diallaid* | saddle |
| *bàgh/bàigh* | bay | *dobhran/dorain* | otter |
| *baile* | town | *dorcha* | dark |
| *bàn* | white/fair | *dorus* | door |
| *bàthach* | byre | *drochaid* | bridge |
| *beag* | small | *druim* | back/ridge |
| *bealach* | mountain pass/col | *dubh* | black |
| *beinn/beinne/bheinn* | mountain | *duinne* | brown |
| *bidean* | pinnacle | *dun* | fortress/mound |
| *bó/bà* | cow | | |
| *bodach/bodaich* | old man | *each* | horse |
| *bruthach* | slope | *eag* | notch |
| *buachaille* | herdsmen | *eaglais* | church |
| *buidhe/bhuidhe* | yellow | *earb* | roe deer |
| | | *eilean* | island |
| *cailleach* | old woman | *eòin* | bird |
| *caisteal* | castle | | |
| *cala* | harbour | *fada* | long |
| *calman/calmain* | dove | *fasgadh* | shelter |
| *caol* | narrows/strait | *feòla* | flesh |
| *caora* | sheep | *feur* | grass |
| *càrn* | cairn or rounded | *fiacaill* | tooth |
| | rocky hill | *fiadh* | deer |
| *cas* | steep | *fionn* | white/holy |
| *cath* | battle | *fithich* | raven |
| *cathair* | chair | *fraoch* | heather |
| *ceann* | end/at the head of | *fuar* | cold |
| | (often anglicised to kin) | | |
| *cearc* | hen | *gabhar* | goat |
| *ceum* | step | *Gaidheal* | Highlander |
| *cìobair* | shepherd | *Gaidhealtach* | Highlands |
| *ciste* | chest | *gaoth* | wind |
| *clach/clachan* | stone/hamlet | *garbh* | rough |
| *cnap* | lump/knob/small hill | *geal* | white |
| *cnoc* | hill | *glas* | grey/green |

| | | | |
|---|---|---|---|
| *gleann* | glen/valley | *poca* | sack |
| *gorm* | blue | *ràmh* | oar |
| | | *rathad* | road |
| *innis* | meadow | *ruadh* | red |
| *iolair* | eagle | | |
| | | *sàil* | heel |
| *lach* | duck | *sgor/sgorr/sgurr* | peak |
| *lairig* | pass/col | *sionnach* | fox |
| *leathann* | broad | *slat* | rod |
| *liath* | grey | *sneachda* | snow |
| *linne* | pool | *spidean* | pinnacle |
| *loch* | lake | *sròn* | nose |
| *lochan* | small lake | *stac* | peak/point |
| | | *stob* | peak/point |
| *machair* | field | *strath* | a long, wide valley |
| *mam* | hill | | |
| *meal/meall* | round hill | *tigh/taigh* | house |
| *monadh* | moor | *tioram* | dry |
| *mor/mhor* | big | *toll* | hole |
| *mullach* | top | *tom* | hillock |
| | | *tràigh* | beach |
| *neul* | cloud | | |
| *nid* | nest | *uaine* | green |
| | | *uamh* | cave |
| *odhar* | dun-coloured | *uiseag* | lark |
| *òigh* | maiden | *uisge* | water |
| *or* | gold | | |

# APPENDIX B – WAYPOINTS

Each GPS waypoint below was taken on the route at the reference number marked on the map as below. This list of GPS waypoints is also available to download from the Trailblazer website – 🖥 trailblazer-guides.com.

| Map | No | GPS Waypoint | Description |
|---|---|---|---|
| A | 001 | N55° 52.203' W04° 16.866' | Entrance to Kelvingrove Park |
| A | 002 | N55° 52.767' W04° 17.119' | Queen Margaret Bridge |
| A | 003 | N55° 53.544' W04° 18.047' | Kelvin Aqueduct |
| B | 004 | N55° 53.924' W04° 18.359' | Bridge across River Kelvin |
| B | 005 | N55° 54.540' W04° 17.877' | Join River Kelvin |
| C | 006 | N55° 55.099' W04° 16.464' | Bridge across River Kelvin |
| C | 007 | N55° 55.670' W04° 16.890' | Path goes under A879 Balmore Rd |
| D | 008 | N55° 55.657' W04° 17.122' | Bridge over Allander Water to north |
| D | 009 | N55° 56.474' W04° 18.849' | Milngavie Railway station |
| 1 | 010 | N55° 56.503' W04° 19.069' | Official start of WHW |
| 1 | 011 | N55° 57.125' W04° 19.252' | Path to car park and Milngavie |
| 1 | 012 | N55° 57.630' W04° 20.105' | Second path off east to Mugdock CP |
| 2 | 013 | N55° 57.825' W04° 20.557' | Gate onto road |
| 2 | 014 | N55° 58.381' W04° 20.989' | Boat shed |
| 2 | 015 | N55° 59.090' W04° 20.817' | Path over stream |
| 3 | 016 | N55° 59.245' W04° 21.180' | Turn right off road; go through gate |
| 3 | 017 | N55° 59.719' W04° 21.425' | Stream |
| 4 | 018 | N56° 00.207' W04° 21.483' | Left off path onto route of old Blane Valley Railway; through gate |
| 4 | 019 | N56° 01.239' W04° 22.256' | Gate before Beech Tree Inn |
| 4 | 020 | N56° 01.375' W04° 22.330' | Double gates |
| 5 | 021 | N56° 01.711' W04° 22.806' | Single gate |
| 5 | 021a | N56° 02.722' W04° 22.315' | Junction in Killearn |
| 5 | 022 | N56° 01.740' W04° 22.853' | Oakwood Garden Centre & Café |
| 6 | 023 | N56° 02.767' W04° 23.974' | Path crosses A81 |
| 6 | 024 | N56° 03.118' W04° 24.245' | Gartness |
| 7 | 025 | N56° 02.966' W04° 25.477' | Bridge across stream |
| 7 | 026 | N56° 03.217' W04° 25.945' | Easter Drumquhassle Farm |
| 8 | 027 | N56° 03.922' W04° 26.341' | Turn off road |
| 8 | 027a | N56° 03.951' W04° 27.155' | Drymen Green |
| 8 | 028 | N56° 04.162' W04° 25.973' | Left through gate; turn away from road |
| 8 | 029 | N56° 05.056' W04° 26.619' | Join road |
| 9 | 030 | N56° 05.369' W04° 28.973' | Gate |
| 10 | 031 | N56° 05.736' W04° 29.477' | Through gate onto open moorland |
| 10 | 032 | N56° 05.970' W04° 30.132' | Bridge |
| 10 | 033 | N56° 05.825' W04° 31.492' | Top of Conic Hill |
| 11 | 034 | N56° 05.406' W04° 31.989' | Kissing gate |
| 11 | 035 | N56° 05.071' W04° 32.650' | Steps off road |
| 11 | 036 | N56° 05.765' W04° 33.352' | Bridge over stream |
| 12 | 037 | N56° 06.003' W04° 33.610' | Path off road |
| 12 | 038 | N56° 06.342' W04° 34.135' | Path crosses track |
| 12 | 039 | N56° 06.634' W04° 34.678' | Path meets road |
| 13 | 040 | N56° 06.766' W04° 34.860' | Bridge over stream |
| 13 | 041 | N56° 07.119' W04° 35.355' | Bridge over Tigh an Laoigh |

| Map | No | GPS Waypoint | Description |
|-----|------|-----------------------------|------------------------------------------|
| 13 | 042 | N56° 07.259' W04° 35.528' | Path leaves road |
| 13 | 043 | N56° 07.617' W04° 36.429' | Car park |
| 14 | 044 | N56° 07.697' W04° 36.813' | Beachside hut |
| 14 | 045 | N56° 08.128' W04° 37.623' | Stone building |
| 14 | 046 | N56° 08.300' W04° 37.768' | Bridge across stream |
| 15 | 047 | N56° 08.966' W04° 38.494' | Rowardennan Hotel |
| 15 | 048 | N56° 09.472' W04° 38.596' | Rowardennan Lodge Youth Hostel |
| 16 | 049 | N56° 10.169' W04° 39.037' | Track to Ptarmigan Lodge |
| 17 | 050 | N56° 11.440' W04° 40.500' | Continue on path for official trail |
| 18 | 051 | N56° 13.179' W04° 40.544' | Bridge by Cailness |
| 19 | 052 | N56° 14.578' W04° 41.100' | Inversnaid |
| 19 | 053 | N56° 15.219' W04° 41.648' | Path to Rob Roy's Cave |
| 20 | 054 | N56° 16.137' W04° 41.524' | Ruin |
| 21 | 055 | N56° 17.557' W04° 41.745' | Doune Byre Bothy |
| 21 | 056 | N56° 18.082' W04° 42.175' | Bridge over stream |
| 21 | 057 | N56° 18.203' W04° 42.248' | Go through wall |
| 22 | 058 | N56° 19.167' W04° 42.742' | Gate |
| 22 | 059 | N56° 19.780' W04° 43.004' | Cross Ben Glas Burn |
| 22 | 060 | N56° 19.902' W04° 43.217' | Bridge over River Falloch |
| 23 | 061 | N56° 20.368' W04° 42.941' | Information board |
| 23 | 062 | N56° 20.602' W04° 42.693' | Junction of paths; turn right |
| 24 | 063 | N56° 21.356' W04° 40.822' | Cross Allt a Chuilinn |
| 24 | 064 | N56° 21.647' W04° 40.185' | Path leaves road (after crossing bridge) |
| 25 | 065 | N56° 22.131' W04° 39.493' | Tunnel under railway line |
| 25 | 066 | N56° 22.797' W04° 38.988' | Gate and stile |
| 26 | 067 | N56° 23.377' W04° 37.956' | Kissing gate before junction |
| 26 | 067a | N56° 23.450' W04° 37.117' | Steps by A82 |
| 26 | 067b | N56° 23.553' W04° 37.036' | Join A85 |
| 26 | 067c | N56° 23.720' W04° 37.679' | Path off A85 towards WHW |
| 27 | 068 | N56° 24.715' W04° 39.581' | Cross railway |
| 27 | 069 | N56° 24.966' W04° 39.802' | Bridge over River Fillan |
| 28 | 070 | N56° 25.127' W04° 39.635' | Bridge by St Fillan's Priory |
| 28 | 071 | N56° 25.407' W04° 40.099' | Gate |
| 28 | 072 | N56° 25.501' W04° 41.601' | Cross Crom Allt |
| 29 | 073 | N56° 26.296' W04° 42.803' | Path meets A85 |
| 29 | 074 | N56° 26.968' W04° 42.528' | Gate after bridge over railway |
| 30 | 075 | N56° 27.826' W04° 42.936' | Narrow tunnel under railway bridge |
| 30 | 076 | N56° 29.013' W04° 43.097' | Gate before junction |
| 31 | 077 | N56° 29.778' W04° 44.631' | Bridge across railway |
| 32 | 078 | N56° 31.005' W04° 45.837' | Gate before railway |
| 32 | 079 | N56° 31.091' W04° 46.277' | Gate into conifer plantation |
| 33 | 080 | N56° 31.913' W04° 47.636' | Lone tree |
| 34 | 081 | N56° 31.968' W04° 48.446' | Inveroran Hotel |
| 34 | 082 | N56° 32.376' W04° 48.820' | Victoria Bridge |
| 34 | 083 | N56° 33.111' W04° 47.917' | Bridge over Allt Bhreacnais |
| 35 | 084 | N56° 33.514' W04° 47.669' | Cross Allt Doire nan Each |
| 35 | 085 | N56° 34.385' W04° 47.640' | Bridge over stream |
| 35 | 086 | N56° 34.889' W04° 47.916' | Bridge over stream |
| 36 | 087 | N56° 35.743' W04° 48.453' | Bà Bridge |
| 36 | 088 | N56° 36.289' W04° 48.458' | Track to Bà Cottage |

| Map | No | GPS Waypoint | Description |
|---|---|---|---|
| 37 | 089 | N56° 36.817' W04° 48.016' | Bridge over stream |
| 37 | 090 | N56° 38.190' W04° 49.444' | Gate |
| 38 | 091 | N56° 38.240' W04° 49.543' | Blackrock Cottage |
| 38 | 092 | N56° 38.590' W04° 49.647' | Gate after crossing road |
| 38 | 093 | N56° 39.068' W04° 50.435' | Bridge by Kings House Hotel |
| 39 | 094 | N56° 39.239' W04° 51.323' | Gate off road |
| 39 | 095 | N56° 39.638' W04° 53.270' | Follow path via gates |
| 40 | 096 | N56° 39.879' W04° 54.190' | Bridge over stream |
| 40 | 097 | N56° 40.554' W04° 54.853' | Highest point of WHW |
| 40 | 098 | N56° 40.852' W04° 55.078' | Stepping stones over stream |
| 41 | 099 | N56° 41.173' W04° 55.001' | First small cairn |
| 41 | 100 | N56° 41.629' W04° 55.209' | Bridge over Allt a'Choire Odhair-mhoir |
| 41 | 101 | N56° 42.042' W04° 56.308' | Junction of path and track |
| 42 | 102 | N56° 41.880' W04° 56.801' | Small reservoir |
| 42 | 103 | N56° 42.729' W04° 57.349' | Cross pipes |
| 42 | 104 | N56° 42.867' W04° 57.625' | Blackwater Hostel |
| 43 | 105 | N56° 43.139' W04° 58.671' | Path crosses lane |
| 43 | 106 | N56° 43.414' W04° 59.661' | Bridge across stream |
| 43 | 107 | N56° 43.570' W05° 00.519' | Cairn |
| 44 | 108 | N56° 43.974' W05° 02.911' | Derelict farmhouses |
| 45 | 109 | N56° 43.803' W05° 04.281' | Lairigmor |
| 45 | 110 | N56° 44.195' W05° 06.313' | Sheepfold |
| 46 | 111 | N56° 44.693' W05° 06.583' | Commemorative cairn |
| 46 | 112 | N56° 45.081' W05° 06.507' | Information board |
| 47 | 113 | N56° 46.240' W05° 05.524' | Gate |
| 47 | 114 | N56° 46.574' W05° 04.835' | Bridge across stream |
| 48 | 115 | N56° 47.176' W05° 04.396' | Join wide track |
| 48 | 116 | N56° 47.411' W05° 04.316' | Turn left onto forest track |
| 48 | 117 | N56° 48.180' W05° 04.781' | Join main track |
| 49 | 118 | N56° 48.466' W05° 04.975' | Path junction: turn right down to road for **official WHW route** to Ft William |
| 49 | 119 | N56° 48.559' W05° 04.641' | Tourist information centre, Glen Nevis |
| 49 | 120 | N56° 49.279' W05° 05.640' | Roundabout Glen Nevis road/A82 |
| 49 | 121 | N56° 49.077' W05° 06.661' | End of WHW via official route |
| 49 | 122 | N56° 48.466' W05° 04.975' | Path junction: turn left up Peat Track for **Peat Track route** into Fort William |
| 49 | 123 | N56° 48.225' W05° 05.826' | Left onto Cow Hill track |
| 49 | 124 | N56° 48.262' W05° 06.574' | Leave track, through gate, follow path |
| 49 | 125 | N56° 48.545' W05° 06.347' | For S end of Ft William turn off here |
| 49 | 126 | N56° 48.788' W05° 06.124' | For centre of Ft William turn left here |
| 49 | 127 | N56° 49.077' W05° 06.661' | End of WHW via Peat Track route |
| 49 | 128 | N56° 48.466' W05° 04.975' | Path junction: ahead for **Around N end of Cow Hill route** into Ft William |
| 49 | 129 | N56° 48.926' W05° 04.788' | Above car park follow Town Ctr path |
| 49 | 130 | N56° 49.169' W05° 05.588' | Path junction: continue ahead |
| 49 | 131 | N56° 49.157' W05° 05.837' | Left to go into town to reach the end |
| 49 | 132 | N56° 49.056' W05° 06.067' | Enter Fort William via Douglas Place. |
| 49 | 133 | N56° 49.077' W05° 06.661' | End of WHW via Around Cow Hill route |

# APPENDIX C – TAKING A DOG

## TAKING A DOG ALONG THE WAY

Many are the rewards that await those prepared to make the extra effort required to bring their best friend along the trail. You shouldn't underestimate the amount of work involved, though. Indeed, just about every decision you make will be influenced by the fact that you've got a dog: how you plan to travel to the start of the trail, where you're going to stay, how far you're going to walk each day, where you're going to rest and where you're going to eat in the evening etc.

If you're also sure your dog can cope with (and, just as importantly, will enjoy) walking 10 miles or more a day for several days in a row, you need to start preparing accordingly. Extra thought also needs to go into your itinerary. The best starting point is to study the village and town facilities table on p31 (and the advice on pp27-8), and plan where to stop and where to buy food.

### Looking after your dog

To begin with, you need to make sure that your own dog is fully **inoculated** against the usual doggy illnesses, and also up to date with regard to **worm pills** (eg Drontal) and **flea preventatives** such as Frontline – they are, after all, following in the pawprints of many a dog before them, some of whom may well have left fleas or other parasites on the trail that now lie in wait for their next meal to arrive. **Pet insurance** is also a very good idea; if you've already got insurance, do check that it will cover a trip such as this.

On the subject of looking after your dog's health, perhaps the most important implement you can take with you is the **plastic tick remover**, available from vets for a couple of quid. These removers, while fiddly, help you to remove the tick safely (ie without leaving its head behind buried under the dog's skin).

Being in unfamiliar territory also makes it more likely that you and your dog could become separated. For this reason, make sure your dog has a **tag with your contact details on it** (a mobile phone number would be best if you are carrying one with you); you could also consider having it **microchipped** for further security.

### When to keep your dog on a lead

● **On mountain tops** It's a sad fact that, every year, a few dogs lose their lives falling over the edge of steep slopes.

● **When crossing farmland**, particularly in the lambing season (around May) when your dog can scare the sheep, causing them to lose their young. Farmers are allowed by law to shoot at and kill any dogs that they consider are worrying their sheep. During lambing, most farmers would prefer it if you didn't bring your dog at all. The exception is if your dog is being attacked by cows. A couple of years ago there were three deaths in the UK caused by walkers being trampled as they tried to rescue their dogs from the attentions of cattle. The advice in this instance is to let go of the lead, head speedily to a position of safety (usually the other side of the field gate or stile) and call your dog to you.

● **Around ground-nesting birds** It's important to keep your dog under control when crossing an area where certain species of birds nest on the ground. Most dogs love foraging around in the woods but make sure you have permission to do so; some woods are used as 'nurseries' for game birds and dogs are only allowed through them if they are on a lead.

**What to pack**

You've probably already got a good idea of what to bring to keep your dog alive and happy, but the following is a checklist:

● **Food/water bowl** Foldable cloth bowls are popular with walkers, being light and take up little room in the rucksack. You can get also get a water-bottle-and-bowl combination, where the bottle folds into a 'trough' from which the dog can drink.

● **Lead and collar** An extendable one is probably preferable for this sort of trip. Make sure both lead and collar are in good condition – you don't want either to snap on the trail, or you may end up carrying your dog through sheep fields until a replacement can be found.

● **Medication** You'll know if you need to bring any lotions or potions.

● **Tick remover** See above

● **Bedding** A simple blanket may suffice, or you can opt for something more elaborate if you aren't carrying your own luggage.

● **Poo bags** Essential.

● **Hygiene wipes** For cleaning your dog after it's rolled in stuff.

● **A favourite toy** Helps prevent your dog from pining for the entire walk.

● **Food/water** Remember to bring treats as well as regular food to keep up the mutt's morale. That said, if your dog is anything like mine the chances are they'll spend most of the walk dining on rabbit droppings and sheep poo anyway.

● **Corkscrew stake** Available from camping or pet shops, this will help you to keep your dog secure in one place while you set up camp/doze.

● **Raingear** It can rain!

● **Old towels** For drying your dog.

When it comes to packing, I always leave an exterior pocket of my rucksack empty so I can put used poo bags in there (for deposit at the first bin we come to). I always like to keep all the dog's kit together and separate from the other luggage (usually inside a plastic bag inside my rucksack). I have also seen several dogs sporting their own 'doggy rucksack', so they can carry their own food, water, poo etc – which certainly reduces the burden on their owner!

**Cleaning up after your dog**

It is extremely important that dog owners behave in a responsible way when walking the path. Dog excrement should be cleaned up. In towns, villages and fields where animals graze or which will be cut for silage, hay etc, you need to pick up and bag the excrement.

**Staying with your dog**

In this guide we have used the symbol 🐾 to denote where a hotel, pub or B&B welcomes dogs. However, this always needs to be arranged in advance and some places may charge extra. Unusually, on the West Highland Way some (but only some) hostels (both SYHA and independent) *do* permit them; smaller campsites tend to accept them, but some of the larger holiday parks do not. Before you turn up always double check whether the place where you would like to stay accepts dogs and whether there is space for them; many places have only one or two rooms suitable for people with dogs.

When it comes to eating, most landlords allow dogs in at least a section of their pubs, though few restaurants do. Make sure you always ask first and ensure your dog doesn't run around the pub but is secured to your table or a radiator.

**Henry Stedman**

# APPENDIX D – DISTANCE CHART

| | Glasgow | Milngavie | Dumgoyne | Gartness | Easter Drumquhassle | Drymen | Balmaha | Cashel | Rowardennan | Inversnaid |
|---|---|---|---|---|---|---|---|---|---|---|
| **Milngavie** | 10 | | | | | | | | | |
| | *16* | | | | | | | | | |
| **Dumgoyne** | 17 | **7** | | | | | | | | |
| | *27* | *11* | | | | | | | | |
| **Gartness** | 20 | **10** | 3 | | | | | | | |
| | *32* | *16* | *5* | | | | | | | |
| **Easter Drumquhassle** | 21 | **11** | 4 | 1 | | | | | | |
| | *33.5* | *17.5* | *6.5* | *1.5* | | | | | | |
| **Drymen** | 22 | **12** | 5 | 2 | 1 | | | | | |
| | *35* | *19* | *8* | *3* | *1.5* | | | | | |
| **Balmaha** | 29 | **19** | 12 | 9 | 8 | 7 | | | | |
| | *46* | *30* | *19* | *14* | *12.5* | *11* | | | | |
| **Cashel** | 32 | **22** | 15 | 12 | 11 | 10 | 3 | | | |
| | *51* | *35* | *24* | *19* | *17.5* | *16* | *5* | | | |
| **Rowardennan** | 36 | **26** | 19 | 16 | 15 | 14 | 7 | 4 | | |
| | *57.5* | *41.5* | *30.5* | *25.5* | *24* | *22.5* | *11.5* | *6.5* | | |
| **Inversnaid** | 43 | **33** | 26 | 23 | 22 | 21 | 14 | 11 | 7 | |
| | *68.5* | *52.5* | *41.5* | *36.5* | *35* | *33.5* | *22.5* | *17.5* | *11* | |
| **Inverarnan** | 49.5 | **39.5** | 32.5 | 29.5 | 28.5 | 27.5 | 20.5 | 17.5 | 13.5 | 6.5 |
| | *78.5* | *62.5* | *51.5* | *46.5* | *44* | *43.5* | *32.5* | *27.5* | *21* | *10* |
| **Crianlarich** | 56 | **46** | 39 | 36 | 35 | 34 | 27 | 24 | 20 | 13 |
| | *88.5* | *72.5* | *61.5* | *56.5* | *55* | *53.5* | *42.5* | *37.5* | *31* | *20* |
| **Strathfillan** | 59.5 | **49.5** | 42.5 | 39.5 | 38.5 | 37.5 | 30.5 | 27.5 | 23.5 | 16.5 |
| | *94.5* | *78.5* | *67.5* | *62.5* | *61* | *59.5* | *48.5* | *43.5* | *37* | *26* |
| **Tyndrum** | 62 | **52** | 45 | 42 | 41 | 40 | 33 | 30 | 26 | 19 |
| | *98.5* | *82.5* | *81.5* | *66.5* | *65* | *63.5* | *52.5* | *47.5* | *42* | *30* |
| **Bridge of Orchy** | 69 | **59** | 52 | 49 | 48 | 47 | 40 | 37 | 33 | 25 |
| | *109.5* | *93.5* | *82.5* | *77.5* | *76* | *74.5* | *63.5* | *58.5* | *52* | *41* |
| **Inveroran** | 72 | **62** | 55 | 52 | 51 | 50 | 43 | 40 | 36 | 29 |
| | *114.5* | *98.5* | *87.5* | *82.5* | *81* | *79.5* | *68.5* | *63.5* | *57* | *46* |
| **Kingshouse** | 82 | **72** | 65 | 62 | 61 | 60 | 53 | 50 | 46 | 39 |
| | *130.5* | *114.5* | *103.5* | *98.5* | *97* | *95.5* | *84.5* | *79.5* | *73* | *62* |
| **Kinlochleven** | 90.5 | **80.5** | 73.5 | 70.5 | 69.5 | 68.5 | 61.5 | 58.5 | 54.5 | 47.5 |
| | *144.5* | *128.5* | *117.5* | *112.5* | *111* | *109.5* | *98.5* | *93.5* | *87* | *76* |
| **Glen Nevis** | 103 | **93** | 86 | 83 | 82 | 81 | 74 | 71 | 67 | 60 |
| | *164.5* | *148.5* | *137.5* | *132.5* | *131* | *129.5* | *118.5* | *113.5* | *107* | *96* |
| **Fort William** | 106 | **96** | 89 | 86 | 85 | 84 | 77 | 74 | 70 | 63 |
| | *169.5* | *154* | *142.5* | *137.5* | *136* | *134.5* | *123.5* | *118.5* | *112* | *101* |

# West Highland Way
## DISTANCE CHART

**(including Glasgow to Milngavie walking route)**

miles/*kilometres* (approx)

| Inverarnan | Crianlarich | Strathfillan | Tyndrum | Bridge of Orchy | Inveroran | Kingshouse | Kinlochleven | Glen Nevis |
|---|---|---|---|---|---|---|---|---|
| 6.5 | | | | | | | | |
| *10* | | | | | | | | |
| 10 | 3.5 | | | | | | | |
| *16* | *6* | | | | | | | |
| 12.5 | 6 | 2.5 | | | | | | |
| *20* | *10* | *4* | | | | | | |
| 19.5 | 13 | 9.5 | 7 | | | | | |
| *31* | *21* | *15* | *11* | | | | | |
| 22.5 | 16 | 12.5 | 10 | 3 | | | | |
| *36* | *26* | *20* | *16* | *5* | | | | |
| 32.5 | 26 | 22.5 | 20 | 13 | 10 | | | |
| *52* | *42* | *36* | *32* | *21* | *16* | | | |
| 41 | 34.5 | 31 | 28.5 | 21.5 | 18.5 | 8.5 | | |
| *66* | *56* | *50* | *46* | *35* | *30* | *14* | | |
| 53.5 | 47 | 43.5 | 41 | 34 | 31 | 21 | 12.5 | |
| *86* | *76* | *70* | *66* | *55* | *50* | *34* | *20* | |
| 56.5 | 50 | 46.5 | 44 | 37 | 34 | 24 | 15.5 | 3 |
| *91* | *81* | *75* | *71* | *60* | *55* | *39* | *25* | *5* |

# APPENDIX E – MAP KEYS

## Trail map key

| | | |
|---|---|---|
| West Highland Way | Plank bridge | Boulders |
| Other path | Bridge | Crags or cliffs |
| 4 x 4 track | Cattle grid | Building or ruin |
| Tarmac road | Water | Accommodation |
| Steps | River | Campsite |
| Slope | Stream | PO Post Office |
| Steep slope | Waterfall | Church |
| Gate | Stone wall | Public telephone |
| Stile | Conifer trees | Water point |
| Stile and gate | Deciduous trees | 014 GPS waypoint |

## Town plan key

| | | |
|---|---|---|
| Where to stay | Tourist information | Map continuation |
| Where to eat & drink | Library/bookstore | Bus stop/station |
| Campsite | Internet | Rail line & station |
| Post office | Museum/gallery | Park |
| Bank/ATM | Church/cathedral | CP Car park |
| Building | Public toilet | Other |
| | | 082 GPS waypoint |

# INDEX

**Page references in bold type refer to maps**

### Peru's Cordilleras Blanca & Huayhuash
### The Hiking & Biking Guide
*Neil & Harriet Pike,* 2nd edn, £17.99
ISBN 978-1-912716-17-3, 242pp, 50 maps, 40 colour photos
This region, in northern Peru, boasts some of the most spectacular scenery in the Andes, and most accessible high mountain
trekking and biking in the world. This practical guide contains
60 detailed route maps and descriptions covering 20 hiking
trails and more than 30 days of paved and dirt road cycling.

### Tour du Mont Blanc
*Jim Manthorpe,* 2nd edn, £13.99
ISBN 978-1-905864-92-8, 204pp, 60 maps, 50 colour photos
At 4807m (15,771ft), Mont Blanc is the highest mountain in west-
ern Europe. The trail (105 miles, 168km) that circumnavigates the
massif, passing through France, Italy and Switzerland, is the most
popular long-distance walk in Europe. Includes day walks. Plus –
Climbing guide to Mont Blanc

### Kilimanjaro – the trekking guide
*Henry Stedman,* 5th edn, £14.99
ISBN 978-1-905864-95-9, 368pp, 40 maps, 50 colour photos
At 5895m (19,340ft) Kilimanjaro is the world's tallest freestand-
ing mountain and one of the most popular destinations for hikers
visiting Africa. Route guides & maps – the 6 major routes. City
guides – Nairobi, Dar-es-Salaam, Arusha, Moshi & Marangu.

### The Inca Trail, Cusco & Machu Picchu
*Alex Stewart & Henry Stedman,* 6th edn, £14.99
ISBN 978-1-905864-88-1, 370pp, 70 maps, 30 colour photos
The Inca Trail from Cusco to Machu Picchu is South America's
most popular trek. This guide includes hiking options from two
days to three weeks. Plus plans of Inca sites, guides to Lima, Cusco
and Machu Picchu. Includes the High Inca Trail, Salkantay Trek
and the Choquequirao Trail. New 6th edition adds two Sacred
Valley treks: Lares Trail and Ausangate Circuit.

### Moroccan Atlas – the trekking guide
*Alan Palmer,* 2nd edn, £14.99
ISBN 978-1-905864-59-1, 420pp, 86 maps, 40 colour photos
The High Atlas in central Morocco is the most dramatic and beautiful section of the entire Atlas range. Towering peaks, deep
gorges and huddled Berber villages enchant all who visit. With 73
detailed maps, 13 town and village guides including Marrakech.

### Trekking in the Everest Region
*Jamie McGuinness* 6th edn, £15.99
ISBN 978-1-905864-81-2, 320pp, 95 maps, 30 colour photos
Sixth edition of this popular guide to the world's most famous
trekking region. Covers not only the classic treks but also the wild
routes. Written by a Nepal-based trek and mountaineering leader.
Includes: 27 detailed route maps and 52 village plans. Plus:
Kathmandu city guide

## TRAILBLAZER'S BRITISH WALKING GUIDES

We've applied to destinations which are closer to home Trailblazer's proven formula for publishing definitive practical route guides for adventurous travellers. Britain's network of long-distance trails enables the walker to explore some of the finest landscapes in the country's best walking areas. These are guides that are user-friendly, practical, informative and environmentally sensitive.

● **Unique mapping features** In many walking guidebooks the reader has to read a route description then try to relate it to the map. Our guides are much easier to use because walking directions, tricky junctions, places to stay and eat, points of interest and walking times are all written onto the maps themselves in the places to which they apply. With their uncluttered clarity, these are not general-purpose maps but fully edited maps drawn by walkers for walkers.

*'The same attention to detail that distinguishes its other guides has been brought to bear here'.*

**THE SUNDAY TIMES**

● **Largest-scale walking maps** At a scale of just under 1:20,000 (8cm or 3¹/₈ inches to one mile) the maps in these guides are bigger than even the most detailed British walking maps currently available in the shops.

● **Not just a trail guide – includes where to stay, where to eat and public transport** Our guidebooks cover the complete walking experience, not just the route. Accommodation options for all budgets are provided (pubs, hotels, B&Bs, campsites, bunkhouses, hostels) as well as places to eat. Detailed public transport information for all access points to each trail means that there are itineraries for all walkers, for hiking the entire route as well as for day or weekend walks.

**Cleveland Way** *Henry Stedman*, 1st edn, ISBN 978-1-905864-91-1, 240pp, 98 maps

**Coast to Coast** *Henry Stedman*, 9th edn, ISBN 978-1-912716-11-1, 268pp, 109 maps

**Cornwall Coast Path (SW Coast Path Pt 2)** *Stedman & Newton*, 7th edn, ISBN 978-1-912716-26-5, 352pp, 142 maps

**Cotswold Way** *Tricia & Bob Hayne,* 4th edn, ISBN 978-1-912716-04-3, 204pp, 53 maps

**Dales Way** *Henry Stedman,* 1st edn, ISBN 978-1-905864-78-2, 192pp, 50 maps

**Dorset & South Devon (SW Coast Path Pt 3)** *Stedman & Newton*, 2nd edn, ISBN 978-1-905864-94-2, 340pp, 97 maps

**Exmoor & North Devon (SW Coast Path Pt I)** *Stedman & Newton*, 3rd edn, ISBN 978-1-9912716-24-1, 224pp, 68 maps

**Glyndŵr's Way** *Chris Scott*, 1st edn, ISBN 978-1-912716-32-6, 220pp, 70 maps **(Spring 2023)**

**Great Glen Way** *Jim Manthorpe*, 2nd edn, ISBN 978-1-912716-10-4, 184pp, 50 maps

**Hadrian's Wall Path** *Henry Stedman*, 6th edn, ISBN 978-1-912716-12-8, 250pp, 60 maps

**London LOOP** *Henry Stedman*, 1st edn, ISBN 978-1-912716-21-0, 236pp, 60 maps

**Norfolk Coast Path & Peddars Way** *Alexander Stewart*, 1st edn, ISBN 978-1-905864-98-0, 224pp, 75 maps

**North Downs Way** *Henry Stedman*, 2nd edn, ISBN 978-1-905864-90-4, 240pp, 98 maps

**Offa's Dyke Path** *Keith Carter*, 5th edn, ISBN 978-1-912716-03-6, 268pp, 98 maps

**Pembrokeshire Coast Path** *Jim Manthorpe*, 6th edn, 978-1-912716-13-5, 236pp, 96 maps

**Pennine Way** *Stuart Greig*, 5th edn, ISBN 978-1-912716-02-9, 272pp, 138 maps

**The Ridgeway** *Nick Hill*, 5th edn, ISBN 978-1-912716-20-3, 208pp, 53 maps

**South Downs Way** *Jim Manthorpe*, 7th edn, ISBN 978-1-912716-23-4, 204pp, 60 maps

**Thames Path** *Joel Newton*, 3rd edn, ISBN 978-1-912716-27-2, 256pp, 99 maps

**West Highland Way** *Charlie Loram*, 8th edn, ISBN 978-1-912716-29-6, 224pp, 60 maps

*'The Trailblazer series stands head, shoulders, waist and ankles above the rest. They are particularly strong on mapping ...'*

**THE SUNDAY TIMES**

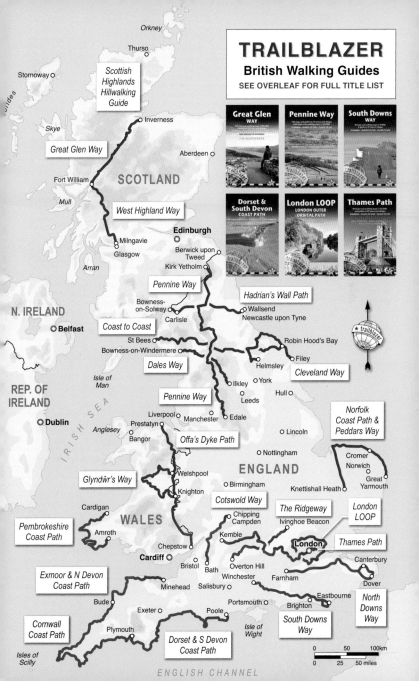

# TRAILBLAZER
## British Walking Guides
SEE OVERLEAF FOR FULL TITLE LIST

Great Glen WAY

Pennine Way

South Downs WAY

Dorset & South Devon COAST PATH

London LOOP LONDON OUTER ORBITAL PATH

Thames Path

Orkney

Thurso

Stornoway

Skye

Scottish Highlands Hillwalking Guide

Inverness

Great Glen Way

Aberdeen

Fort William

SCOTLAND

Mull

West Highland Way

Arran

Milngavie

Glasgow

Edinburgh

Berwick upon Tweed

Kirk Yetholm

N. IRELAND

Belfast

Pennine Way

Bowness-on-Solway

Carlisle

Wallsend

Newcastle upon Tyne

Hadrian's Wall Path

Coast to Coast

St Bees

Bowness-on-Windermere

Robin Hood's Bay

Filey

Dales Way

Ilkley

Helmsley

York

Cleveland Way

REP. OF IRELAND

Dublin

Isle of Man

Pennine Way

Leeds

Hull

IRISH SEA

Liverpool

Manchester

Edale

Anglesey

Prestatyn

Bangor

Lincoln

Offa's Dyke Path

Nottingham

Norfolk Coast Path & Peddars Way

Glyndŵr's Way

Welshpool

Knighton

ENGLAND

Birmingham

Knettishall Heath

Cromer

Norwich

Great Yarmouth

Cardigan

Pembrokeshire Coast Path

Amroth

Cotswold Way

Chipping Campden

The Ridgeway

Ivinghoe Beacon

London LOOP

WALES

Kemble

Chepstow

Cardiff

Bristol

Bath

Overton Hill

London

Thames Path

Canterbury

Exmoor & N Devon Coast Path

Minehead

Salisbury

Winchester

Farnham

Dover

North Downs Way

Bude

Exeter

Portsmouth

Eastbourne

Brighton

Cornwall Coast Path

Plymouth

Poole

Isle of Wight

South Downs Way

Isles of Scilly

Dorset & S Devon Coast Path

| 0 | 50 | 100km |
| 0 | 25 | 50 miles |

ENGLISH CHANNEL

# TRAILBLAZER TITLE LIST

For more information about Trailblazer and our
expanding range of guides, for guidebook updates or
for credit card mail order sales visit our website:

## www.trailblazer-guides.com

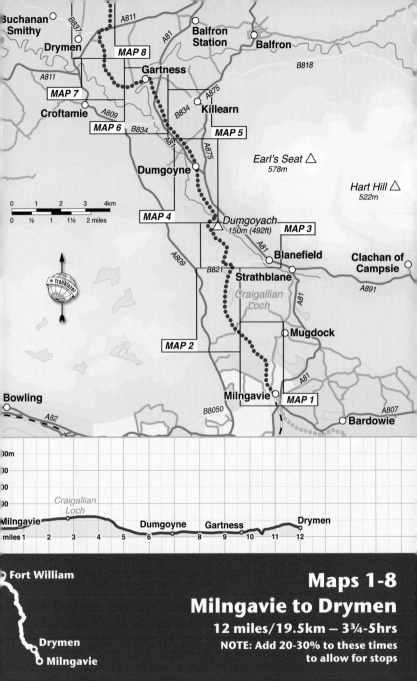

Buchanan
Smithy

Drymen

A811

A811

B837

A811

**Balfron
Station**

**Balfron**

B818

**MAP 8**

Gartness

A81

**MAP 7**

Croftamie

A809

B834

**MAP 6**

B834

A875

A875

**Killearn**

**MAP 5**

A81

Earl's Seat △
578m

Hart Hill △
522m

Dumgoyne

A875

**MAP 4**

A809

△ Dumgoyach
150m (492ft)

**MAP 3**

A81

**Blanefield**

**Clachan of
Campsie**

B821

A891

**Strathblane**

A81

Craigallian
Loch

★ trailblazer

0   1   2   3   4km
0   ½   1   1½   2 miles

**MAP 2**

**Mugdock**

A81

**Bowling**

A82

B8050

**Milngavie**

**MAP 1**

A807

**Bardowie**

)0m

)0

)0

)0

Craigallian
Loch

Milngavie     Dumgoyne     Gartness     Drymen

miles 1   2   3   4   5   6   7   8   9   10   11   12

◦ **Fort William**

◦ **Drymen**
◦ **Milngavie**

# Maps 1-8
## Milngavie to Drymen
### 12 miles/19.5km — 3¾-5hrs
**NOTE: Add 20-30% to these times
to allow for stops**

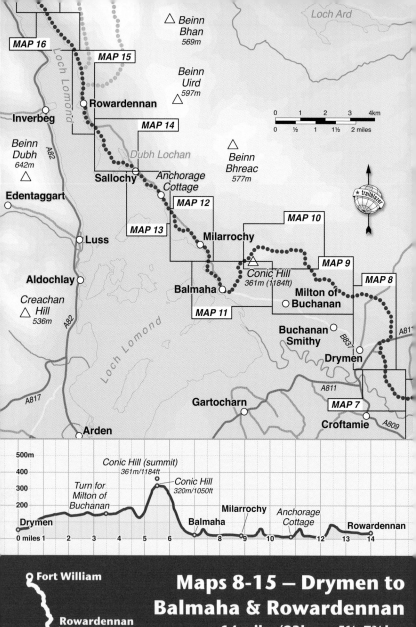

MAP 16

MAP 15

*Loch Ard*

△ *Beinn Bhan 569m*

*Loch Lomond*

*Beinn Uird 597m* △

**Rowardennan**

MAP 14

**Inverbeg**

A82

*Beinn Dubh 642m* △

*Dubh Lochan*

△ *Beinn Bhreac 577m*

**Sallochy**

*Anchorage Cottage*

MAP 12

**Edentaggart**

MAP 13

**Milarrochy**

MAP 10

**Luss**

MAP 9

**Aldochlay**

△ *Conic Hill 361m (1184ft)*

MAP 8

*Creachan Hill 536m* △

**Balmaha**

**Milton of Buchanan**

A82

MAP 11

A81

*Loch Lomond*

**Buchanan Smithy**

B837

**Drymen**

A811

A817

**Gartocharn**

A811

MAP 7

**Arden**

**Croftamie**

A809

0  1  2  3  4km
0  ½  1  1½  2 miles

★ trailblazer

---

500m
400
300
200
100

*Conic Hill (summit) 361m/1184ft*

*Conic Hill 320m/1050ft*

*Turn for Milton of Buchanan*

**Milarrochy**

*Anchorage Cottage*

**Drymen**

**Balmaha**

**Rowardennan**

0 miles 1    2    3    4    5    6    7    8    9    10    11    12    13    14

---

○ **Fort William**

○ **Rowardennan**
○ **Balmaha**
○ **Drymen**
○ **Milngavie**

# Maps 8-15 — Drymen to Balmaha & Rowardennan

## 14 miles/23km — 5¼-7¾hrs

**NOTE: Add 20-30% to these times to allow for stops**

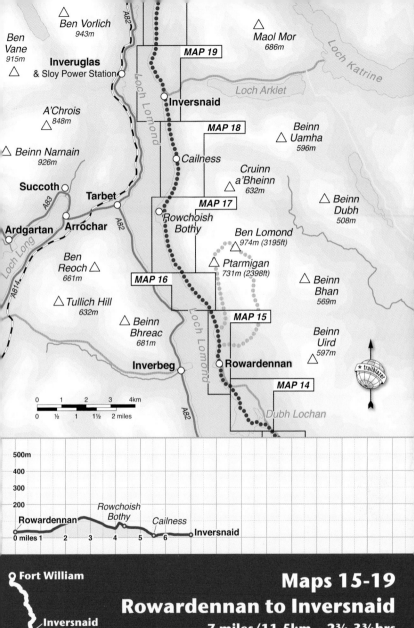

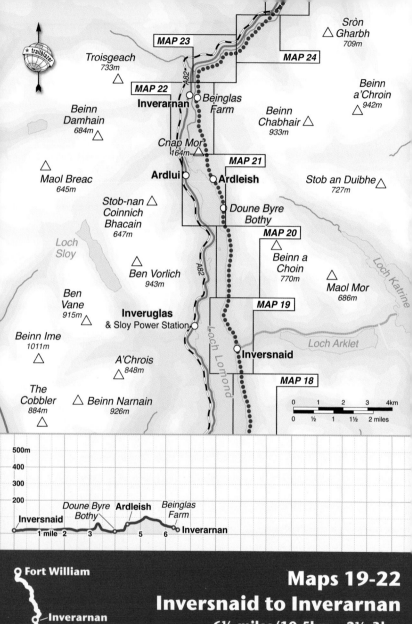

**Maps 19-22**
**Inversnaid to Inverarnan**
6½ miles/10.5km – 2½-3hrs
NOTE: Add 20-30% to these times
to allow for stops

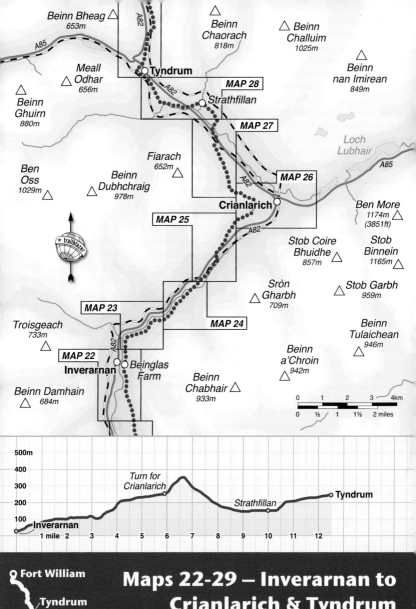

# Maps 22-29 – Inverarnan to Crianlarich & Tyndrum

12½ miles/20.5km – 4-5hrs

NOTE: Add 20-30% to these times to allow for stops

Beinn Bheag
653m

A82

A85

Beinn
Chaorach
818m

Beinn
Challuim
1025m

Meall
Odhar
656m

Tyndrum

Beinn
nan Imirean
849m

MAP 28

A82

Strathfillan

Beinn
Ghuirn
880m

MAP 27

Loch
Lubhair

A85

Fiarach
652m

Ben
Oss
1029m

Beinn
Dubhchraig
978m

A82

MAP 26

Crianlarich

Ben More
1174m
(3851ft)

MAP 25

A82

Stob Coire
Bhuidhe
857m

Stob
Binnein
1165m

Sròn
Gharbh
709m

Stob Garbh
959m

MAP 23

MAP 24

Beinn
Tulaichean
946m

Troisgeach
733m

A82

MAP 22

Beinglas
Farm

Beinn
a'Chroin
942m

Inverarnan

Beinn Damhain
684m

Beinn
Chabhair
933m

0    1    2    3    4km
0    ½    1    1½    2 miles

500m
400
300
200
100

Turn for
Crianlarich

Tyndrum

Strathfillan

Inverarnan

1 mile  2    3    4    5    6    7    8    9    10    11    12

Fort William

Tyndrum
Crianlarich
Inverarnan

Milngavie

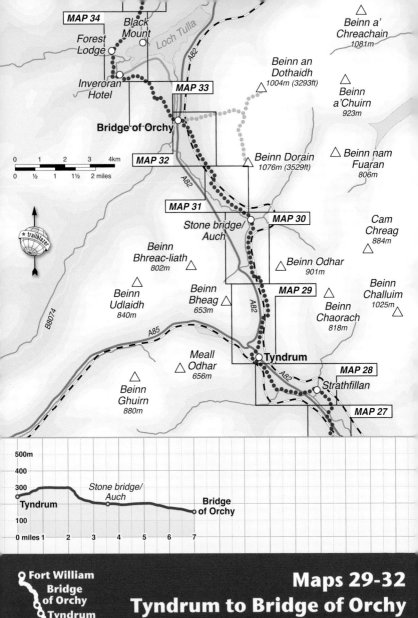

**Maps 29-32**
**Tyndrum to Bridge of Orchy**
7 miles/11.5km – 1¾-2¼hrs
NOTE: Add 20-30% to these times
to allow for stops

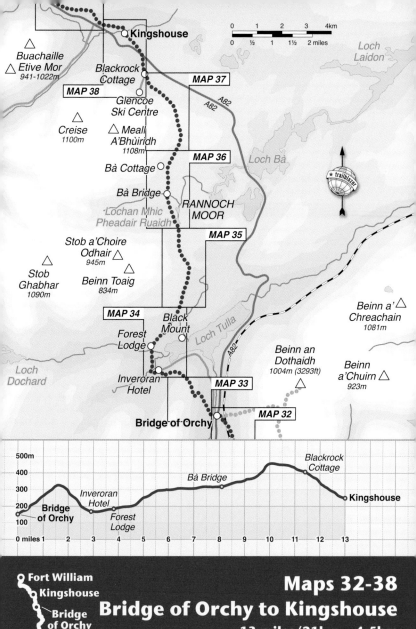

**MAP 37**

**MAP 38**

**MAP 36**

**MAP 35**

**MAP 34**

**MAP 33**

**MAP 32**

Kingshouse

Buachaille
Etive Mor
*941-1022m*

Blackrock
Cottage

Glencoe
Ski Centre

Creise
*1100m*

Meall
A'Bhùiridh
*1108m*

Loch
Laidon

A82

A82

Loch Bà

★ trailblazer

Bà Cottage

Bà Bridge

*Lochan Mhic
Pheadair Ruaidh*

RANNOCH
MOOR

Stob a'Choire
Odhair
*945m*

Beinn a'
Chreachain
*1081m*

Stob
Ghabhar
*1090m*

Beinn Toaig
*834m*

Black
Mount

Loch Tulla

Beinn an
Dothaidh
*1004m (3293ft)*

Beinn
a'Chuirn
*923m*

Forest
Lodge

A82

Loch
Dochard

Inveroran
Hotel

Bridge of Orchy

---

500m
400
300
200
100

Bridge
of Orchy

Inveroran
Hotel

Forest
Lodge

Bà Bridge

Blackrock
Cottage

Kingshouse

0 miles 1   2   3   4   5   6   7   8   9   10   11   12   13

---

Fort William
Kingshouse
Bridge of Orchy

Milngavie

# Maps 32-38
## Bridge of Orchy to Kingshouse
### 13 miles/21km – 4-5hrs
**NOTE: Add 20-30% to these times
to allow for stops**

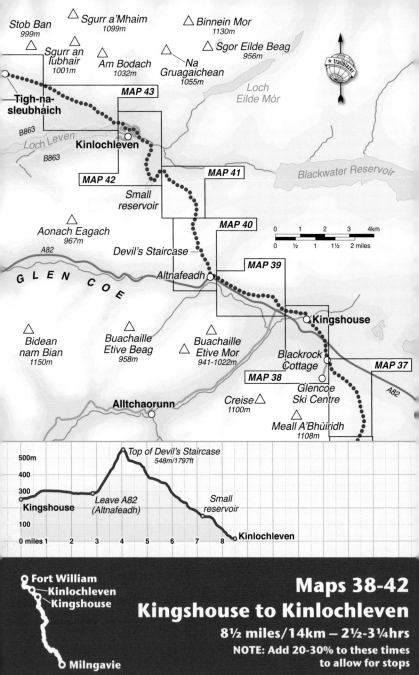

Stob Ban 999m
△ Sgurr a'Mhaim 1099m
△ Binnein Mor 1130m
△ Sgor Eilde Beag 956m

△ Sgurr an Iubhair 1001m
△ Am Bodach 1032m
△ Na Gruagaichean 1055m

Tigh-na-sleubhaich

B863
Loch Leven
B863

Loch Eilde Mòr

**MAP 43**

**Kinlochleven**

**MAP 42**

**MAP 41**

Small reservoir

Blackwater Reservoir

△ Aonach Eagach 967m

A82

**MAP 40**

Devil's Staircase

G L E N   C O E

Altnafeadh

**MAP 39**

**Kingshouse**

△ Bidean nam Bian 1150m
△ Buachaille Etive Beag 958m
△ Buachaille Etive Mor 941-1022m

Blackrock Cottage

**MAP 37**

**MAP 38**

**Alltchaorunn**

△ Creise 1100m

Glencoe Ski Centre

A82

△ Meall A'Bhùiridh 1108m

0  1  2  3  4km
0  ½  1  1½  2 miles

500m
400
300
100
**Kingshouse**
Leave A82 (Altnafeadh)
Top of Devil's Staircase 548m/1797ft
Small reservoir
**Kinlochleven**
0 miles 1  2  3  4  5  6  7  8

○ **Fort William**
○ **Kinlochleven**
○ **Kingshouse**

○ **Milngavie**

# Maps 38-42
## Kingshouse to Kinlochleven
### 8½ miles/14km – 2½-3¼hrs
**NOTE: Add 20-30% to these times to allow for stops**

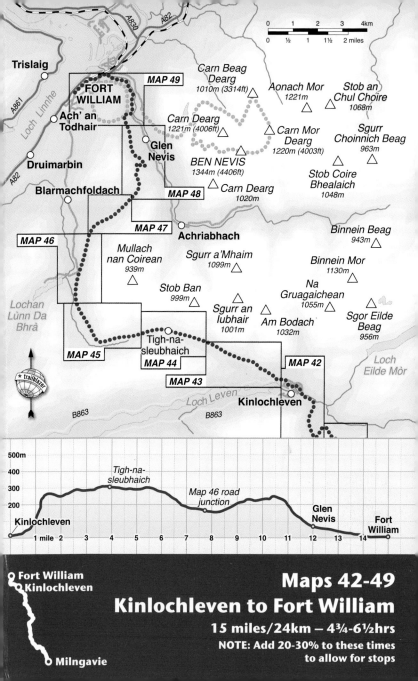

Trislaig

A830
A82

FORT WILLIAM

**MAP 49**

Carn Beag Dearg
*1010m (3314ft)*

Aonach Mor
*1221m*

Stob an Chul Choire
*1068m*

Ach' an Todhair

Carn Dearg
*1221m (4006ft)*

Glen Nevis

Carn Mor Dearg
*1220m (4003ft)*

Sgurr Choinnich Beag
*963m*

Druimarbin

A82

Loch Linnhe

A861

BEN NEVIS
*1344m (4406ft)*

Blarmachfoldach

**MAP 48**

Carn Dearg
*1020m*

Stob Coire Bhealaich
*1048m*

**MAP 47**

Achriabhach

**MAP 46**

Mullach nan Coirean
*939m*

Sgurr a'Mhaim
*1099m*

Binnein Beag
*943m*

Binnein Mor
*1130m*

Lochan Lùnn Da Bhrà

Stob Ban
*999m*

Na Gruagaichean
*1055m*

Sgor Eilde Beag
*956m*

Sgurr an Iubhair
*1001m*

Am Bodach
*1032m*

Tigh-na-sleubhaich

**MAP 45**

**MAP 44**

**MAP 43**

**MAP 42**

Loch Eilde Mòr

B863

Loch Leven

B863

Kinlochleven

*trailblazer*

500m
400
300
200

Tigh-na-sleubhaich

Map 46 road junction

Glen Nevis

Fort William

Kinlochleven

1 mile  2   3   4   5   6   7   8   9   10   11   12   13   14

Fort William
Kinlochleven

Milngavie

# Maps 42-49
# Kinlochleven to Fort William
### 15 miles/24km – 4¾-6½hrs
**NOTE: Add 20-30% to these times to allow for stops**

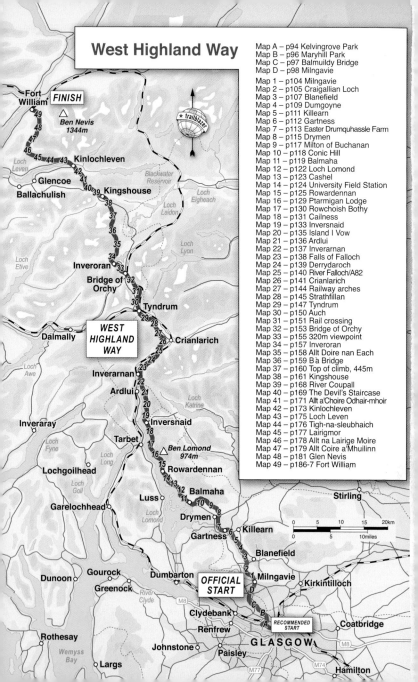

# West Highland Way

Marsh Marigold
*Caltha palustris*

Meadow Buttercup
*Ranunculus acris*

Gorse
*Ulex europaeus*

Tormentil
*Potentilla erecta*

Birdsfoot-trefoil
*Lotus corniculatus*

Ox-eye Daisy
*Leucanthemum vulgare*

St John's Wort
*Hypericum perforatum*

Primrose
*Primula vulgaris*

Cowslip
*Primula veris*

Common Ragwort
*Senecio jacobaea*

Hemp-nettle
*Galeopsis speciosa*

Cotton Grass
*Eriophorum angustifolium*

Common Butterwort
*Pinguicula vulgaris*

Early Purple Orchid
*Orchis mascula*

Spear Thistle
*Cirsium vulgare*

Bell Heather
*Erica cinerea*

Heather (Ling)
*Calluna vulgaris*

Wood Sorrel
*Oxalis acetosella*

Rosebay Willowherb
*Epilobium angustifolium*

Common Vetch
*Vicia sativa*

Common Fumitory
*Fumaria officinalis*

Meadow Cranesbill
*Geranium pratense*

Water Avens
*Geum rivale*

Red Campion
*Silene dioica*

Lobbying groups, such as the **Association for the Protection of Rural Scotland** (🖳 aprs.scot), also play a vital role in environmental protection by raising public awareness and occasionally co-operate with government agencies such as NatureScot when policy needs to be formulated. A huge increase in membership over the last 20 years and a general understanding that environmental issues can't be left to government 'experts' is creating a new and powerful lobbying group; an informed electorate.

## BEYOND CONSERVATION

*… we are not safe in assuming that we can preserve wildness by making wilderness reserves. Those of us who see that wildness and wilderness need to be preserved are going to have to understand the dependence of these things upon our domestic economy and our domestic behaviour.*  **Wendell Berry** *Standing on Earth*

The ideas embodied in nature conservation have served us well over the last century. Without the multitude of designations which protect wildlife and landscape there is no doubt that the countryside of Scotland would be far more impoverished than it is today. However, in some respects the creation of nature reserves and other protected areas is an admission that we are not looking after the rest of our environment properly.

If we can't keep the soil, air and water free from contamination or prevent man's activities from affecting the world's climate, nature reserves will have little lasting value. Similarly, if decisions made by national government, the European Union (EU) or the World Trade Organisation (WTO) continue to fragment communities and force farmers, foresters and fishermen to adopt unsustainable practices, those who are best placed to protect the land and wildlife end up destroying it. Those who care about Scotland's wildlife and countryside now need to step beyond the narrow focus of conservation. We need to find ways to reconnect with the natural world and relearn how to live in balance with it. This not only demands action on a personal level, for which walking in the wild is surely an ideal tutor, but also a wholesale rethink of the basic assumptions underlying the political and economic policies that created our critical situation in the first place. Wendell Berry in *Standing on Earth* puts it more bluntly:

*The wildernesses we are trying to preserve are standing squarely in the way of our present economy, and the wildernesses cannot survive if our economy does not change.*

# Flora and fauna

## FLOWERS

### Hedgerows

On the southern part of the Way the hedgerows and wood margins along the trail provide the best displays of wild flowers. In early summer look out for the pink flowers of **red campion** (*Silene dioica*), **wood cranesbill** (*Geranium sylvaticum*) and the more fragile **herb robert** (*Geranium robertianum*) along with the bright yellow displays of **creeping** and **meadow buttercup** (*Ranunculus repens* and *R. acris*). In summer **broad-leaved willowherb** (*Epilobium montanum*) and **foxgloves** (*Digitalis purpurea*) make an appearance in hedges and woods while **rosebay willowherb** (*Chamerion angustifolium*) often colonises the sides of footpaths and waste ground.

The tall white-flowering heads of plants such as **sweet cicely** (*Myrrhis odorata*), **cow parsley** (*Anthriscus sylvestris*) and **hogweed** (*Heracleum sphondylium*) are another familiar sight along verges. In the autumn the hedgerows produce their edible harvest of delicious blackberries which can be eaten straight from the thorny **bramble** (*Rubus fruticosus*) and rose-hips of the **dog rose** (*Rosa canina*), best made into a syrup which provides 20 times the vitamin C of oranges.

## Grassland

There is much overlap between the hedge/woodland-edge habitat and that of pastures and meadows. You will come across **common birdsfoot-trefoil** (*Lotus corniculatus*), **germander speedwell** (*Veronica chamaedrys*), **tufted** and **bush vetch** (*Vicia cracca* and *V. sepium*) and **meadow vetchling** (*Lathyrus pratensis*) in both.

Often the only species you will see in heavily grazed pastures are the most resilient. The emblem of Scotland, the thistle, is one of these. The three most common species are **creeping thistle**, **spear thistle** and **marsh thistle** (*Cirsium arvense*, *C. vulgare* and *C. palustre*). Among them you may find **common ragwort** (*Senecio jacobaea*), **yarrow** (*Achillea millefolium*), **sheep's** and **common sorrel** (*Rumex acetosella* and *R. acetosa*), and **white** and **red clover** (*Trifolium repens* and *T. pratense*).

Other widespread grassland species include **Scottish bluebell** (*Campanula rotundifolia*), known as harebell in England, delicate yellow **tormentil** (*Potentilla erecta*) which will often spread up onto the lower slopes of mountains along with **devil's-bit scabious** (*Succisa pratensis*). Also keep an eye out for orchids such as the **fragrant orchid** (*Gymnadenia conopsea*) and **early purple orchid** (*Orchis mascula*).

## Woodland

Springtime is when the lowland woods are at their best. In birch and oak woods during May and June the floor will be dotted with **primroses** (*Primula vulgaris*), **wood anemones** (*Anemone nemorosa*), **dog's mercury** (*Mercurialis perennis*), **lesser celandine** (*Ranunculus ficaria*), **wood sorrel** (*Oxalis acetosella*), **wild hyacinth** (*Hyacinthoides non-scripta*, called bluebell in England), **common** and **small cow-wheat** (*Melapyrum pratense* and *M. sylvaticum*) and **common dog-violets** (*Viola riviniana*).

## Moorland

Common **heather** (*Calluna vulgaris*), or ling, is the flower most often associated with the Scottish moors, bursting into purple blooms at the end of summer. Its natural habitat is the native pine woods but the regular burning of the moors as part of their management for grouse shooting keeps it regenerating on open ground. **Bell heather** (*Erica cinerea*) has larger flowers and is usually found on